Contents

Cambridge School Shakespeare

This edition of *Antony and Cleopatra* is part of the *Cambridge School Shakespeare* series. Like every other play in the series, it has been specially prepared to help all students in schools and colleges.

This *Antony and Cleopatra* aims to be different from other editions of the play. It invites you to bring the play to life in your classroom, hall or drama studio through enjoyable activities that will increase your understanding. Actors have created their different interpretations of the play over the centuries. Similarly, you are encouraged to make up your own mind about *Antony and Cleopatra*, rather than having someone else's interpretation handed down to you.

Cambridge School Shakespeare does not offer you a cut-down or simplified version of the play. This is Shakespeare's language, filled with imaginative possibilities. You will find on every left-hand page: a summary of the action, an explanation of unfamiliar words, a choice of activities on Shakespeare's language, characters and stories.

Between each act and in the pages at the end of the play, you will find notes, illustrations and activities. This will help to increase your understanding of the whole play.

There are a large number of activities to give you the widest choice to suit your own particular needs. Please don't think you have to do every one. Choose the activities that will help you most.

This edition will be of value to you whether you are studying for an examination, reading for pleasure, or thinking of putting on the play to entertain others. You can work on the activities on your own or in groups. Many of the activities suggest a particular group size, but don't be afraid to make up larger or smaller groups to suit your own purposes.

Although you are invited to treat *Antony and Cleopatra* as a play, you don't need special dramatic or theatrical skills to do the activities. By choosing your activities, and by exploring and experimenting, you can make your own interpretations of Shakespeare's language, characters and stories. Whatever you do, remember that Shakespeare wrote his plays to be acted, watched and enjoyed.

Rex Gibson

This edition of *Antony and Cleopatra* uses the text of the play established by David Bevington in *The New Cambridge Shakespeare*.

CAMBRIDGE SCHOOL·

Shakespeare

CAMBRIDGE UNIVERSITY PRESS

CAMBRIDGE UNIVERSITY PRESS
Cambridge, New York, Melbourne, Madrid, Cape Town, Singapore,
São Paulo, Delhi, Dubai, Tokyo, Mexico City

Cambridge University Press
The Edinburgh Building, Cambridge CB2 8RU, UK

www.cambridge.org
Information on this title: www.cambridge.org/9780521445849

First published 1994
11th printing 2011

Printed in the United Kingdom at the University Press, Cambridge

A catalogue record for this publication is available from the British Library

ISBN 978-0-521-44584-9 Paperback

Prepared for publication by Stenton Associates
Designed by Richard Morris, Stonesfield Design
Picture research by Callie Kendall
Cover illustration by Elizabeth Kerr
Illustration by Margaret Jones

Thanks are due to the following for permission to reproduce photographs:

6, 10, 54, 140, 190*t*, 226, 235*l*, Shakespeare Centre Library, Stratford-upon-Avon/Joe Cocks
Studio Collection; 16, 32, 41*b*. 130, 149, 164, 188, 216, 231, 235*tr*, Clive Barda/Performing
Arts Library; 26, 34, 41*t*, 112, 184, 220, Mark Williamson; 72, 170, 190*b*, 202, 206, BBC
Photograph Library/photo: David Green; 44, 86, 88, 92, 98, 116, 182, 192, 224, Reg Wilson;
66, Mansell Collection; 154, Archivi Alinari; 176, SCALA/Museo Nazionale Napoli; 235*br*,
John Haynes/courtesy of National Theatre Press Office.

List of characters

Egypt

CLEOPATRA   Queen of Egypt

CHARMIAN ⎱
IRAS ⎰ her personal attendants

ALEXAS her minister   MARDIAN a eunuch
SELEUCUS her treasurer   DIOMEDES a servant
                           CLOWN a simple country man

Rome

MARK ANTONY ⎫
OCTAVIUS CAESAR ⎬ joint rulers of
LEPIDUS ⎭ the Roman world

OCTAVIA sister of Octavius Caesar and wife of Antony

SEXTUS POMPEIUS (POMPEY) leader of the faction opposed
to the Triumvirate

Mark Antony's followers and officers

DOMITIUS ENOBARBUS   DEMETRIUS   PHILO
VENTIDIUS   SILIUS   CANIDIUS
EROS   DERCETUS   SCARUS
SCHOOLMASTER   SOOTHSAYER

Octavius Caesar's followers and officers

MAECENAS   AGRIPPA   TAURUS
THIDIAS   DOLABELLA   GALLUS
PROCULEIUS

Sextus Pompeius's followers and officers

MENAS and MENECRATES pirates   VARRIUS

Messengers, servants, officers, soldiers, sentries, guards, watchmen

The play is set in Egypt, Rome and several places
in the Roman provinces.

Antony regrets Fulvia's death. He resolves to leave Cleopatra and tells Enobarbus of his decision to return to Rome. Enobarbus says Cleopatra will react passionately to his departure.

1 Conflicting emotions (in pairs)

a When Fulvia was alive, Antony had often wished her dead. Now she is dead, he wishes her alive again (lines 119–24). Is Antony a hypocrite, or can you justify his change of mind?

b In this conversation, Enobarbus expresses both a genuine admiration and a cynical awareness of Cleopatra's 'cunning'. List examples of each. Does Antony also show contradictory attitudes towards Cleopatra?

c There is much talk of dying in this scene. Antony muses on Fulvia's death, then Enobarbus remarks (lines 136–40) how easily and often Cleopatra dies. 'To die' in Elizabethan English could mean 'to reach sexual orgasm'. Do you think Enobarbus is hinting at this with his repeated references to dying, or does he mean something else?

Which line best fits this moment from the 1992 Royal Shakespeare Company production?

Forbear me leave me
What our contempts ... ours again we only appreciate something when it is gone
By revolution lowering in time loses its attraction
could pluck would like to pull

enchanting bewitching
upon ... moment for far more trivial reasons
mettle strength, spirit
celerity quickness
discredited your travel been a serious gap in your education

ANTONY   Forbear me.

[*Exit Messenger*]

There's a great spirit gone! Thus did I desire it.
What our contempts doth often hurl from us,   120
We wish it ours again. The present pleasure,
By revolution lowering, does become
The opposite of itself. She's good, being gone;
The hand could pluck her back that shoved her on.
I must from this enchanting queen break off.   125
Ten thousand harms more than the ills I know
My idleness doth hatch. – How now, Enobarbus!

Enter ENOBARBUS

ENOBARBUS What's your pleasure, sir?

ANTONY I must with haste from hence.

ENOBARBUS Why then we kill all our women. We see how mortal an   130
unkindness is to them; if they suffer our departure, death's the
word.

ANTONY I must be gone.

ENOBARBUS Under a compelling occasion, let women die. It were
pity to cast them away for nothing, though between them and a   135
great cause they should be esteemed nothing. Cleopatra, catching
but the least noise of this, dies instantly; I have seen her die
twenty times upon far poorer moment. I do think there is mettle
in death, which commits some loving act upon her, she hath
such a celerity in dying.   140

ANTONY She is cunning past man's thought.

ENOBARBUS Alack, sir, no, her passions are made of nothing but
the finest part of pure love. We cannot call her winds and waters
sighs and tears; they are greater storms and tempests than
almanacs can report. This cannot be cunning in her; if it be,   145
she makes a shower of rain as well as Jove.

ANTONY Would I had never seen her!

ENOBARBUS O sir, you had then left unseen a wonderful piece of
work, which not to have been blest withal would have discredited
your travel.   150

17

Enobarbus jokingly consoles Antony about Fulvia's death, saying that Antony can easily find another wife. Antony declares they must return to Rome to counter the threat of Pompey.

1 Enobarbus's tribute to Fulvia (in pairs)

Antony's wife is dead. Enobarbus offers consolation. The gods are the world's tailors, constantly fashioning new people to replace the old and worn-out (lines 156–63). Antony should rejoice that he has his 'new petticoat' (Cleopatra) to replace his 'old smock' (Fulvia).

In lines 151–70, Enobarbus makes several bawdy puns: 'members' could mean the male sexual organs; 'cut' (a blow, misfortune) and 'case' could refer to the female sexual organs. Decide what prompts him to speak like this (for example, cynicism, matter-of-factness, genuine concern for Antony). Decide how Antony responds.

2 The threat to the Triumvirate

There was an uneasy relationship in Rome between the ruling classes and the people. Antony calls them 'Our slippery people'. Sextus Pompeius, the son of Pompey the Great (see page 240), is using the prestige of his father's name to gather support (lines 176–89).

'Like the courser's hair' (line 186). Elizabethans believed that the hair of a horse ('courser'), when placed in water, would grow into a serpent. Draw cartoons with captions illustrating the growing threat to the Triumvirate of 'Pompey the Serpent'.

3 'No more light answers' (in large groups)

As Antony concerns himself with Roman affairs, his language becomes ever more formal and public. One person reads lines 169–90. When Antony uses 'our'/'we'/'us', the rest echo it, adding 'as a leader of Rome'. Check back to discover if Antony has used the formal royal 'we' before in the play.

---

broachèd stirred up
abode staying here
break impart
expedience immediate departure
touches reasons, motives
Petition us at home beg me to come home

stands up … soldier lays claim to being the greatest soldier
whose … danger if allowed to thrive, he will endanger the Empire
Say … hence tell my followers that we leave at once

ANTONY Fulvia is dead.

ENOBARBUS Sir?

ANTONY Fulvia is dead.

ENOBARBUS Fulvia?

ANTONY Dead.   155

ENOBARBUS Why, sir, give the gods a thankful sacrifice. When it
pleaseth their deities to take the wife of a man from him, it shows
to man the tailors of the earth; comforting therein, that when old
robes are worn out, there are members to make new. If there
were no more women but Fulvia, then had you indeed a cut, and   160
the case to be lamented. This grief is crowned with consolation;
your old smock brings forth a new petticoat, and indeed the tears
live in an onion that should water this sorrow.

ANTONY The business she hath broachèd in the state
Cannot endure my absence.   165

ENOBARBUS And the business you have broached here cannot
be without you, especially that of Cleopatra's, which wholly
depends on your abode.

ANTONY No more light answers. Let our officers
Have notice what we purpose. I shall break   170
The cause of our expedience to the queen
And get her leave to part. For not alone
The death of Fulvia, with more urgent touches,
Do strongly speak to us, but the letters too
Of many our contriving friends in Rome   175
Petition us at home. Sextus Pompeius
Hath given the dare to Caesar and commands
The empire of the sea. Our slippery people,
Whose love is never linked to the deserver
Till his deserts are past, begin to throw   180
Pompey the Great and all his dignities
Upon his son, who – high in name and power,
Higher than both in blood and life – stands up
For the main soldier; whose quality, going on,
The sides o'th'world may danger. Much is breeding,   185
Which, like the courser's hair, hath yet but life
And not a serpent's poison. Say our pleasure,
To such whose place is under us, requires
Our quick remove from hence.

ENOBARBUS I shall do't.   *[Exeunt]*   190

*Cleopatra sends a provoking message to Antony. Charmian attempts,
without success, to advise her mistress on how best to keep Antony's love.
Antony enters and Cleopatra turns on him.*

1 How to keep a man (in groups of three)

Cleopatra and Charmian disagree radically about how best to keep a
man's love. Read lines 1–12 and try the following:

a Who is right, Charmian or Cleopatra? Take sides and argue the
case. Then present a TV chat show in which two distinguished
women are questioned about how they keep their men. One of
you advocates Charmian's view, one of you advocates Cleopatra's.
The third person is the chat show host.

b What can you infer about the character of each woman from this
brief exchange?

2 A stormy relationship (in groups of eight)

The deteriorating political situation in Rome requires Antony's
immediate return, but Cleopatra will use every trick she knows to keep
him from going. In this scene, the 'balance of power' between them
shifts and changes.

Two of you take the parts of Antony and Cleopatra and read aloud
lines 13–106. The others decide who is controlling the discussion at
each point. If Cleopatra is dominating, the listeners speak Cleopatra's
words with her. If Antony dominates, they echo his lines to show his
control.

Decide if there is a particular line where either one or the other
capitulates.

since recently	**sullen** in low spirits
sad in a serious mood	**give breathing to** speak of
hold the method use the right	**It cannot be thus long** I cannot
tactics	last long at this rate
I do not that I am not doing	**the sides of nature** my body
Tempt vex	**stand farther from me** give me air
I wish I wish you would	**the married woman** your wife

ACT 1 SCENE 3
Alexandria Cleopatra's palace

Enter CLEOPATRA, CHARMIAN, ALEXAS, *and* IRAS

CLEOPATRA Where is he?
CHARMIAN   I did not see him since.
CLEOPATRA *[To Alexas]*
    See where he is, who's with him, what he does.
    I did not send you. If you find him sad,
    Say I am dancing; if in mirth, report
    That I am sudden sick. Quick, and return.   5

                                              [Exit Alexas]
CHARMIAN Madam, methinks if you did love him dearly,
    You do not hold the method to enforce
    The like from him.
CLEOPATRA   What should I do I do not?
CHARMIAN In each thing give him way. Cross him in nothing.
CLEOPATRA Thou teachest like a fool: the way to lose him.   10
CHARMIAN Tempt him not so too far. I wish, forbear;
    In time we hate that which we often fear.

                    Enter ANTONY

    But here comes Antony.
CLEOPATRA   I am sick and sullen.
ANTONY I am sorry to give breathing to my purpose –
CLEOPATRA Help me away, dear Charmian, I shall fall.   15
    It cannot be thus long; the sides of nature
    Will not sustain it.
ANTONY   Now, my dearest queen –
CLEOPATRA Pray you, stand farther from me.
ANTONY   What's the matter?
CLEOPATRA I know by that same eye there's some good news.
    What, says the married woman you may go?   20
    Would she had never given you leave to come!
    Let her not say 'tis I that keep you here.
    I have no power upon you; hers you are.

21

Cleopatra does not give Antony a chance to talk about his departure. Eventually, he is able to tell her of the desperate situation in Rome, of the civil wars and the power of Sextus Pompeius.

1 'She is cunning past man's thought' (in pairs)

So said Antony to Enobarbus in the previous scene. 'Cunning' could mean both 'skilled' and 'deceitful'. Can you decide whether Cleopatra is genuinely angry or just play-acting? Take it in turns to be Cleopatra and explore lines 17–44 in the following ways:

a As Cleopatra speaks, Antony must attempt to interrupt whenever he can (not just where shown in the script). She must make sure that he says no more than what is in the script.

b 'Eternity was in our lips and eyes.' Cleopatra's use of 'our' (lines 35–7) possibly refers to herself (using the royal 'we'). As Cleopatra speaks, she must very firmly point to herself on every appropriate word (for example, 'I', 'me', 'my', 'queen', 'Egypt') and prod Antony even more firmly on every appropriate word (for example, 'thou', 'you', 'that eye', 'soldier', 'liar'). Afterwards talk together about what this pointing activity tells you about Cleopatra's mood.

c 'He is purposeful, so she is weak, pretending to faint; he is tender, she asks him to move away; he is puzzled, and she mocks him, attacking him for his infidelity to both Fulvia and herself.' This is how one critic described Cleopatra at this point. Present a version of lines 17–44 which shows the quickness and 'cunning' of her responses to Antony's words.

---

mouth-made not truly meant
no colour no excuse, pretext
sued staying begged to stay
brows' bent curve of the eyebrows
none our parts so poor none of my qualities, however poor
a race of heaven of divine origin

civil swords civil war
scrupulous faction petty squabbles
Upon ... state under our government
quietness ... change peace grows sick and must be purged by the blood-letting of war
safe safeguard

ANTONY The gods best know –
CLEOPATRA   O, never was there queen
　　　　So mightily betrayed! Yet at the first   25
　　　　I saw the treasons planted.
ANTONY   Cleopatra –
CLEOPATRA Why should I think you can be mine, and true,
　　　　Though you in swearing shake the thronèd gods,
　　　　Who have been false to Fulvia? Riotous madness,
　　　　To be entangled with those mouth-made vows,   30
　　　　Which break themselves in swearing!
ANTONY   Most sweet queen –
CLEOPATRA Nay, pray you, seek no colour for your going,
　　　　But bid farewell and go. When you sued staying,
　　　　Then was the time for words. No going then.
　　　　Eternity was in our lips and eyes,   35
　　　　Bliss in our brows' bent; none our parts so poor
　　　　But was a race of heaven. They are so still,
　　　　Or thou, the greatest soldier of the world,
　　　　Art turned the greatest liar.
ANTONY   How now, lady?
CLEOPATRA I would I had thy inches. Thou shouldst know   40
　　　　There were a heart in Egypt.
ANTONY   Hear me, queen:
　　　　The strong necessity of time commands
　　　　Our services awhile, but my full heart
　　　　Remains in use with you. Our Italy
　　　　Shines o'er with civil swords; Sextus Pompeius   45
　　　　Makes his approaches to the port of Rome;
　　　　Equality of two domestic powers
　　　　Breed scrupulous faction; the hated, grown to strength,
　　　　Are newly grown to love; the condemned Pompey,
　　　　Rich in his father's honour, creeps apace   50
　　　　Into the hearts of such as have not thrived
　　　　Upon the present state, whose numbers threaten;
　　　　And quietness, grown sick of rest, would purge
　　　　By any desperate change. My more particular,
　　　　And that which most with you should safe my going,   55
　　　　Is Fulvia's death.

Learning of Fulvia's death, Cleopatra begins a fresh outburst against Antony, seeing in his lack of grief for Fulvia a sign that his love for her will also be false. Antony becomes increasingly angry.

1 Unspoken thoughts (in groups of four)

Cleopatra and Antony mean much more than they actually say. Explore the nature of their complex emotional relationship in lines 57–106.

a *Alter egos*

Two of you are Cleopatra and Antony, the others are their *alter egos* (inner thoughts). As each character pauses at the end of his/her speech, the *alter egos* say what their character thinks. Try this several times until you are happy with the combination of inner thoughts and outer words. Show your version to the class.

b Pushing and pulling (in pairs)

Cleopatra chides, taunts and cajoles in her desire to make Antony stay. She pushes him away, then pulls him back. One moment she scornfully calls him 'this herculean Roman' (Antony's family claimed to be descended from the Greek hero Hercules). The next moment she cries 'O, my oblivion is a very Antony'. Antony also does his share of emotional/verbal pushing and pulling.

Feel the scornful or taunting 'pushing-words' and the cajoling or pleading 'pulling-words'. Hold the script in one hand and grasp your partner's shoulder with the other. As you read lines 60–106, push your partner away on the 'pushing-words' and pull him/her towards you on the 'pulling-words'.

Do this activity several times, then use the following questions to analyse your view of their relationship: How much pushing and pulling does Antony do? Where do they both pull together? Who is winning the emotional war of words?

---

garboils commotions, troubles
vials (the Romans placed bottles of tears into tombs of loved ones)
which are, or cease which will proceed or not
fire … slime sun that fertilises the mud of the Nile valley
thou affects you desire

lace tightly-laced clothing
trial test
meetly good acting
target shield
mends improves
does become … chafe acts the part of an angry man

CLEOPATRA Though age from folly could not give me freedom,
    It does from childishness. Can Fulvia die?
ANTONY She's dead, my queen.
                  [*He offers letters*]
    Look here, and at thy sovereign leisure read   60
    The garboils she awaked; at the last, best,
    See when and where she died.
CLEOPATRA   O most false love!
    Where be the sacred vials thou shouldst fill
    With sorrowful water? Now I see, I see,
    In Fulvia's death how mine received shall be.   65
ANTONY Quarrel no more, but be prepared to know
    The purposes I bear, which are, or cease,
    As you shall give th'advice. By the fire
    That quickens Nilus' slime, I go from hence
    Thy soldier, servant, making peace or war   70
    As thou affects.
CLEOPATRA   Cut my lace, Charmian, come!
    But let it be; I am quickly ill, and well,
    So Antony loves.
ANTONY   My precious queen, forbear,
    And give true evidence to his love which stands
    An honourable trial.
CLEOPATRA   So Fulvia told me.   75
    I prithee, turn aside and weep for her,
    Then bid adieu to me, and say the tears
    Belong to Egypt. Good now, play one scene
    Of excellent dissembling, and let it look
    Like perfect honour.
ANTONY   You'll heat my blood. No more.   80
CLEOPATRA You can do better yet; but this is meetly.
ANTONY Now by my sword –
CLEOPATRA   And target. Still he mends.
    But this is not the best. Look, prithee, Charmian,
    How this herculean Roman does become
    The carriage of his chafe.   85

Cleopatra searches for a suitable farewell to say to Antony. She asks forgiveness for her mood changes and wishes him victory and success.

1 Cleopatra's moods (in pairs)

In this scene, Cleopatra pretends indifference, feigns illness and deliberately goads Antony. She seems by turns reproachful, angry, scornful, sarcastic, helpless and humble. Copy and continue the chart below to show the range of Cleopatra's moods, tactics and motives in Scene 3.

Tactic	*Lines which show mood*	*Intention / effect*
Pretend to be ill and miserable	'I am sick and sullen.' 'Help me away, dear Charmian, I shall fall.'	To gain sympathy and worry Antony

Which moment do you think this production photograph shows?

my oblivion ... forgotten my forgetful memory, like Antony, has deserted me
But that ... subject if you weren't the queen of foolishness
'Tis sweating labour it is as painful as giving birth
bear ... so near the heart feel such foolishness so sincerely
becomings graces or changes
Eye appear
laurel victory the laurel wreath of victory

ANTONY I'll leave you, lady.

CLEOPATRA Courteous lord, one word.
        Sir, you and I must part, but that's not it;
        Sir, you and I have loved, but there's not it;
        That you know well. Something it is I would –   90
        O, my oblivion is a very Antony,
        And I am all forgotten.

ANTONY   But that your royalty
        Holds idleness your subject, I should take you
        For idleness itself.

CLEOPATRA   'Tis sweating labour
        To bear such idleness so near the heart
        As Cleopatra this. But sir, forgive me,   95
        Since my becomings kill me when they do not
        Eye well to you. Your honour calls you hence;
        Therefore be deaf to my unpitied folly,
        And all the gods go with you! Upon your sword   100
        Sit laurel victory, and smooth success
        Be strewed before your feet!

ANTONY   Let us go. Come;
        Our separation so abides and flies
        That thou, residing here, goes yet with me,
        And I, hence fleeting, here remain with thee.   105
        Away!

                    Exeunt

Octavius Caesar condemns Antony's indulgent and debauched life in Alexandria. Lepidus is kinder in his judgements of Antony's character. Caesar blames Antony for neglecting his duty to Rome.

1 First impressions (in pairs)

First words often reveal character. Speak lines 1–15 to each other and describe the kind of men you think Antony's partners are. Then list the differences in their manner of speech compared with Antony and Cleopatra's manner in Act 1 Scenes 1 and 3.

2 Octavius Caesar's criticisms of Antony
   (in groups of four)

Lepidus attempts to defend Antony, saying that it is because of his great virtues that his faults appear so terrible (lines 10–15). But Octavius Caesar states his case against Antony:

lines 16–23 Let us grant that Antony's behaviour is no significant blemish on his character ('composure'), though that is questionable.

lines 23–5 However, it is inexcusable that he should behave like that when we are left to cope with such difficulties in his absence.

lines 25–8 If his pleasure-seeking ('lightness', 'voluptuousness') was reserved only for his leisure time ('vacancy'), he would deserve no more than the unpleasant consequences of stomach disorders ('Full surfeits') and the symptoms of sexually transmitted disease ('dryness of his bones').

lines 28–33 But to waste ('confound') time when the fate of the whole Triumvirate is at stake is to deserve to be told off like a boy who, old enough to know better, deliberately seeks his own immediate ('present') pleasure and ignores his better judgement.

How far do you agree or sympathise with Caesar's arguments?

---

competitor partner
Ptolemy the Egyptian monarchy
gave audience listened to our
   messengers
find there read in the letter
abstract perfect example
spots of heaven stars

purchased gained by experience
stand the buffet exchange blows
foils disgraces, blemishes
drums him calls him to arms
speaks … ours proclaims that his
   and our survival is at stake
rate scold, tell off

ACT 1 SCENE 4
Rome

Enter CAESAR reading a letter, LEPIDUS, and their train

CAESAR You may see, Lepidus, and henceforth know,
　　　　It is not Caesar's natural vice to hate
　　　　Our great competitor. From Alexandria
　　　　This is the news: he fishes, drinks, and wastes
　　　　The lamps of night in revel; is not more manlike　　5
　　　　Than Cleopatra, nor the queen of Ptolemy
　　　　More womanly than he; hardly gave audience, or
　　　　Vouchsafed to think he had partners. You shall find there
　　　　A man who is the abstract of all faults
　　　　That all men follow.

LEPIDUS 　　　　　　　　I must not think there are　　10
　　　　Evils enough to darken all his goodness.
　　　　His faults in him seem as the spots of heaven,
　　　　More fiery by night's blackness, hereditary
　　　　Rather than purchased, what he cannot change
　　　　Than what he chooses.　　　　　　　　　　　15

CAESAR You are too indulgent. Let's grant it is not
　　　　Amiss to tumble on the bed of Ptolemy,
　　　　To give a kingdom for a mirth, to sit
　　　　And keep the turn of tippling with a slave,
　　　　To reel the streets at noon, and stand the buffet　　20
　　　　With knaves that smells of sweat. Say this becomes him –
　　　　As his composure must be rare indeed
　　　　Whom these things cannot blemish – yet must Antony
　　　　No way excuse his foils when we do bear
　　　　So great weight in his lightness. If he filled　　25
　　　　His vacancy with his voluptuousness,
　　　　Full surfeits and the dryness of his bones
　　　　Call on him for't. But to confound such time
　　　　That drums him from his sport and speaks as loud
　　　　As his own state and ours, 'tis to be chid　　30
　　　　As we rate boys who, being mature in knowledge,
　　　　Pawn their experience to their present pleasure
　　　　And so rebel to judgement.

> *Messengers report the growing threat of Sextus Pompeius as many*
> *ordinary Romans switch their allegiance to him. Pompey's allies, the*
> *pirates Menecrates and Menas, threaten the coasts of Italy.*

1 Great leaders? (in small groups)

Government of the Roman Republic was largely in the hands of the patricians (nobility), but whoever sought to control Rome needed the support of the ordinary citizens ('This common body'), who now seem to be switching their allegiance from the Triumvirate to Pompey.

Caesar the patrician compares the common people to a reed ('flag') in a river, swaying back and forth with the tide (lines 44–7). He couples two other images to this ('vagabond' = tramp or beggar and 'lackeying' = following like a servile servant). Turn to page 19, line 178, to see another patrician make a similarly contemptuous remark about the Roman people.

Improvise a conversation between a group of ordinary Roman citizens as they talk about the current political situation and the actions of their great leaders. These citizens may be aware of their leaders' opinions, but may well have reasons for questioning them.

2 'Menecrates and Menas, famous pirates'

The map on page 3 shows how important sea power was in the struggle for control of the Roman world. Events in the play are very much concerned with the command of the sea.

As you read on, note down all the words and images to do with the sea.

---

discontents disaffected people
Give him say he is
from the primal state since the earliest society
ebbed man man who has lost power
Comes … lacked is valued when no longer there

ear plough
keels ships
borders maritime coastal areas
Lack … on't turn pale at the thought
flush youth vigorous young men
Than could … resisted than an actual attack could ever do

Enter a MESSENGER

LEPIDUS   Here's more news.

MESSENGER Thy biddings have been done, and every hour,
          Most noble Caesar, shalt thou have report   35
          How 'tis abroad. Pompey is strong at sea,
          And it appears he is beloved of those
          That only have feared Caesar. To the ports
          The discontents repair, and men's reports
          Give him much wronged.   [*Exit*]
CAESAR   I should have known no less.   40
          It hath been taught us from the primal state
          That he which is was wished until he were;
          And the ebbed man, ne'er loved till ne'er worth love,
          Comes deared by being lacked. This common body,
          Like to a vagabond flag upon the stream,   45
          Goes to and back, lackeying the varying tide
          To rot itself with motion.

                [*Enter a second* MESSENGER]

MESSENGER Caesar, I bring thee word
          Menecrates and Menas, famous pirates,
          Makes the sea serve them, which they ear and wound   50
          With keels of every kind. Many hot inroads
          They make in Italy; the borders maritime
          Lack blood to think on't, and flush youth revolt.
          No vessel can peep forth but 'tis as soon
          Taken as seen; for Pompey's name strikes more   55
          Than could his war resisted.   [*Exit*]

Caesar recalls how great a general Antony once was: courageous and unafraid of hardship. He hopes Antony will leave his easy life in Egypt to support his partners in their war against Pompey.

1 Antony's past greatness (in small groups)

After the assassination of Julius Caesar, Antony faced many enemies. The consuls Hirtius and Pansa were sent by the Roman Senate to drive Antony out of Italy. Although the two consuls were killed in battle, Antony was nevertheless forced to retreat across the Alps. From Caesar's account of Antony's retreat (lines 56–72), write down the phrases which you think express genuine admiration and those which you think are ambiguous. What do you think is Caesar's real opinion of Antony?

Compare this picture of Caesar with those on pages 54 and 92.
What kind of man do they portray?

---

wassails drunken revelling	**So ... lanked not** did not even grow thin
whom (refers to 'famine')	
daintily elegantly	**show ... i'th'field** prepare for battle
stale urine	
gilded covered with yellow scum	**front** confront
deign not reject	**stirs** events, happenings
rudest wildest	**knew ... bond** am aware it is my duty
sheets covers	

CAESAR   Antony,
        Leave thy lascivious wassails. When thou once
        Was beaten from Modena, where thou slew'st
        Hirtius and Pansa, consuls, at thy heel
        Did famine follow, whom thou fought'st against,   60
        Though daintily brought up, with patience more
        Than savages could suffer. Thou didst drink
        The stale of horses and the gilded puddle
        Which beasts would cough at. Thy palate then did deign
        The roughest berry on the rudest hedge.   65
        Yea, like the stag when snow the pasture sheets,
        The barks of trees thou browsèd. On the Alps
        It is reported thou didst eat strange flesh,
        Which some did die to look on. And all this –
        It wounds thine honour that I speak it now –   70
        Was borne so like a soldier that thy cheek
        So much as lanked not.
LEPIDUS 'Tis pity of him.
CAESAR Let his shames quickly
        Drive him to Rome. 'Tis time we twain   75
        Did show ourselves i'th'field, and to that end
        Assemble we immediate council. Pompey
        Thrives in our idleness.
LEPIDUS   Tomorrow, Caesar,
        I shall be furnished to inform you rightly
        Both what by sea and land I can be able   80
        To front this present time.
CAESAR   Till which encounter,
        It is my business too. Farewell.
LEPIDUS Farewell, my lord. What you shall know meantime
        Of stirs abroad, I shall beseech you, sir,
        To let me be partaker.   85
CAESAR Doubt not, sir, I knew it for my bond.
                                        Exeunt [*separately*]

Cleopatra seeks to while away the time until Antony returns. She jokes with her eunuch servant about his sexual impotence, and wonders what Antony is doing at that moment in Rome.

1 Contrast Rome and Egypt (in groups of six)

Act out Scene 4, lines 74–86, immediately followed by Scene 5, lines 1–22. Contrast Caesar and Lepidus's hasty preparations for military action with Cleopatra's drowsy lethargy. Does Cleopatra's 'Ha, ha!' in line 3 suggest a laugh, or some other reaction or sound?

As you read through the rest of Scene 5, be aware of other glimpses of Egyptian attitudes and values.

'O Charmian,/ Where think'st thou he is now?'

mandragora plant with strong narcotic qualities

'tis treason that's a treacherous remark!

eunuch castrated male servant

aught anything

unseminared castrated

of Egypt from Egypt

affections passions, desires

Venus goddess of love (who seduced Mars, the god of war)

ACT 1   SCENE 5
Alexandria   Cleopatra's palace

Enter CLEOPATRA, CHARMIAN, IRAS, *and* MARDIAN

CLEOPATRA Charmian!

CHARMIAN Madam?

CLEOPATRA Ha, ha! Give me to drink mandragora.

CHARMIAN Why, madam?

CLEOPATRA That I might sleep out this great gap of time   5
    My Antony is away.

CHARMIAN You think of him too much.

CLEOPATRA O, 'tis treason!

CHARMIAN   Madam, I trust not so.

CLEOPATRA Thou, eunuch Mardian!

MARDIAN   What's your highness' pleasure?

CLEOPATRA Not now to hear thee sing. I take no pleasure   10
    In aught an eunuch has. 'Tis well for thee
    That, being unseminared, thy freer thoughts
    May not fly forth of Egypt. Hast thou affections?

MARDIAN Yes, gracious madam.

CLEOPATRA Indeed?   15

MARDIAN Not in deed, madam, for I can do nothing
    But what indeed is honest to be done.
    Yet have I fierce affections, and think
    What Venus did with Mars.

CLEOPATRA   O Charmian,
    Where think'st thou he is now? Stands he, or sits he?   20
    Or does he walk? Or is he on his horse?
    O happy horse, to bear the weight of Antony!

Cleopatra day-dreams about Antony's heroic qualities and recalls how she enchanted both Julius Caesar and Gnaeus Pompey. Alexas brings Cleopatra a pearl from Antony with his promise to extend her empire.

1 Your thoughts about Cleopatra (in groups of three)

Cleopatra's day-dreams and reminiscences are revealing:

Her sexuality Cleopatra recalls the great men who have been her lovers (lines 30–5). To 'stand', 'grow' and 'die' all suggest sexual arousal. List other words and phrases in this scene which might have erotic or sexual connotations.

Her love for Antony Some people see a passionate intensity in Cleopatra's vision of Antony. List the words and phrases which express her intense passion. Are they the words of a woman truly in love?

Her love of power 'Power is a great aphrodisiac', remarked one twentieth-century politician. Is there any evidence in this scene that this is true for Cleopatra?

Her cruelty Find the barbed comments and threats Cleopatra makes towards Mardian, Alexas and Charmian. Are these spoken good-naturedly, or is there a sadistic streak in her words?

Her elusiveness Cleopatra describes herself as 'wrinkled deep in time' (line 30). Is she being serious or self-mocking, or is she searching for compliments? Find other lines in this scene where you are uncertain whether Cleopatra is genuinely serious or play-acting.

Her contradictions 'Now I feed myself/With most delicious poison', says Cleopatra as she imagines Antony thinking of her (lines 27–8). Talk about how Cleopatra's dreams might be 'delicious' yet also 'poison'. This pairing of two contradictory ideas is termed an oxymoron. Create another oxymoron to describe Cleopatra's character.

Do bravely act proudly
wot'st thou do you know
Atlas god who supported the world on his shoulders
burgonet helmet, protector
Phoebus god of the sun
Broad-fronted with broad forehead

aspect gaze
tinct influence
mend improve
piece add to
arm-gaunt battle-hardened
beastly ... him obliterated by the noise of the horse

36

Do bravely, horse, for wot'st thou whom thou mov'st?
The demi-Atlas of this earth, the arm
And burgonet of men. He's speaking now,   25
Or murmuring 'Where's my serpent of old Nile?'
For so he calls me. Now I feed myself
With most delicious poison. Think on me,
That am with Phoebus' amorous pinches black
And wrinkled deep in time. Broad-fronted Caesar,   30
When thou wast here above the ground I was
A morsel for a monarch. And great Pompey
Would stand and make his eyes grow in my brow;
There would he anchor his aspect, and die
With looking on his life.   35

Enter ALEXAS *from Antony*

ALEXAS Sovereign of Egypt, hail!
CLEOPATRA How much unlike art thou Mark Antony!
    Yet coming from him, that great med'cine hath
    With his tinct gilded thee.
    How goes it with my brave Mark Antony?   40
ALEXAS Last thing he did, dear queen,
    He kissed – the last of many doubled kisses –
    This orient pearl. His speech sticks in my heart.
CLEOPATRA Mine ear must pluck it thence.
ALEXAS   'Good friend', quoth he,
    'Say the firm Roman to great Egypt sends   45
    This treasure of an oyster; at whose foot,
    To mend the petty present, I will piece
    Her opulent throne with kingdoms. All the East,
    Say thou, shall call her mistress.' So he nodded,
    And soberly did mount an arm-gaunt steed,   50
    Who neighed so high that what I would have spoke
    Was beastly dumbed by him.

Cleopatra praises Antony's balanced personality and determines to send him yet another letter. When Charmian praises Julius Caesar, Cleopatra threatens violence and dismisses her own youthful passion.

1 Alexas – a skilled politician?

According to the Greek historian Plutarch (see page 243), the historical Alexas was a skilled politician. Shakespeare's Alexas is also astute enough to make sure he tells Cleopatra what she wants to hear.

Write Alexas's diary entry in which he frankly describes his meetings with Antony and Cleopatra, and speculates on their political future. Does Alexas believe Cleopatra is impressed by Antony's message (lines 44–52)?

2 Catch the quicksilver Cleopatra (in groups of three)

Does Cleopatra ever stay still long enough for you to be certain just who she really is? Take parts and read lines 53–81.

a Identify each of Cleopatra's shifts of emotion, thought or attitude.

b In lines 73–5, Cleopatra threatens to give Charmian 'bloody teeth' for praising Julius Caesar. It may be friendly banter or genuine anger. Speak lines 66–81 both ways, then talk about Cleopatra's mood and the nature of her relationship with Charmian.

c 'My salad days' (days of youthful inexperience). Line 76 has become a familiar expression in English. Read pages 240–2 and decide if you think the historical Cleopatra was ever 'green in judgement'.

d Compare the Cleopatra of this scene with the Cleopatra of the first three scenes.

---

sad serious
well-divided well-balanced
'tis the man that's exactly what he's like
make their looks take their mood
violence of either wholehearted expression of either emotion

thee becomes suits you
several separate
paragon compare
I sing but after you I am only copying you
unpeople Egypt kill everyone, or send everyone as messengers

CLEOPATRA What, was he sad, or merry?
ALEXAS Like to the time o'th'year between the extremes
  Of hot and cold, he was nor sad nor merry.   55
CLEOPATRA O well-divided disposition! Note him,
  Note him, good Charmian, 'tis the man; but note him.
  He was not sad, for he would shine on those
  That make their looks by his; he was not merry,
  Which seemed to tell them his remembrance lay   60
  In Egypt with his joy; but between both.
  O heavenly mingle! Be'st thou sad or merry,
  The violence of either thee becomes,
  So does it no man else. – Met'st thou my posts?
ALEXAS Ay, madam, twenty several messengers.   65
  Why do you send so thick?
CLEOPATRA   Who's born that day
  When I forget to send to Antony
  Shall die a beggar. Ink and paper, Charmian.
  Welcome, my good Alexas. Did I, Charmian,
  Ever love Caesar so?
CHARMIAN   O, that brave Caesar!
CLEOPATRA Be choked with such another emphasis!   70
  Say, 'the brave Antony'.
CHARMIAN   The valiant Caesar!
CLEOPATRA By Isis, I will give thee bloody teeth
  If thou with Caesar paragon again
  My man of men.
CHARMIAN   By your most gracious pardon,
  I sing but after you.   75
CLEOPATRA   My salad days,
  When I was green in judgement, cold in blood,
  To say as I said then. But come, away,
  Get me ink and paper.
  He shall have every day a several greeting,
  Or I'll unpeople Egypt.   80

                                                   Exeunt

                          39

Looking back at Act 1
Activities for groups or individuals

1 Mini-saga
Tell the events of Act 1 as a mini-saga, a story of exactly fifty words.

2 A very public private affair
List the events in Act 1 that would interest a political journalist, then list the events that would interest a gossip columnist. Use your lists to present a dialogue between the two journalists as they prepare to write their articles.

3 The worlds of Egypt and Rome
What kind of gulf separates these two worlds? Think of at least six key words or phrases to describe the culture and values of each society (for example, Egypt 'pleasure-loving', Rome 'disciplined').

a For each location design stage sets which highlight the contrasts you see between the two worlds. Write notes to accompany each design, giving your reasons for presenting each world in that way.

b Create your own Egyptian tableau from Act 1. Photograph it if you can. Do the same for a Roman tableau.

4 Conflicting viewpoints
Many different views of Antony and Cleopatra are expressed in Act 1. Collect some of the positive and negative words and images used by other characters to describe them, and also words and images that Antony and Cleopatra use to describe themselves. Record them in a diagram like this:

Positive pictures of		Negative pictures of	
Antony	*Cleopatra*	*Antony*	*Cleopatra*
'demi–Atlas' 'firm Roman'	'great Egypt'	'strumpet's fool'	'cunning'

Use your diagram to write a paragraph on each character expressing *your* view of Antony and Cleopatra.

Two Egyptian moments.
Identify where you think
they come from in Act 1.

5 The to-and-fro of messengers (in small groups)

How differently do Antony, Cleopatra and Caesar deal with their
messengers? Rehearse each messenger's entrance and exit, then show
them in sequence at great speed to give an impression of how differently
each messenger is received.

6 Octavius Caesar

Caesar's name intrudes into the world of Egypt many times before he
appears in person. What impression do you have of him?

a Collect everything that people say about Caesar in Scenes 1–3.
What picture does this create of Antony's political partner?

b Compare this picture of Caesar with how he appears in Scene 4.
Then write a paragraph expressing *your* opinion of Caesar.

Pompey waits for a sign from the gods that he should make his bid for power. He comments on the divisions between Antony, Caesar and Lepidus and hopes Cleopatra's charms will keep Antony in Egypt.

1 Another player in the power game (in small groups)

Pompey is confident: 'If the great gods be just, they shall (must surely) assist/The deeds (efforts) of justest men' (lines 1–2). Find six reasons why he thinks his chance has come to strike against the Triumvirate.

2 Who's who? (in groups of seven)

Arrange three sets of chairs as Rome, Egypt and Sicily. Two of you sit 'in Egypt' as Antony and Cleopatra; two sit opposite 'in Rome' as Caesar and Lepidus (use name labels if it helps). Pompey, Menecrates and Menas are in the middle 'in Sicily'. As you speak, point, gesture or move to show whom you are talking about and what you think of them. For example:

> Pompey: ... 'I (point to self) shall do well/The people (gesture to audience) love me (point to self), and the sea is mine (point to self)/... Mark Antony (move towards Antony and gesture)/In Egypt sits (indicate Antony) at dinner...'.

Whenever Antony, Cleopatra, Caesar and Lepidus are pointed out, they must behave as Pompey describes them.

3 Cleopatra's power and Antony's weakness

Make a list of the words and phrases Pompey uses in lines 20–7 to describe Cleopatra's charms and Antony's sensuality. To help you:

line 24 Epicurus was a philosopher whose teachings were interpreted as recommending a life of sensual pleasure.
line 27 Lethe was a river in Hades (hell) from which the dead drank and totally forgot their past life.

---

what they ... deny a delay in answering prayers is not a refusal
Whiles ... sue for even as we plead, what we ask for is losing its value
Beg ... harms beg for things which will harm us
crescent growing (like the moon)

auguring prophesying
without doors outside Egypt
Salt lustful
waned faded
fuming befuddled with alcohol
cloyless ever mouth-watering
prorogue suspend, postpone

ACT 2 SCENE 1
Sicily Pompey's headquarters

Enter POMPEY, MENECRATES, *and* MENAS, *in battledress*

POMPEY If the great gods be just, they shall assist
　　　The deeds of justest men.
MENAS 　　　　　　　　　Know, worthy Pompey,
　　　That what they do delay they not deny.
POMPEY Whiles we are suitors to their throne, decays
　　　The thing we sue for.
MENAS 　　　　　　　　We, ignorant of ourselves,　　5
　　　Beg often our own harms, which the wise powers
　　　Deny us for our good; so find we profit
　　　By losing of our prayers.
POMPEY 　　　　　　　　I shall do well.
　　　The people love me, and the sea is mine;
　　　My powers are crescent, and my auguring hope　　10
　　　Says it will come to th'full. Mark Antony
　　　In Egypt sits at dinner, and will make
　　　No wars without doors. Caesar gets money where
　　　He loses hearts. Lepidus flatters both,
　　　Of both is flattered; but he neither loves,　　15
　　　Nor either cares for him.
MENAS 　　　　　　　　Caesar and Lepidus
　　　Are in the field. A mighty strength they carry.
POMPEY Where have you this? 'Tis false.
MENAS 　　　　　　　　From Silvius, sir.
POMPEY He dreams. I know they are in Rome together
　　　Looking for Antony. But all the charms of love,　　20
　　　Salt Cleopatra, soften thy waned lip!
　　　Let witchcraft joined with beauty, lust with both,
　　　Tie up the libertine in a field of feasts,
　　　Keep his brain fuming. Epicurean cooks,
　　　Sharpen with cloyless sauce his appetite,　　25
　　　That sleep and feeding may prorogue his honour
　　　Even till a Lethe'd dullness –　　　　*Enter* VARRIUS

　　　　　　　　How now, Varrius?

Varrius reports that Antony will soon be in Rome. Pompey is dismayed. He knows that Antony is a far better soldier than the others. Pompey suspects that the Triumvirate may now unite against him.

This is how the 1972 Royal Shakespeare Company production portrayed Pompey (right) and Menas (one of the 'famous pirates' described in Act 1 Scene 4, line 49). Mediterranean pirates were the scourge of merchant ships in Elizabethan as well as Roman times. Look at what Menas says in this scene. How does he speak – like a pirate or a trained military officer?

'**tis ... travel** he could have travelled even further in the time
amorous surfeiter excessively lustful man
donned his helm put on his helmet
rear ... our opinion think highly of ourselves

well greet meet as friends
did trespasses to harmed
moved incited, encouraged
pregnant obvious
square quarrel
It only ... upon our lives depend upon it

VARRIUS This is most certain that I shall deliver:
　　　　Mark Antony is every hour in Rome
　　　　Expected. Since he went from Egypt 'tis   30
　　　　A space for farther travel.
POMPEY I could have given less matter
　　　　A better ear. Menas, I did not think
　　　　This amorous surfeiter would have donned his helm
　　　　For such a petty war. His soldiership   35
　　　　Is twice the other twain. But let us rear
　　　　The higher our opinion, that our stirring
　　　　Can from the lap of Egypt's widow pluck
　　　　The ne'er-lust-wearied Antony.
MENAS　　　　　　　　　　　　I cannot hope
　　　　Caesar and Antony shall well greet together.   40
　　　　His wife that's dead did trespasses to Caesar;
　　　　His brother warred upon him, although, I think,
　　　　Not moved by Antony.
POMPEY　　　　　　　　　I know not, Menas,
　　　　How lesser enmities may give way to greater.
　　　　Were't not that we stand up against them all,   45
　　　　'Twere pregnant they should square between themselves,
　　　　For they have entertainèd cause enough
　　　　To draw their swords. But how the fear of us
　　　　May cement their divisions and bind up
　　　　The petty difference, we yet not know.   50
　　　　Be't as our gods will have't! It only stands
　　　　Our lives upon to use our strongest hands.
　　　　Come, Menas.

Exeunt

ACT 2   SCENE 2
Rome

Enter ENOBARBUS and LEPIDUS

LEPIDUS Good Enobarbus, 'tis a worthy deed,
　　　　And shall become you well, to entreat your captain
　　　　To soft and gentle speech.

Enobarbus refuses Lepidus's request to urge Antony to restrain his anger when he meets Caesar. Antony and Caesar enter from opposite sides. Lepidus pleads for co-operation and friendship.

1 Enobarbus and Lepidus – what's their tone? (in pairs)

At this vital meeting of the three self-appointed governors of the Roman world, Lepidus wants to heal the rift between Antony and Caesar. Enobarbus wants Antony to stand firm. The two men pick up and echo each other's words in lines 1–14 ('entreat', 'time', 'matter', 'small'). Try speaking these lines in different ways, for example:

- Lepidus: flattering, friendly, stern, cautioning
- Enobarbus: defiant, blustering, politely disagreeing.

Afterwards, decide which tones you think are most appropriate and why.

2 Entrances and political posturing (in groups of seven)

The atmosphere is tense for the meeting of the Triumvirate. When Antony and Caesar enter they do not even greet each other until Lepidus pleads with them to discuss things calmly.

Prepare a presentation of lines 1–34. Show the different groupings, the entrances from opposite sides, the tensions, and the action which could accompany Antony's words 'I should do thus'. Which leader seems most at ease with himself as they sit ready to talk?

Finish your presentation with a tableau (a 'frozen moment'). Make each character's position and expression reflect his thoughts. Hold the tableau for about thirty seconds. As each character in turn 'unfreezes', he must speak his thoughts in role.

---

look over Caesar's head stand tall
Mars god of war
Jupiter king of the gods
private stomaching personal resentments
compose well reach a satisfactory agreement
leaner action rend us less important reason divide us

What's amiss whatever is wrong
The rather for all the more because
Nor curstness ... matter let us not become bitter
and to fight and about to fight
Nay, then well, if you insist

ENOBARBUS   I shall entreat him
    To answer like himself. If Caesar move him,
    Let Antony look over Caesar's head   5
    And speak as loud as Mars. By Jupiter,
    Were I the wearer of Antonio's beard,
    I would not shave't today.
LEPIDUS 'Tis not a time for private stomaching.
ENOBARBUS Every time serves for the matter that is then born in't.   10
LEPIDUS But small to greater matters must give way.
ENOBARBUS Not if the small come first.
LEPIDUS Your speech is passion; but pray you stir
    No embers up. Here comes the noble Antony.

    Enter ANTONY *and* VENTIDIUS [*in conversation*]

ENOBARBUS And yonder Caesar.   15

    Enter CAESAR, MAECENAS, *and* AGRIPPA [*by another door,*
            also in conversation]

ANTONY If we compose well here, to Parthia.
    Hark, Ventidius.
                [*They confer apart*]
CAESAR I do not know, Maecenas. Ask Agrippa.
LEPIDUS Noble friends:
    That which combined us was most great, and let not   20
    A leaner action rend us. What's amiss,
    May it be gently heard. When we debate
    Our trivial difference loud, we do commit
    Murder in healing wounds. Then, noble partners,
    The rather for I earnestly beseech,   25
    Touch you the sourest points with sweetest terms,
    Nor curstness grow to th'matter.
ANTONY   'Tis spoken well.
    Were we before our armies, and to fight,
    I should do thus.
                Flourish
CAESAR Welcome to Rome.   30
ANTONY Thank you.
CAESAR Sit.
ANTONY Sit, sir.
CAESAR Nay, then.   [*They sit*]

Caesar claims that Antony's brother and wife made war against him, incited by Antony himself. Antony denies all responsibility for his family's actions, claiming that Fulvia was impossible to control.

1 Accusations, rebuttals, reconciliation (in groups of five)

Antony and Caesar meet face to face for the first time in the play. They have explanations to give and rifts to heal. To gain a first impression of their confrontation, take parts and read aloud lines 35–182.

Script an edited version of these lines (maximum length fifty lines). Include all of Caesar's complaints, Antony's responses and the final reconciliation. Rehearse your parts and perform your edited version.

2 Accusation and defence (in small groups)

In lines 44–5, Caesar says that Antony, while in Egypt, attempted to undermine Caesar's power ('you there/Did practise on my state').

What reasons does Caesar give for his accusation and what does Antony say in his defence (lines 47–77)? The following will help you:

'Catch at mine intent' = guess what I mean

'Was theme for you' = was all about you

'urge me in his act' = use my name as an excuse for his acts

'learning' = information

'reports/That drew their swords with you' = reporters who were your supporters

'Discredit my authority with yours' = injure both of us

'stomach' = inclination

'alike your cause' = as much reason as you

'did satisfy you' = gave you full information.

Decide whether you think Antony's tone changes when he moves from talking about his brother (lines 51–67) to talking about his wife (lines 67–70).

Chiefly i'th'world of all people
derogately dismissively
question business, concern
As matter ... with and pretend to have genuine grievances
laying defects ... to me accusing me of defects of judgement

lack/Very necessity ... thought have failed to understand
with ... attend condone
fronted opposed
snaffle ... easy you can easily control with a light bridle-bit

ANTONY I learn you take things ill which are not so,   35
Or, being, concern you not.
CAESAR   I must be laughed at
If or for nothing or a little, I
Should say myself offended, and with you
Chiefly i'th'world; more laughed at that I should
Once name you derogately, when to sound your name   40
It not concerned me.
ANTONY My being in Egypt, Caesar, what was't to you?
CAESAR No more than my residing here at Rome
Might be to you in Egypt. Yet if you there
Did practise on my state, your being in Egypt   45
Might be my question.
ANTONY   How intend you, 'practised'?
CAESAR You may be pleased to catch at mine intent
By what did here befall me. Your wife and brother
Made wars upon me, and their contestation
Was theme for you; you were the word of war.   50
ANTONY You do mistake your business. My brother never
Did urge me in his act. I did enquire it,
And have my learning from some true reports
That drew their swords with you. Did he not rather
Discredit my authority with yours,
And make the wars alike against my stomach,   55
Having alike your cause? Of this, my letters
Before did satisfy you. If you'll patch a quarrel,
As matter whole you have to make it with,
It must not be with this.
CAESAR   You praise yourself   60
By laying defects of judgement to me, but
You patched up your excuses.
ANTONY   Not so, not so.
I know you could not lack – I am certain on't –
Very necessity of this thought, that I,
Your partner in the cause 'gainst which he fought,   65
Could not with graceful eyes attend those wars
Which fronted mine own peace. As for my wife,
I would you had her spirit in such another;
The third o'th'world is yours, which with a snaffle
You may pace easy, but not such a wife.   70

Antony offers further excuses in response to Caesar's accusations, but denies breaking his oath of support. Fulvia's intrigues and his own neglect had prevented him from supplying Caesar with the promised aid.

---

1 Who's to blame? (in small groups)

Antony is very much on the defensive. List the charges that Caesar makes against him in lines 77–105. How often does Antony: (1) blame other people or 'circumstances'; (2) accept the blame himself; (3) convincingly answer Caesar's charges? It may help you decide if one person reads Antony's replies, pausing at each punctuation mark or sense unit. In the pauses, the others say 'someone else's fault' or 'his/her fault'. Repeat the process, but in the pauses the group now says 'my fault'. Which answers ring true?

Do you think Caesar has genuine grievances, or is he trying to 'patch' (manufacture) a quarrel, as Antony suggests in lines 58–60?

2 Wary manoeuvrings (in groups of four)

There is a subtle fluctuating tension in this scene. You can capture some of this in diagram form using thought bubbles:

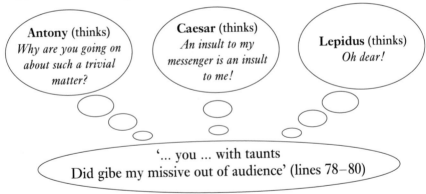

Show three other moments from lines 71–105 using similar diagrams.

---

garboils disturbances, revolts
not wanted ... too were not
  without political cunning either
rioting debauching yourself
missive messenger
ere admitted without permission
did want ... i'th'morning had a
  hangover

article exact terms
bound me ... knowledge drugged
  me so I didn't know what I was
  doing
mine honesty ... without it I
  shall be honest in whatever I do
motive cause (of her actions)

ENOBARBUS Would we had all such wives, that the men might go to
    wars with the women!
ANTONY So much uncurbable, her garboils, Caesar,
    Made out of her impatience – which not wanted
    Shrewdness of policy too – I grieving grant   75
    Did you too much disquiet. For that you must
    But say I could not help it.
CAESAR   I wrote to you
    When rioting in Alexandria; you
    Did pocket up my letters, and with taunts
    Did gibe my missive out of audience.   80
ANTONY Sir, he fell upon me ere admitted, then;
    Three kings I had newly feasted, and did want
    Of what I was i'th'morning. But next day
    I told him of myself, which was as much
    As to have asked him pardon. Let this fellow   85
    Be nothing of our strife; if we contend,
    Out of our question wipe him.
CAESAR   You have broken
    The article of your oath, which you shall never
    Have tongue to charge me with.
LEPIDUS Soft, Caesar!
                                          90
ANTONY No, Lepidus, let him speak.
    The honour is sacred which he talks on now,
    Supposing that I lacked it. But on, Caesar –
    The article of my oath.
CAESAR To lend me arms and aid when I required them,   95
    The which you both denied.
ANTONY   Neglected, rather;
    And then when poisoned hours had bound me up
    From mine own knowledge. As nearly as I may
    I'll play the penitent to you, but mine honesty
    Shall not make poor my greatness, nor my power   100
    Work without it. Truth is that Fulvia,
    To have me out of Egypt, made wars here,
    For which myself, the ignorant motive, do
    So far ask pardon as befits mine honour
    To stoop in such a case.
LEPIDUS   'Tis noble spoken.   105

Enobarbus suggests that Antony and Caesar should pretend friendship until Pompey is defeated. Caesar thinks reconciliation is impossible. Agrippa proposes a solution – Caesar's sister, Octavia.

1 How sincere is this reconciliation? (in groups of six)

Antony apologises (lines 96–105) for his neglect of duty and for his wife's interference. Lepidus and Maecenas both urge friendship, but Enobarbus and Caesar have reservations. Take parts and read lines 106–32. Then talk together about whether you think Antony and Caesar genuinely wish to be reconciled (at least for the time being).

2 Has Caesar planned this moment? (in groups of eight)

Agrippa suggests that a marriage between Octavia and Antony would cement a new alliance. Did Caesar instruct Agrippa to do this when they entered deep in conversation at line 15? Divide into two groups and present two versions of the reconciliation (lines 121–62).

Group 1 (four students): your Caesar has earlier instructed Agrippa to suggest a marriage. Devise moves and actions which hint at a conspiracy between the two. One student is Caesar's *alter ego* who interrupts proceedings and reveals Caesar's true intentions.

Group 2 (four students): your Caesar is surprised by Agrippa's suggestion and needs time to think. Show this. Caesar's *alter ego* should reveal his surprise and hasty thought processes before Caesar finally agrees to the marriage.

Present your two versions and decide which is the more convincing.

---

griefs grievances
quite completely
present need current crisis
Speaks argues powerfully
atone reconcile
soldier only ignorant of politics
presence distinguished company
Go to, then very well then

considerate thinking (he may be silent but he can still think!)
conditions temperaments
hoop metal band around a barrel
staunch firmly together
your reproof ... rashness you would deserve to be rebuked

MAECENAS If it might please you to enforce no further
          The griefs between ye; to forget them quite
          Were to remember that the present need
          Speaks to atone you.
LEPIDUS   Worthily spoken, Maecenas.
ENOBARBUS Or, if you borrow one another's love for the instant,   110
    you may, when you hear no more words of Pompey, return it
    again. You shall have time to wrangle in when you have nothing
    else to do.
ANTONY Thou art a soldier only. Speak no more.
ENOBARBUS That truth should be silent I had almost forgot.   115
ANTONY You wrong this presence, therefore speak no more.
ENOBARBUS Go to, then; your considerate stone.
CAESAR I do not much dislike the matter, but
          The manner of his speech; for't cannot be
          We shall remain in friendship, our conditions   120
          So differing in their acts. Yet if I knew
          What hoop should hold us staunch, from edge to edge
          O'th'world I would pursue it.
AGRIPPA Give me leave, Caesar.
CAESAR Speak, Agrippa.
AGRIPPA Thou hast a sister by the mother's side,   125
          Admired Octavia. Great Mark Antony
          Is now a widower.
CAESAR   Say not so, Agrippa.
          If Cleopatra heard you, your reproof
          Were well deserved of rashness.   130
ANTONY I am not married, Caesar. Let me hear
          Agrippa further speak.

Agrippa suggests marriage between Antony and Caesar's sister, Octavia, to end all dispute between the two men. Caesar and Antony agree. Caesar hopes the marriage will seal their alliance.

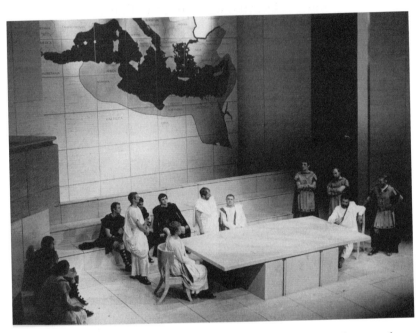

Tense negotiations. Above and on page 92 are production photographs taken at different points in the meeting between Caesar and Antony. Identify the characters in each photograph. Say which lines you think are being spoken at these moments and give reasons for your choices.

amity friendship
take Antony let Antony take
jealousies suspicions
import bring
Truths ... tales reports of your
  quarrels will seem merely rumours
present unconsidered

By duty ruminated born out of
  my loyal concern
touched/With affected by
impediment objecting
never ... loves may our friendship
  never desert us

AGRIPPA To hold you in perpetual amity,
       To make you brothers, and to knit your hearts
       With an unslipping knot, take Antony   135
       Octavia to his wife, whose beauty claims
       No worse a husband than the best of men,
       Whose virtue and whose general graces speak
       That which none else can utter. By this marriage
       All little jealousies, which now seem great,   140
       And all great fears, which now import their dangers,
       Would then be nothing. Truths would be tales,
       Where now half tales be truths. Her love to both
       Would each to other and all loves to both
       Draw after her. Pardon what I have spoke,   145
       For 'tis a studied, not a present thought,
       By duty ruminated.
ANTONY   Will Caesar speak?
CAESAR Not till he hears how Antony is touched
       With what is spoke already.
ANTONY What power is in Agrippa   150
       If I would say, 'Agrippa, be it so',
       To make this good?
CAESAR   The power of Caesar, and
       His power unto Octavia.
ANTONY   May I never
       To this good purpose, that so fairly shows,
       Dream of impediment! Let me have thy hand   155
       Further this act of grace; and from this hour
       The heart of brothers govern in our loves
       And sway our great designs!
CAESAR   There's my hand.
              [*They clasp hands*]
       A sister I bequeath you whom no brother
       Did ever love so dearly. Let her live   160
       To join our kingdoms and our hearts; and never
       Fly off our loves again!
LEPIDUS   Happily, amen!

Lepidus warns that Pompey must be confronted before he has time to strike. The Triumvirs agree to move against Pompey after the marriage. Maecenas and Agrippa question Enobarbus about Egypt.

1 Honour and reputation (in small groups)

Honour and reputation matter greatly to these men of power. There have been problems even with which man sits down first (lines 30–4). Now, as they prepare to fight Pompey, Antony's sense of honour requires him to remember to thank his enemy, Pompey, for his recent kindnesses ('strange courtesies and great')! Antony must not be thought ungrateful ('Lest my remembrance suffer ill report').

Find other lines in this scene where Antony talks of honour and decide what prompts his remarks. Do you think Caesar is equally concerned about personal honour and reputation?

2 'The business we have talked of' (in groups of three)

The 'business' is Antony's marriage to Octavia, an event which will significantly affect future events. What do you think is uppermost in each of the Triumvir's minds in lines 163–82: the campaign against Pompey, or the marriage between Antony and Octavia?

3 A change of mood

The leaders' departure allows their officers to relax and indulge in some gossip. Advise the actors playing Enobarbus, Maecenas and Agrippa on what they might do at line 182 to create a different atmosphere.

---

strange remarkable
only at least
At heel of immediately after
presently at once
So is the fame so it is reported
spoke together joined battle
Half the heart close friend

digested settled
stayed well by't had a great time
day ... countenance all through
 the day
by an eagle compared to an eagle
square to accurate about
devised invented

ANTONY I did not think to draw my sword 'gainst Pompey,
    For he hath laid strange courtesies and great
    Of late upon me. I must thank him only,   165
    Lest my remembrance suffer ill report;
    At heel of that, defy him.
LEPIDUS   Time calls upon's.
    Of us must Pompey presently be sought,
    Or else he seeks out us.
ANTONY Where lies he?   170
CAESAR About the Mount Misena.
ANTONY What is his strength by land?
CAESAR Great and increasing;
    But by sea he is an absolute master.
ANTONY So is the fame.   175
    Would we had spoke together! Haste we for it.
    Yet, ere we put ourselves in arms, dispatch we
    The business we have talked of.
CAESAR   With most gladness,
    And do invite you to my sister's view,
    Whither straight I'll lead you.   180
ANTONY Let us, Lepidus, not lack your company.
LEPIDUS Noble Antony, not sickness should detain me.
    Flourish. Exeunt [Caesar, Antony, Lepidus, and Ventidius].
          Enobarbus, Agrippa, Maecenas remain
MAECENAS Welcome from Egypt, sir.
ENOBARBUS Half the heart of Caesar, worthy Maecenas! My hon-
    ourable friend Agrippa!   185
AGRIPPA Good Enobarbus!
MAECENAS We have cause to be glad that matters are so well
    digested. You stayed well by't in Egypt.
ENOBARBUS Ay, sir, we did sleep day out of countenance, and made
    the night light with drinking.   190
MAECENAS Eight wild boars roasted whole at a breakfast, and but
    twelve persons there. Is this true?
ENOBARBUS This was but as a fly by an eagle. We had much more
    monstrous matter of feast, which worthily deserved noting.
MAECENAS She's a most triumphant lady, if report be square to her.   195
ENOBARBUS When she first met Mark Antony, she pursed up his
    heart upon the river of Cydnus.
AGRIPPA There she appeared indeed, or my reporter devised well
    for her.

Enobarbus describes the magnificent spectacle of Antony and Cleopatra's first meeting. Cleopatra's royal barge, with its dazzling queen, sailed up the River Cydnus. Antony was enchanted.

1 'It beggared all description' (in small groups)

Even the cynical Enobarbus has to admit to the power of Cleopatra's appearance. To describe it exhausts ('beggars') the powers of language. Not even the famous portrait of Venus – where the artist's 'fancy' (imagination) created a vision far more powerful than anything in nature – can match Cleopatra's art (lines 210–11).

a Plan a film version. As Enobarbus speaks lines 200–36, flashbacks will show key moments of Antony and Cleopatra's first meeting. Choose the lines you want to use for flashbacks and *either* storyboard these sections, with sketches of the flashbacks to be shown; *or* create a tableau for each flashback moment, with Enobarbus moving around the frozen pictures pointing to each detail as he speaks.

b Speak it! Learn sections and speak them in different ways. Experiment with choral speaking, echoing, whispering and other methods.

c Cleopatra the politician. Why should she have gone to so much trouble to impress Antony? A possible answer is on page 241.

d An artist at work. Cleopatra's arrival on the River Cydnus was magnificently stage-managed. Find quotations to show how she designed the spectacle to appeal to Antony's five senses (sight, sound, taste, smell and touch).

cloth ... tissue very rich fabric
Cupids gods of love
divers-coloured iridescent
Nereides sea-nymphs
tended ... eyes attended to her
  every glance or nod
bends bowing movements

tackle ropes, rigging
yarely ... office nimbly perform
  their tasks
upon her because of her
but for vacancy but for the fact
  that nature abhors a vacuum
his ordinary the price of his meal

ENOBARBUS I will tell you.   200
  The barge she sat in, like a burnished throne
  Burned on the water. The poop was beaten gold;
  Purple the sails, and so perfumèd that
  The winds were lovesick with them. The oars were silver,
  Which to the tune of flutes kept stroke, and made   205
  The water which they beat to follow faster,
  As amorous of their strokes. For her own person,
  It beggared all description: she did lie
  In her pavilion – cloth of gold, of tissue –
  O'erpicturing that Venus where we see   210
  The fancy outwork nature. On each side her
  Stood pretty dimpled boys, like smiling Cupids,
  With divers-coloured fans, whose wind did seem
  To glow the delicate cheeks which they did cool,
  And what they undid did.
AGRIPPA   O rare for Antony!   215
ENOBARBUS Her gentlewomen, like the Nereides,
  So many mermaids, tended her i'th'eyes,
  And made their bends adornings. At the helm
  A seeming mermaid steers. The silken tackle
  Swell with the touches of those flower-soft hands,   220
  That yarely frame the office. From the barge
  A strange invisible perfume hits the sense
  Of the adjacent wharfs. The city cast
  Her people out upon her; and Antony,
  Enthroned i'th'market-place, did sit alone,   225
  Whistling to th'air, which, but for vacancy,
  Had gone to gaze on Cleopatra too,
  And made a gap in nature.
AGRIPPA   Rare Egyptian!
ENOBARBUS Upon her landing, Antony sent to her,
  Invited her to supper. She replied,   230
  It should be better he became her guest,
  Which she entreated. Our courteous Antony,
  Whom ne'er the word of 'No' woman heard speak,
  Being barbered ten times o'er, goes to the feast,
  And for his ordinary pays his heart   235
  For what his eyes ate only.

Agrippa and Enobarbus tell of Cleopatra's escapades. Maecenas believes Antony must now abandon her for Octavia, but Enobarbus knows she will always fascinate Antony. In Scene 3, Antony promises to reform.

1 Cleopatra's 'infinite variety' (in small groups)

Maecenas and Agrippa are fascinated by the goings-on in Egypt, but perhaps do not understand Cleopatra's real power. Agrippa sees it as merely sexual attraction (lines 236–8). Work out the metaphor in which he refers to 'sword', 'ploughed' and 'cropped'. But perhaps he does sense something of Cleopatra's magic when he calls her 'Royal wench' (line 235). Which two contradictory qualities does this phrase suggest?

Enobarbus sees much more. Even Cleopatra's faults are bewitching charms. How many of Cleopatra's 'beguiling faults' does he mention in lines 236–55? Talk together about what you think Enobarbus means when he talks of Cleopatra's 'infinite variety'.

2 Antony, Octavia and Cleopatra (in groups of six)

The two women in Antony's life are presented in quick sequence: Cleopatra by report in Scene 2; Octavia directly in Scene 3. Present the opposite page so that Scene 3 follows quickly on from Scene 2. Compare Octavia's first appearance with Cleopatra's in Act 1 Scene 1. Do you think Octavia will 'settle/The heart of Antony' as Maecenas hopes?

3 'Enter ANTONY, CAESAR, OCTAVIA between them' (in groups of three)

This stage direction suggests that Octavia is a woman caught between two powerful men. As you rehearse lines 1–9, focus on Octavia's point of view. How should she say lines 2–4? Whom does she look at as she speaks?

Caesar Julius Caesar (see page 240)

cropped gave birth (to Caesar's son, Caesarion)

breathless ... forth her very breathlessness is charming

cloy dull, satiate, deaden

Become themselves make themselves attractive

riggish lustful

lottery prize, gift of fortune

Read not ... report don't believe what people say of me

kept my square behaved properly

AGRIPPA   Royal wench!
        She made great Caesar lay his sword to bed;
        He ploughed her, and she cropped.
ENOBARBUS   I saw her once
        Hop forty paces through the public street,
        And having lost her breath, she spoke, and panted,   240
        That she did make defect perfection
        And, breathless, power breathe forth.
MAECENAS Now Antony must leave her utterly.
ENOBARBUS Never. He will not.
        Age cannot wither her, nor custom stale   245
        Her infinite variety. Other women cloy
        The appetites they feed, but she makes hungry
        Where most she satisfies. For vilest things
        Become themselves in her, that the holy priests
        Bless her when she is riggish.   250
MAECENAS If beauty, wisdom, modesty can settle
        The heart of Antony, Octavia is
        A blessèd lottery to him.
AGRIPPA   Let us go.
        Good Enobarbus, make yourself my guest
        Whilst you abide here.
ENOBARBUS   Humbly, sir, I thank you.   *Exeunt* 255

ACT 2   SCENE 3
Rome   Caesar's house

Enter ANTONY, CAESAR, OCTAVIA *between them*

ANTONY The world, and my great office, will sometimes
        Divide me from your bosom.
OCTAVIA   All which time
        Before the gods my knee shall bow my prayers
        To them for you.
ANTONY   Good night, sir. My Octavia,
        Read not my blemishes in the world's report.   5
        I have not kept my square, but that to come
        Shall all be done by th'rule. Good night, dear lady.
OCTAVIA Good night, sir.
CAESAR Good night.
                                        Exit [*with Octavia*]

61

The Soothsayer advises Antony to return to Egypt, because if he stays with Caesar he will be overshadowed. Antony recognises the truth of this warning and determines to return to Cleopatra.

1 Supernatural warnings (in groups of six)

This is not the first time that characters in the play believe supernatural forces are at work (remember Act 1 Scene 2 and Act 2 Scene 1).

- Warn Antony. Two of you are Antony and the Soothsayer. The others encircle them. Read lines 10–42 aloud. When the Soothsayer speaks a warning, the whole group echoes it. Make the warnings very real and urgent.

- Daemons and angels. The Soothsayer sees Antony's 'daemon/ angel' (guardian spirit) losing its power beside Caesar's spirit. For Antony, this explains all too well his ill-luck in contests against Caesar. To enact what the Soothsayer sees, two of you slowly read aloud lines 15–39. The rest perform a dumb-show, or mime, showing Antony and Caesar with their invisible 'daemons/angels'.

2 A divided mind (in small groups)

Moments after promising Octavia, his newly betrothed bride, that he will mend his ways, Antony resolves to return to Cleopatra ('I'th'East my pleasure lies').

Either: imagine you are Ventidius, Antony's trusted lieutenant. Antony has asked you to advise him on future policy. Write an official report assessing the merits of Antony's two options: to remain in Rome or return to the East.

Or: write Ventidius's private diary entry, commenting on his commander and the decisions he has made.

---

thither to Egypt
in my motion intuitively
hie you go quickly
keeps safeguards
Where Caesar's is not when not
  near Caesar's guardian spirit
and of that and because of that

lustre thickens brilliance dims
art or hap skill or mere luck
cunning skill
speeds wins
cocks/quails fighting birds
inhooped in the fighting area

Enter SOOTHSAYER

ANTONY Now, sirrah: you do wish yourself in Egypt?   10
SOOTHSAYER Would I had never come from thence, nor you thither!
ANTONY If you can, your reason?
SOOTHSAYER I see it in my motion, have it not in my tongue; but yet
    hie you to Egypt again.
ANTONY Say to me, whose fortunes shall rise higher,   15
    Caesar's or mine?
SOOTHSAYER Caesar's.
    Therefore, O Antony, stay not by his side.
    Thy daemon – that thy spirit which keeps thee – is
    Noble, courageous, high unmatchable,   20
    Where Caesar's is not. But near him thy angel
    Becomes afeard, as being o'erpowered; therefore
    Make space enough between you.
ANTONY   Speak this no more.
SOOTHSAYER To none but thee; no more but when to thee.
    If thou dost play with him at any game,   25
    Thou art sure to lose; and of that natural luck
    He beats thee 'gainst the odds. Thy lustre thickens
    When he shines by. I say again, thy spirit
    Is all afraid to govern thee near him;
    But, he away, 'tis noble.
ANTONY   Get thee gone.   30
    Say to Ventidius I would speak with him.
                             Exit [Soothsayer]
    He shall to Parthia. – Be it art or hap,
    He hath spoken true. The very dice obey him,
    And in our sports my better cunning faints
    Under his chance. If we draw lots, he speeds;   35
    His cocks do win the battle still of mine
    When it is all to naught, and his quails ever
    Beat mine, inhooped, at odds. I will to Egypt;
    And though I make this marriage for my peace,
    I'th'East my pleasure lies.

Enter VENTIDIUS

                  O, come, Ventidius.   40
    You must to Parthia; your commission's ready.
    Follow me and receive't.   *Exeunt*

Maecenas and Agrippa prepare to join their generals at Misena to fight Pompey. Lepidus will take a longer route. In Alexandria, Cleopatra moodily awaits Antony's return.

1 Hastening and waiting (in groups of seven)

Rome is a world of business-like activity as Lepidus urges Maecenas and Agrippa to hurry after Antony and Caesar. The Egyptian court in Alexandria, by contrast, seeks to entertain a bored and listless Cleopatra. Form two groups and work through the script opposite as follows:

Group 1: prepare a presentation of Scene 4. Learn the lines and block your moves (decide where characters stand). Create a sense of pace and urgency.

Group 2: prepare a presentation of Scene 5 (lines 1–9). Think about the atmosphere, the music and the sexual jokes. Block your moves and learn your lines.

Present your versions to the class so that one scene flows quickly into the next to establish the contrast between the two worlds.

2 Smiles and storms (the whole class)

Pity the poor messenger who must bring Cleopatra the news of Antony's marriage! Her moods swing swiftly, violently and savagely during Scene 5. Three of you take the parts of Cleopatra, Charmian and the Messenger. The rest form two groups, one on each side of the queen. Read through the whole scene. As the three characters speak their lines:

Group 1: echo every 'kindly' thing Cleopatra says. You are her calm and charming side, full of smiling promises and gifts.

Group 2: echo violently every insult and threat. You are her fiery and cruel side.

---

e'en but kiss just kiss
th'Mount Mount Misenum (Misena)
do draw ... about cause me to take a longer route
win ... upon me gain two days on me

moody melancholy
that trade in who engage in
good will good intention, or sexual desire
I'll none now I won't play now

ACT 2 SCENE 4
Rome

Enter LEPIDUS, MAECENAS, *and* AGRIPPA

LEPIDUS Trouble yourselves no further. Pray you hasten
    Your generals after.
AGRIPPA   Sir, Mark Antony
    Will e'en but kiss Octavia, and we'll follow.
LEPIDUS Till I shall see you in your soldiers' dress,
    Which will become you both, farewell.
MAECENAS   We shall,   5
    As I conceive the journey, be at th'Mount
    Before you, Lepidus.
LEPIDUS   Your way is shorter;
    My purposes do draw me much about.
    You'll win two days upon me.
MAECENAS, AGRIPPA   Sir, good success!
LEPIDUS Farewell.   *Exeunt*   10

ACT 2 SCENE 5
Alexandria   Cleopatra's palace

Enter CLEOPATRA, CHARMIAN, IRAS, *and* ALEXAS

CLEOPATRA Give me some music; music, moody food
    Of us that trade in love.
ALL   The music, ho!

Enter MARDIAN *the eunuch*

CLEOPATRA Let it alone. Let's to billiards. Come, Charmian.
CHARMIAN My arm is sore. Best play with Mardian.
CLEOPATRA As well a woman with an eunuch played   5
    As with a woman. Come, you'll play with me, sir?
MARDIAN As well as I can, madam.
CLEOPATRA And when good will is showed, though't come too short,
    The actor may plead pardon. I'll none now.

The thought of fishing reminds Cleopatra of the tricks and amorous games that she has played with Antony. A Messenger brings news from Rome. Cleopatra senses that something is wrong.

1 'Like a Fury crowned with snakes'

The Furies were spirits of vengeance from the Underworld. They wore black and bloody garments and had writhing serpents instead of hair. They held a burning torch in one hand and a whip of scorpions in the other.

Hercules in women's clothes. Romans satirised Antony's affair with Cleopatra by showing him as Hercules bewitched by Omphale. According to legend, she dressed him in her clothes and gave him wool to spin (a woman's task), while she wore his lion skin and helmet and wielded his club (see lines 22–3).

---

angle fishing rod
betray deceive, trick
salt dried, preserved
ninth hour 9.00 a.m.
tires head-dresses, or robes
Philippan (named after the Battle of Philippi – see page 241)

yield grant, or report
sirrah (mode of address to inferiors)
we use / To say we often say
Bring it to that if you mean that
tart a favour sour an expression
formal human

Give me mine angle; we'll to the river. There,   10
My music playing far off, I will betray
Tawny-finned fishes. My bended hook shall pierce
Their slimy jaws, and as I draw them up
I'll think them every one an Antony
And say, 'Aha! You're caught.'

CHARMIAN   'Twas merry when   15
You wagered on your angling, when your diver
Did hang a salt fish on his hook, which he
With fervency drew up.

CLEOPATRA   That time? – O times! –
I laughed him out of patience; and that night
I laughed him into patience, and next morn,   20
Ere the ninth hour, I drunk him to his bed;
Then put my tires and mantles on him, whilst
I wore his sword Philippan.

Enter a MESSENGER

                              O, from Italy!
Ram thou thy fruitful tidings in mine ears,
That long time have been barren.

MESSENGER   Madam, madam –   25

CLEOPATRA Antonio's dead! If thou say so, villain,
Thou kill'st thy mistress; but well and free,
If thou so yield him, there is gold, and here
My bluest veins to kiss – a hand that kings
Have lipped, and trembled kissing.   30

MESSENGER First, madam, he is well.

CLEOPATRA Why, there's more gold. But, sirrah, mark, we use
To say the dead are well. Bring it to that,
The gold I give thee will I melt and pour
Down thy ill-uttering throat.   35

MESSENGER Good madam, hear me.

CLEOPATRA Well, go to, I will.
But there's no goodness in thy face, if Antony
Be free and healthful – so tart a favour
To trumpet such good tidings! If not well,   40
Thou shouldst come like a Fury crowned with snakes,
Not like a formal man.

MESSENGER   Will't please you hear me?

When Cleopatra finally hears the news of Antony's marriage to Octavia, she explodes, striking the Messenger to the floor and dragging him by the hair.

---

1 The volcano erupts (in pairs)

Do you find Cleopatra's behaviour savage, irrational, undignified or comic? Or do your sympathies lie with the deserted queen? Try speaking lines 23–108 in different ways:

a Cleopatra as cruel, threatening, violent and sadistic.

b Cleopatra as anxious and frightened. Her violent anger is a manifestation of her great love for Antony, whom she fears she has lost.

How might the Messenger react to these two Cleopatras? Will he smirk at the mention of 'bed' and 'married' (lines 60–1), or will he be almost too terrified to utter them? How do Charmian and Iras react?

2 'I'll set thee in a shower of gold' (in small groups)

The gold and pearls that Cleopatra promises to shower on the Messenger in lines 46–7 may refer to the custom of sprinkling eastern monarchs with pearls and gold dust at their coronation.

Cleopatra's language in this scene is full of hyperbole (exaggerated statements or images). Copy out the table below and list the extravagant statements she makes in lines 25–108:

Hyperbole of abuse and threat	Hyperbole of compliment and reward

---

ere before
does allay ... precedence spoils what has begun so promisingly
Fie upon shame upon
malefactor criminal
Pour ... mine ear tell me everything

bound obliged, or married
turn favour
spurn kick
hales drags by the hair
ling'ring long-lasting
pickle preserving fluid, brine

CLEOPATRA I have a mind to strike thee ere thou speak'st.
　　　　　Yet if thou say Antony lives, is well,
　　　　　Or friends with Caesar, or not captive to him,　　　　　45
　　　　　I'll set thee in a shower of gold and hail
　　　　　Rich pearls upon thee.
MESSENGER　　　　　　　　　Madam, he's well.
CLEOPATRA　　　　　　　　　　　　　Well said.
MESSENGER And friends with Caesar.
CLEOPATRA　　　　　　　　　Thou'rt an honest man.
MESSENGER Caesar and he are greater friends than ever.
CLEOPATRA Make thee a fortune from me.
MESSENGER　　　　　　　　　　　But yet, madam –　　　50
CLEOPATRA I do not like 'But yet'; it does allay
　　　　　The good precedence. Fie upon 'But yet'!
　　　　　'But yet' is as a gaoler to bring forth
　　　　　Some monstrous malefactor. Prithee, friend,
　　　　　Pour out the pack of matter to mine ear,　　　　　55
　　　　　The good and bad together: he's friends with Caesar,
　　　　　In state of health, thou say'st, and, thou say'st, free.
MESSENGER Free, madam? No! I made no such report.
　　　　　He's bound unto Octavia.
CLEOPATRA　　　　　　　　For what good turn?
MESSENGER For the best turn i'th'bed.
CLEOPATRA　　　　　　　　　　I am pale, Charmian.　　　60
MESSENGER Madam, he's married to Octavia.
CLEOPATRA The most infectious pestilence upon thee!
　　　　　　　　　　　Strikes him down
MESSENGER Good madam, patience.
CLEOPATRA　　　　　　　　　What say you?
　　　　　　　　　　Strikes him
　　　　　　　　　　　　　　Hence,
　　　　　Horrible villain, or I'll spurn thine eyes
　　　　　Like balls before me! I'll unhair thy head!　　　　　65
　　　　　　　　She hales him up and down
　　　　　Thou shalt be whipped with wire, and stewed in brine,
　　　　　Smarting in ling'ring pickle!
MESSENGER　　　　　　　　Gracious madam,
　　　　　I that do bring the news made not the match.

Despite Cleopatra's anger, the Messenger confirms that Antony has married. Cleopatra threatens him with a knife. He flees. When summoned to return, the Messenger is again interrogated.

1 'Melt Egypt into Nile' (in small groups)

Cleopatra's rage and despair at losing Antony (line 79) echo closely Antony's equally extravagant language in the opening scene of the play ('Let Rome in Tiber melt...', line 35). Talk about the pictures and the meanings their 'melting' images create.

2 'Since I myself / I have given myself the cause'

Why should Cleopatra think she has been the cause of her own misfortune (lines 84–5)? Be alert for the moments later in this scene where she again blames herself, but also blames Antony.

3 Narcissus and Echo

In Greek mythology, Narcissus was a young man who was so beautiful that he fell in love with his own reflection. The nymph Echo fell in love with him, but because she had offended the goddess Hera, she was punished by only being able to repeat what was said to her.

Use this information to work out the meaning of Cleopatra's words in lines 98–9. Does Cleopatra echo any of the Messenger's words elsewhere in this scene?

---

make thy peace make up for
boot thee make amends to you
what gift whatever gift
Thy modesty a man of your modest expectations
keep ... yourself contain yourself
kindly possessing good, natural qualities

meaner of inferior class
gracious pleasing
let ... tell / Themselves let people find out bad news for themselves
hold ... still stick to that story
So half even if half

CLEOPATRA Say 'tis not so, a province I will give thee
          And make thy fortunes proud. The blow thou hadst   70
          Shall make thy peace for moving me to rage,
          And I will boot thee with what gift beside
          Thy modesty can beg.
MESSENGER   He's married, madam.
CLEOPATRA Rogue, thou hast lived too long! *Draw a knife*
MESSENGER   Nay then, I'll run.
          What mean you, madam? I have made no fault.   *Exit*   75
CHARMIAN Good madam, keep yourself within yourself.
          The man is innocent.
CLEOPATRA Some innocents scape not the thunderbolt.
          Melt Egypt into Nile, and kindly creatures
          Turn all to serpents! Call the slave again.   80
          Though I am mad, I will not bite him. Call!
CHARMIAN He is afeard to come.
CLEOPATRA   I will not hurt him.
                 [*The Messenger is sent for*]
          These hands do lack nobility, that they strike
          A meaner than myself, since I myself
          Have given myself the cause.

               Enter the MESSENGER *again*

                              Come hither, sir.   85
          Though it be honest, it is never good
          To bring bad news. Give to a gracious message
          An host of tongues, but let ill tidings tell
          Themselves when they be felt.
MESSENGER I have done my duty.   90
CLEOPATRA Is he married?
          I cannot hate thee worser than I do
          If thou again say 'Yes'.
MESSENGER   He's married, madam.
CLEOPATRA The gods confound thee, dost thou hold there still?
MESSENGER Should I lie, madam?
CLEOPATRA   O, I would thou didst,   95
          So half my Egypt were submerged and made
          A cistern for scaled snakes! Go, get thee hence.
          Hadst thou Narcissus in thy face, to me
          Thou wouldst appear most ugly. He is married?

71

Cleopatra acknowledges the injustice of punishing the Messenger for Antony's faults, but nevertheless dismisses him with a curse. She sends Alexas to find out details of Octavia's age and appearance.

Decide which line is being spoken here. Is it a threat, a promise, or both?

1 Both Mars and the Gorgon (in groups of three)

Popular in Elizabethan times were trick paintings which showed different images according to the angle from which they were viewed. Cleopatra sees the faithless Antony as the Gorgon, Medusa (crowned with snakes like the Fury) who turned all who saw her into stone. Yet she also sees him as Mars, the magnificent god of war.

The surging, conflicting emotions that overwhelm Cleopatra in this scene suggest why Antony finds her such an exciting woman. Take parts as Cleopatra, Charmian and the Messenger, and read lines 100–21. How many different emotions seem to engulf Cleopatra here?

that I would not because I do not wish to
much unequal most unjust
his fault Antony's fault
knave villain
That art ... sure of! who are not in yourself hateful like the news you bring

Lie they ... by 'em! may your 'merchandise' (news) lie unsold and ruin you
feature physical appearance
inclination disposition, character

MESSENGER I crave your highness' pardon.
CLEOPATRA   He is married?   100
MESSENGER Take no offence that I would not offend you;
    To punish me for what you make me do
    Seems much unequal. He's married to Octavia.
CLEOPATRA O, that his fault should make a knave of thee,
    That art not what thou'rt sure of! Get thee hence.   105
    The merchandise which thou hast brought from Rome
    Are all too dear for me. Lie they upon thy hand,
    And be undone by 'em!
                                        [Exit Messenger]
CHARMIAN   Good your highness, patience.
CLEOPATRA In praising Antony, I have dispraised Caesar.
CHARMIAN Many times, madam.   110
CLEOPATRA I am paid for't now. Lead me from hence;
    I faint. O Iras, Charmian! – 'Tis no matter.
    Go to the fellow, good Alexas. Bid him
    Report the feature of Octavia, her years,
    Her inclination. Let him not leave out   115
    The colour of her hair. Bring me word quickly.
                                        [Exit Alexas]
    Let him for ever go! – Let him not, Charmian.
    Though he be painted one way like a Gorgon,
    The other way's a Mars. [To Mardian] Bid you Alexas
    Bring me word how tall she is. – Pity me, Charmian,   120
    But do not speak to me. Lead me to my chamber.
                                        Exeunt

Caesar asks Pompey if he is ready to agree peace terms. Pompey states his case for taking up arms. Antony dismisses Pompey's naval strength and stresses the Triumvirate's strength on land.

1 The ghosts of Pompey the Great, Julius Caesar, Brutus and Cassius

There have been many power struggles leading up to this confrontation between Pompey and the Triumvirate (see pages 240–2).

List Pompey's grievances (lines 8–29). Are they genuine? Look back at Pompey's more confidential remarks on page 43 to help you decide.

2 Squaring up to each other (the whole class)

The stage directions show that both sides have come prepared to fight. There is a 'Flourish' (fanfare of trumpets) to mark the entrance of armed men with 'Drum and Trumpet' (drummers and trumpeters). But first they talk. Separate into two groups and prepare lines 1–48.

Group 1 (Pompey's group): select a leader to speak Pompey's lines. Rehearse giving him vocal support. For example, you might echo his gibe at Antony (lines 26–9), when he comments on how Antony, like a cuckoo, took over a house that did not belong to him.

Group 2 (the Triumvirs): select your leaders to speak the Triumvirs' lines. Rehearse giving them your vocal support, and express your disapproval of Pompey's accusations. For example, you might comment appreciatively on Caesar's clever manipulation or Antony's reminders of your side's supremacy on land.

When the opposing sides have prepared for the meeting, Pompey leads in his supporters from one side, while the Triumvirate marches in from the other. When the hostilities cease, let cheers break out all round.

meet fitting	**honest** honourable
purposes proposals	**courtiers** lovers
tall gallant	**drench** drown (in the murdered
senators alone sole leaders	Julius Caesar's blood)
factors agents	**fear us** frighten us
want lack	**speak with** fight with
ghosted visited as a ghost	**o'ercount** outnumber, or cheat

ACT 2   SCENE 6
Italy   Near Misena

Flourish. Enter POMPEY *and* MENAS *at one door, with Drum and Trumpet; at another,* CAESAR, LEPIDUS, ANTONY, ENOBARBUS, MAECENAS, AGRIPPA, *with soldiers marching*

POMPEY Your hostages I have, so have you mine,
        And we shall talk before we fight.
CAESAR   Most meet
        That first we come to words, and therefore have we
        Our written purposes before us sent,
        Which if thou hast considered, let us know   5
        If 'twill tie up thy discontented sword
        And carry back to Sicily much tall youth
        That else must perish here.
POMPEY   To you all three,
        The senators alone of this great world,
        Chief factors for the gods: I do not know   10
        Wherefore my father should revengers want,
        Having a son and friends, since Julius Caesar,
        Who at Philippi the good Brutus ghosted,
        There saw you labouring for him. What was't
        That moved pale Cassius to conspire? And what   15
        Made th'all-honoured, honest Roman, Brutus,
        With the armed rest, courtiers of beauteous freedom,
        To drench the Capitol, but that they would
        Have one man but a man? And that is it
        Hath made me rig my navy, at whose burden   20
        The angered ocean foams, with which I meant
        To scourge th'ingratitude that despiteful Rome
        Cast on my noble father.
CAESAR   Take your time.
ANTONY Thou canst not fear us, Pompey, with thy sails.
        We'll speak with thee at sea. At land thou know'st   25
        How much we do o'ercount thee.
POMPEY   At land indeed
        Thou dost o'ercount me of my father's house;
        But since the cuckoo builds not for himself,
        Remain in't as thou mayst.

*Pompey is prepared to agree peace terms but is angry that Antony has
not acknowledged his past kindness to Antony's mother. Antony's
generous apology reconciles Pompey and peace is made.*

1 Has Pompey made a big mistake? (in small groups)

'Since I saw you last,/There's a change upon you', remarks Caesar to
Pompey (lines 52–3). In reply, Pompey says that Fortune may have
left her accounting marks upon his face ('counts' = tally marks, 'casts'
= calculates), but she will never take ownership of his heart. Is it a
failure of nerve that prompts Pompey to make peace? Talk about the
kind of pressure the Triumvirate put on Pompey in lines 1–39, and the
different negotiating styles of Caesar, Antony and Lepidus.

Then consider the peace terms that Pompey accepts (lines 34–9).
Later in this scene, Menas claims that 'Pompey doth this day laugh
away his fortune' (lines 103–4). Decide why Menas should be so
unhappy with the treaty.

The achievements of Pompey's father earned him the title of Pompey
the Great. Decide on the title you think the great man's son deserves.

2 'The beds i'th'East are soft' (in pairs)

Antony shakes Pompey's hand and thanks him for drawing him away
from the soft pleasures of Egyptian beds (lines 48–52).

Greet each other in different ways with Antony's words. Does
Antony speak of Egypt dismissively, jokingly, ruefully, contemptuously,
or in some other way?

---

from the present beside the point
Which do ... embraced don't
regard this as an entreaty, but
consider what you will gain if you
accept
what may ... fortune how
disastrous it may be to try to win
more

'greed upon agreed
targes undinted shields undented
well studied for fully prepared to
give
timelier than my purpose earlier
than I had intended
gained by't profited by it
vassal slave

LEPIDUS   Be pleased to tell us –
    For this is from the present – how you take   30
    The offers we have sent you.
CAESAR   There's the point.
ANTONY Which do not be entreated to, but weigh
    What it is worth embraced.
CAESAR   And what may follow
    To try a larger fortune.
POMPEY   You have made me offer
    Of Sicily, Sardinia; and I must   35
    Rid all the sea of pirates; then, to send
    Measures of wheat to Rome. This 'greed upon,
    To part with unhacked edges and bear back
    Our targes undinted.
CAESAR, ANTONY, LEPIDUS That's our offer.
POMPEY   Know then
    I came before you here a man prepared   40
    To take this offer. But Mark Antony
    Put me to some impatience. Though I lose
    The praise of it by telling, you must know,
    When Caesar and your brother were at blows,
    Your mother came to Sicily, and did find   45
    Her welcome friendly.
ANTONY   I have heard it, Pompey,
    And am well studied for a liberal thanks
    Which I do owe you.
POMPEY   Let me have your hand.
    [They shake hands]
    I did not think, sir, to have met you here.
ANTONY The beds i'th'East are soft; and thanks to you,   50
    That called me timelier than my purpose hither,
    For I have gained by't.
CAESAR   Since I saw you last,
    There's a change upon you.
POMPEY   Well, I know not
    What counts harsh fortune casts upon my face,
    But in my bosom shall she never come   55
    To make my heart her vassal.

Pompey asks for the treaty to be signed before they feast. He tactlessly talks of Julius Caesar, Cleopatra's former lover, and then invites his former enemies to feast on his galley.

1 What does Pompey think of his new allies?
(in groups of five)

There is to be no war. Pompey suggests that they 'feast each other' before they part, to celebrate their new alliance, but is he really reconciled? Take parts and read lines 48–85 in different ways:

- Pompey is genuinely pleased to have made the treaty.
- Pompey smiles, laughs and shakes everyone's hands, but there is tension and mistrust just below the surface.
- Pompey is openly disrespectful and malicious (for example, in reminding Antony of the incident when Cleopatra was secretly brought by Apollodorus to Julius Caesar).

Then each student writes a soliloquy in role as Pompey, revealing his true feelings about the treaty and his new allies. Read each other's soliloquies and talk together about them.

2 'Near him thy angel / Becomes afeard' (in small groups)

The Soothsayer warned Antony to leave Rome. In the presence of Caesar, Antony's 'angel' or 'daemon' (guardian spirit) would quickly be overpowered (Act 2 Scene 3, lines 17–22). Do you think Antony is now overshadowed by Caesar?

---

composition agreement
That will I I'll go first
take the lot accept the decision of the lottery, or draw lots
have / The fame have the glory
I have fair meanings I don't mean to be insulting

fair words elegantly smooth words
Apollodorus (see Activity 1 above)
toward coming up
Enjoy continue to practise
plainness blunt frankness

LEPIDUS   Well met here.
POMPEY I hope so, Lepidus. Thus we are agreed.
          I crave our composition may be written
          And sealed between us.
CAESAR   That's the next to do.
POMPEY We'll feast each other ere we part, and let's   60
          Draw lots who shall begin.
ANTONY   That will I, Pompey.
POMPEY No, Antony, take the lot. But, first or last,
          Your fine Egyptian cookery shall have
          The fame. I have heard that Julius Caesar
          Grew fat with feasting there.   65
ANTONY You have heard much.
POMPEY I have fair meanings, sir.
ANTONY And fair words to them.
POMPEY Then so much have I heard.
          And I have heard Apollodorus carried –   70
ENOBARBUS No more of that. He did so.
POMPEY   What, I pray you?
ENOBARBUS A certain queen to Caesar in a mattress.
POMPEY I know thee now. How far'st thou, soldier?
ENOBARBUS   Well,
          And well am like to do, for I perceive
          Four feasts are toward.
POMPEY   Let me shake thy hand.   75
          I never hated thee. I have seen thee fight
          When I have envied thy behaviour.
ENOBARBUS   Sir,
          I never loved you much, but I ha' praised ye
          When you have well deserved ten times as much
          As I have said you did.
POMPEY   Enjoy thy plainness;   80
          It nothing ill becomes thee.
          Aboard my galley I invite you all.
          Will you lead, lords?
CAESAR, ANTONY, LEPIDUS Show's the way, sir.
POMPEY   Come.
                    Exeunt. Enobarbus and Menas remain

79

*Enobarbus and Menas, former enemies, praise each other's fighting skills
and talk of the falseness of women. Menas is unhappy about the treaty.
Enobarbus doubts the strength of Antony and Caesar's new alliance.*

1 More handshaking (in pairs)

Menas and Enobarbus know each other by reputation. Enobarbus's
face is familiar to Menas ('You and I have known, sir'). Take parts and
read lines 84–115. Are you wary, hostile, genuinely friendly, admiring
of your enemy, or do you have some other attitude?

2 Write a Shakespeare Chorus (in groups of four)

In ancient Greek drama, the Chorus acted as watchers of the stage
action, commenting at intervals on events, or expressing their fears,
hopes and judgements. Sometimes they would predict future events.

Shakespeare sometimes uses a Chorus-figure in his plays. In *Romeo
and Juliet*, a Chorus begins the play. He speaks of the feud between the
Montagues and the Capulets, and how it will lead to the lovers' death:

> From forth the fatal loins of these two foes
> A pair of star-crossed lovers take their life;
> Whose misadventured piteous overthrows
> Doth with their death bury their parents' strife.

Menas and Enobarbus fulfil a similar role here.

Your director wants to replace this Menas–Enobarbus episode (lines
99–131) with a Chorus. List the comments both men make about
events and their predictions for the future. Use the information in your
list to write a script of eight to fourteen lines for the Chorus, who will
comment on events and prophesy the future. Write in blank verse if
you can (see page 246).

---

deny ... service claim exemption
from military service, or deny that
I have been a thief
had authority power of arrest
take two thieves/ kissing arrest
two handshaking villains
true (lines 99–100) honest, or
without cosmetics

whatsome'er ... are whatever their
actions may be
No slander that's not entirely
slanderous
Pray ye, sir? is that so?
divine of prophesy about

MENAS [*Aside*] Thy father, Pompey, would ne'er have made this
    treaty. – You and I have known, sir.   85
ENOBARBUS At sea, I think.
MENAS We have, sir.
ENOBARBUS You have done well by water.
MENAS And you by land.
ENOBARBUS I will praise any man that will praise me, though it   90
    cannot be denied what I have done by land.
MENAS Nor what I have done by water.
ENOBARBUS Yes, something you can deny for your own safety: you
    have been a great thief by sea.
MENAS And you by land.   95
ENOBARBUS There I deny my land service. But give me your hand,
    Menas. If our eyes had authority, here they might take two thieves
    kissing.
MENAS All men's faces are true, whatsome'er their hands are.
ENOBARBUS But there is never a fair woman has a true face.   100
MENAS No slander, they steal hearts.
ENOBARBUS We came hither to fight with you.
MENAS For my part, I am sorry it is turned to a drinking. Pompey
    doth this day laugh away his fortune.
ENOBARBUS If he do, sure he cannot weep't back again.   105
MENAS You've said, sir. We looked not for Mark Antony here. Pray
    you, is he married to Cleopatra?
ENOBARBUS Caesar's sister is called Octavia.
MENAS True, sir. She was the wife of Caius Marcellus.
ENOBARBUS But she is now the wife of Marcus Antonius.   110
MENAS Pray ye, sir?
ENOBARBUS 'Tis true.
MENAS Then is Caesar and he for ever knit together.
ENOBARBUS If I were bound to divine of this unity, I would not
    prophesy so.   115

Enobarbus and Menas agree that Antony's marriage will inevitably be a cause of strife between Antony and Caesar. On board Pompey's ship, servants comment on Lepidus's drunkenness.

1 Perceptive words from Enobarbus (in small groups)

Enobarbus tells Menas what he thinks will come of Antony's marriage to Octavia. Work out how Enobarbus uses images of coldness, heat and food to describe the complex relationships between Octavia and Antony, Octavia and Caesar, and Antony and Cleopatra.

2 Frank words from the servants (in groups of three)

In Scene 7, the ordinary man has a chance to say what he thinks of Lepidus, one of the rulers of the world.

a Sarcastic word-play

Lines 1–2 play on the two meanings of 'plants'. The servant could be referring to planted trees or the soles of the feet. Talk about the two images which the servant's remark conjures up.

b 'As they pinch one another by the disposition'

Lines 5–7 might mean either 'while his colleagues try to hold back in their drinking, Lepidus insists on drinking even more', or 'to stop his colleagues from arguing, Lepidus keeps calling for them to raise their glasses and so has to keep drinking toasts'. Which gives the better picture of Lepidus?

c Reeds and partisans (lines 10–12)

A partisan is a long-handled, two-headed spear. What image of Lepidus do these lines suggest to you?

d Cosmic inadequacy (lines 13–15)

Lepidus is like a star that cannot keep its 'sphere' (orbit), or a face with empty eye sockets. Look out for other mingled human and cosmic images later in the play.

---

policy political considerations
made more played more of a role
still conversation quiet manner
author ... variance cause of their falling out
use ... it is get his pleasure where he now enjoys it (in Egypt)

but his occasion merely to suit his political ends
health toast
alms-drink left-over drink
a name a name only
had as lief would just as soon
disaster ruin, disfigure

MENAS I think the policy of that purpose made more in the marriage
than the love of the parties.

ENOBARBUS I think so, too. But you shall find the band that seems
to tie their friendship together will be the very strangler of their
amity: Octavia is of a holy, cold, and still conversation. 120

MENAS Who would not have his wife so?

ENOBARBUS Not he that himself is not so, which is Mark Antony.
He will to his Egyptian dish again. Then shall the sighs of Octavia
blow the fire up in Caesar, and, as I said before, that which is the
strength of their amity shall prove the immediate author of their 125
variance. Antony will use his affection where it is. He married
but his occasion here.

MENAS And thus it may be. Come, sir, will you aboard? I have a
health for you.

ENOBARBUS I shall take it, sir. We have used our throats in Egypt. 130

MENAS Come, let's away.

Exeunt

ACT 2   SCENE 7
Aboard Pompey's galley

Music plays. Enter two or three SERVANTS *with a banquet*

1 SERVANT Here they'll be, man. Some o'their plants are ill-rooted
already; the least wind i'th'world will blow them down.

2 SERVANT Lepidus is high-coloured.

1 SERVANT They have made him drink alms-drink.

2 SERVANT As they pinch one another by the disposition, he cries 5
out, 'No more', reconciles them to his entreaty, and himself to
the drink.

1 SERVANT But it raises the greater war between him and his
discretion.

2 SERVANT Why, this it is to have a name in great men's fellowship. 10
I had as lief have a reed that will do me no service as a partisan
I could not heave.

1 SERVANT To be called into a huge sphere, and not to be seen to
move in't, are the holes where eyes should be, which pitifully
disaster the cheeks. 15

83

Lepidus gets more and more drunk and the others have fun at his expense. Menas tries to call his commander Pompey aside for a private conversation.

1 Pyramids and crocodiles (in groups of four)

Antony explains to Caesar how the height of the Nile is calculated by graduated marks on the pyramids, and how these calculations help determine whether it will be a time of plenty or famine. When the befuddled Lepidus interrupts with remarks about the Nile serpent and crocodile, Antony gives a straight-faced, but meaningless, description of the crocodile's marvellous properties.

Present Antony's crocodile story (lines 38–45) as a comedy sketch, with Antony as the smart half of a comic double act.

2 Was Antony the first post-structuralist?

Post-structuralist philosophers maintain that 'there is nothing outside the text'. Language is merely a chain of words, each word pointing to another word, with no reference to 'reality'.

Antony's crocodile description may be light-heartedly exploiting this self-referential quality of language. But where in lines 16–48 does he also use language in a more practical and down-to-earth way?

Think back over the play so far. Write an essay on the proposition that 'there is as much "real life" in *Antony and Cleopatra* as there is in real life'.

---

sennet fanfare of trumpets
scales i' measuring marks on
dearth/Or foison famine or plenty
Your serpent ... your sun
  (this use of 'your' is still colloquial
  and everyday)
ne'er out not refuse to drink
pyramises (the drunken plural!)

Forbear ... anon wait a moment
elements (of life)
transmigrates takes on another
  life form
it own its own
epicure one who believes only in
  earthly existence

A sennet sounded. Enter CAESAR, ANTONY, POMPEY, LEPIDUS,
AGRIPPA, MAECENAS, ENOBARBUS, MENAS, *with other Captains*
[*and a* BOY]

ANTONY [*To Caesar*] Thus do they, sir: they take the flow o'th'Nile
    By certain scales i'th'Pyramid; they know,
    By the height, the lowness, or the mean if dearth
    Or foison follow. The higher Nilus swells,
    The more it promises; as it ebbs, the seedsman   20
    Upon the slime and ooze scatters his grain,
    And shortly comes to harvest.
LEPIDUS You've strange serpents there.
ANTONY Ay, Lepidus.
LEPIDUS Your serpent of Egypt is bred now of your mud by the   25
    operation of your sun; so is your crocodile.
ANTONY They are so.
POMPEY Sit – and some wine. A health to Lepidus!
                [*They sit and drink*]
LEPIDUS I am not so well as I should be, but I'll ne'er out.
ENOBARBUS Not till you have slept; I fear me you'll be in till then.   30
LEPIDUS Nay, certainly, I have heard the Ptolemies' pyramises are
    very goodly things. Without contradiction I have heard that.
MENAS [*Aside to Pompey*] Pompey, a word.
POMPEY [*Aside to Menas*]   Say in mine ear, what is't?
MENAS (*Whispers in's ear*) Forsake thy seat, I do beseech thee, captain,
    And hear me speak a word.   35
POMPEY [*Aside to Menas*] Forbear me till anon. – This wine for
        Lepidus!
LEPIDUS What manner o'thing is your crocodile?
ANTONY It is shaped, sir, like itself, and it is as broad as it hath
    breadth. It is just so high as it is, and moves with it own organs. It
    lives by that which nourisheth it, and the elements once out of it,   40
    it transmigrates.
LEPIDUS What colour is it of?
ANTONY Of it own colour too.
LEPIDUS 'Tis a strange serpent.
ANTONY 'Tis so, and the tears of it are wet.   45
CAESAR Will this description satisfy him?
ANTONY With the health that Pompey gives him, else he is a very
    epicure.

Menas offers to cut the throats of Antony, Lepidus and Caesar. Pompey refuses to conspire in such a deed, although he would have applauded the act if Menas had done it without his knowledge.

Choose a line from page 85 that Lepidus (left) might be saying to Antony.

1 'Wilt thou be lord of all the world?' (in pairs)

Had the faithful Menas killed the Triumvirate without Pompey's knowledge, Menas would have deserved praise ('In me 'tis villainy;/In thee't had been good service'). But the demands of honour cannot allow Pompey to sanction the deed now that Menas has told him of his plan.

Talk together about what you think of Pompey's concept of honour and loyalty in lines 69–76. Would Pompey have reacted like this if he hadn't been drinking?

---

merit my good service
ever ... fortunes served you loyally
quicksands (perhaps Lepidus is sinking!)
But entertain it just grant the possibility
Jove king of the gods (Jupiter)

pales encloses
inclips embraces
competitors partners
are put off have put to sea
All there all that they possess
Mine honour, it my honour comes before my personal profit

[Menas whispers again]

POMPEY *[Aside to Menas]* Go hang, sir, hang! Tell me of that? Away!
    Do as I bid you. – Where's this cup I called for?   50

MENAS *[Aside to Pompey]* If for the sake of merit thou wilt hear me,
    Rise from thy stool.

POMPEY *[Aside to Menas]*   I think thou'rt mad.
         [He rises, and they walk aside]
                           The matter?

MENAS I have ever held my cap off to thy fortunes.

POMPEY Thou hast served me with much faith. What's else to say? –
    Be jolly, lords.

ANTONY   These quicksands, Lepidus,   55
    Keep off them, for you sink.
         [Menas and Pompey speak aside]

MENAS Wilt thou be lord of all the world?

POMPEY   What say'st thou?

MENAS Wilt thou be lord of the whole world? That's twice.

POMPEY How should that be?

MENAS   But entertain it,
    And, though thou think me poor, I am the man   60
    Will give thee all the world.

POMPEY   Hast thou drunk well?

MENAS No, Pompey, I have kept me from the cup.
    Thou art, if thou dar'st be, the earthly Jove.
    Whate'er the ocean pales or sky inclips
    Is thine, if thou wilt ha't.

POMPEY   Show me which way.   65

MENAS These three world-sharers, these competitors,
    Are in thy vessel. Let me cut the cable,
    And when we are put off, fall to their throats.
    All there is thine.

POMPEY   Ah, this thou shouldst have done
    And not have spoke on't! In me 'tis villainy;   70
    In thee't had been good service. Thou must know,
    'Tis not my profit that does lead mine honour;
    Mine honour, it. Repent that e'er thy tongue
    Hath so betrayed thine act. Being done unknown,
    I should have found it afterwards well done,   75
    But must condemn it now. Desist, and drink.
         [He returns to the feast]

Menas decides to desert Pompey for missing his opportunity for seizing power. The drunken Lepidus is carried out. Caesar criticises their drunkenness, but Antony calls for wine and dancing.

1 The first desertion

Menas is angry that Pompey has lost the opportunity to become sole ruler of the world. Write a monologue for Menas to speak at the end of the scene, explaining why he is deserting Pompey.

The masters of the world. Identify the characters in this 1972 Royal Shakespeare Company production, and suggest which moment you think is being presented here.

palled decayed, weakened
pledge ... him drink the toast
till ... be hid to overflowing
A bears he carries
go on wheels go smoothly, or whirl dizzily
reels people staggering, or fun
Strike the vessels open the casks
I ... forbear't I'd rather not
wash my brain drink
Be a child o'th'time let yourself go!
Possess ... answer be master of the situation, I say
Bacchanals drunken dances
Lethe river of forgetfulness

MENAS [*Aside*] For this, I'll never follow thy palled fortunes more.
        Who seeks and will not take when once 'tis offered
        Shall never find it more.
POMPEY   This health to Lepidus!
ANTONY Bear him ashore. I'll pledge it for him, Pompey.   80
ENOBARBUS Here's to thee, Menas!
                [*They drink*]
MENAS   Enobarbus, welcome!
POMPEY Fill till the cup be hid.
ENOBARBUS There's a strong fellow, Menas.
        [*He points to the Servant who carries off Lepidus*]
MENAS   Why?
ENOBARBUS   A bears
        The third part of the world, man; see'st not?
MENAS The third part, then, is drunk. Would it were all,   85
        That it might go on wheels!
ENOBARBUS Drink thou; increase the reels.
MENAS Come.
POMPEY This is not yet an Alexandrian feast.
ANTONY It ripens towards it. Strike the vessels, ho!   90
        Here's to Caesar.
CAESAR   I could well forbear't.
        It's monstrous labour when I wash my brain
        And it grow fouler.
ANTONY   Be a child o'th'time.
CAESAR Possess it, I'll make answer;
        But I had rather fast from all, four days,   95
        Than drink so much in one.
ENOBARBUS [*To Antony*]   Ha, my brave emperor,
        Shall we dance now the Egyptian Bacchanals,
        And celebrate our drink?
POMPEY Let's ha't, good soldier.
ANTONY Come, let's all take hands,   100
        Till that the conquering wine hath steeped our sense
        In soft and delicate Lethe.

Enobarbus leads the company in a drunken song and dance. Caesar has had enough. As the leaders make their unsteady way ashore, Menas orders a military salute.

1 Drunken revels (in large groups)

Prepare your own version of lines 77–129. Remember before you start that portraying drunks on stage is a skill that needs careful thought and rehearsal. Actors work out their every move. Though it may *look* rowdy, everyone is in full control. The language must always be clear to the audience. Consider as you rehearse:

- Where Lepidus collapses and how the servant carries him out.
- How Caesar shows his disapproval of all the drunkenness.
- Even now, Antony and Caesar cannot help but come into conflict. 'Be a child o'th'time', cries Antony. 'Possess it', answers Caesar (lines 93–4). How will you present this exchange?
- The boy's song (lines 107–12), which is often performed as a chorus where everyone joins in. Make up your own tune. Will there be drums or musical accompaniment?
- The way in which each leader exits. Remember the military salutes (*'flourish, with drums'*) that Menas calls for in lines 125–7 as the generals leave the ship.

Present your version to the rest of the class and talk together about your impressions of the four leaders of the Roman world.

2 Hangovers (in small groups)

Write the thoughts of each man when he wakes up the following morning. Do not just give their thoughts about the drunken party. What is each man's sober assessment of the recent summit negotiations?

Make battery to assault, pound
holding ... bear every man shall
 sing the chorus
Bacchus Roman god of wine
eyne eyes
fats vats (of wine)
Cup us fill our cups

Good brother Antony
request you off ask you to come
 ashore
wild disguise drunken behaviour
Anticked us turned us into fools
try you test your drinking ability
Neptune god of the ocean

ENOBARBUS   All take hands.
Make battery to our ears with the loud music,
The while I'll place you; then the boy shall sing.
The holding every man shall bear as loud   105
As his strong sides can volley.
Music plays. Enobarbus places them hand in hand

The Song

BOY [*Sings*] Come thou monarch of the vine,
Plumpy Bacchus with pink eyne!
In thy fats our cares be drowned,
With thy grapes our hairs be crowned.   110
ALL   Cup us till the world go round,
Cup us till the world go round.
CAESAR What would you more? Pompey, good night. Good brother,
Let me request you off. Our graver business
Frowns at this levity. Gentle lords, let's part;   115
You see we have burnt our cheeks. Strong Enobarb
Is weaker than the wine, and mine own tongue
Splits what it speaks. The wild disguise hath almost
Anticked us all. What needs more words? Good night.
Good Antony, your hand.
POMPEY   I'll try you on the shore.   120
ANTONY And shall, sir. Give's your hand.
POMPEY   O Antony,
You have my father's house. But what? We are friends.
Come down into the boat.
ENOBARBUS   Take heed you fall not.
                    [*Exeunt all but Enobarbus and Menas*]
Menas, I'll not on shore.
MENAS   No, to my cabin.
These drums, these trumpets, flutes! What!   125
Let Neptune hear we bid a loud farewell
To these great fellows. Sound and be hanged, sound out!
                    Sound a flourish, with drums
ENOBARBUS Hoo! says a. There's my cap.
                    [*He flings his cap in the air*]
MENAS Hoo! Noble captain, come.

                                        Exeunt

Looking back at Act 2
Activities for groups or individuals

1 A united front – but what lies beneath?

Imagine that Antony, Caesar and Lepidus have organised a public press conference to reassure the citizens of Rome that the Triumvirate is truly united, and that there are no internal divisions.

Either : Create a tableau to show their united front. Photograph it if you can, and write the caption to be released alongside the photograph.

Or: Imagine you are the Roman artist commissioned to draw a picture showing the Triumvirate's unity. Draw the picture, adding a suitable title.

Add thought bubbles to your drawing or photograph, and in each bubble write what each member of the Triumvirate might be thinking.

2 Mini-act

Write and perform a five-minute edited version of Act 2.

3 What do the subordinates think?

In Act 2, Enobarbus is close to Antony as he negotiates, concludes his marriage agreement, prepares for war and celebrates the peace treaty. Similarly, Agrippa keeps close by Caesar, and Menas close by Pompey.

As either Enobarbus, Agrippa or Menas, make notes about your commander's actions, character and behaviour. Prepare a speech saying what you think of your commander and his affairs. Speak in role to the class and answer their questions.

4 ... And the women?

Write an extra scene in the play in which Charmian and Iras gossip together about what happened between the Messenger and their mistress. What might they say about Cleopatra's future?

5 The Soothsayer speaks again

Fate and prophecy play their part in this act. The Soothsayer has already spoken of the fate of Charmian and Iras in Act 1 Scene 2. In Act 2 Scene 3, he warns Antony to beware of Caesar. Imagine the Soothsayer ends Act 2 with predictions for Antony, Cleopatra, Caesar and Lepidus. Write his prophetic words.

6 Both Mars and the Gorgon

When Cleopatra hears of Antony's marriage to Octavia, she compares her conflicting emotions to a trick perspective painting in which Antony's image shifts and changes. One moment it is frighteningly ugly, the next god-like and magnificent (see page 72). Draw this 'two-faced' Antony. Under the Mars half, write the reasons Cleopatra has to love and admire him. Under the Gorgon half, put her reasons for hating him.

7 Hold a presidential election

If Pompey, Lepidus, Caesar and Antony were in a democracy, they would have to appeal to the people for their vote in order to gain power. Choose either Pompey, Caesar, Antony or Lepidus and prepare a campaign to get your candidate elected. You will need to write your candidate's speech to the voters (praising himself and attacking the opposition), prepare handouts, posters and slogans, and design a political broadcast for television.

*Antony's lieutenant, Ventidius, has avenged the defeat and murder of the
Roman Consul Marcus Crassus. He is reluctant to pursue the fleeing
Parthians because too much success might arouse Antony's displeasure.*

1 Roman legions versus 'darting Parthia'
(in small groups)

The Parthians were brilliant mounted soldiers and a formidable enemy.
They would first hurl their 'darts' (javelins), then, as they retreated,
turn in the saddle to fire their arrows at their pursuers.

The phrase 'a Parthian shot' is now part of the language. Work out
what you think it means. Check your guess in a good dictionary.

The 1978 Royal Shakespeare Company production showed the
savagery of this campaign by having Pacorus executed on stage as
Ventidius speaks. Talk together about how you would stage this scene
to create an image of Roman military power.

2 Don't do better than your boss! (in pairs)

Sir Thomas North's translation of Plutarch remarks that Antony and
Caesar 'were always more fortunate when they made war by their
lieutenants, than by themselves'. North also mentions Sossius and
Canidius as serving Antony well.

a Take parts and read this scene through. Find the lines where
   Shakespeare echoes North's words and also identify the reward
   that Sossius received for his loyal service to Antony (you will find
   out later in this act what happens to Canidius).

b Silius urges Ventidius to follow up his victory and push the
   Parthians back into their home territories, but Ventidius disagrees
   (lines 11–27). What does his reply tell you of the dangers of
   working for powerful men?

Pacorus son of King Orodes
Orodes King of Parthia
garlands crown of victory
lower ... act a subordinate may be
  too successful for his own safety
by th'minute continually, rapidly

rather makes ... him prompts a
  soldier to accept a loss rather than
  a gain which displeases his superior
his offence his displeasure
Thou hast ... distinction you
  have discretion (which makes a
  soldier more than just a sword)

ACT 3 SCENE 1
A plain in Syria

Enter in triumph VENTIDIUS, SILIUS, *and other Romans, officers and Soldiers, the dead body of Pacorus borne before them*

VENTIDIUS Now, darting Parthia, art thou struck, and now
    Pleased Fortune does of Marcus Crassus' death
    Make me revenger. Bear the king's son's body
    Before our army. Thy Pacorus, Orodes,
    Pays this for Marcus Crassus.
SILIUS   Noble Ventidius,   5
    Whilst yet with Parthian blood thy sword is warm,
    The fugitive Parthians follow. Spur through Media,
    Mesopotamia, and the shelters whither
    The routed fly. So thy grand captain, Antony,
    Shall set thee on triumphant chariots and   10
    Put garlands on thy head.
VENTIDIUS   O Silius, Silius,
    I have done enough. A lower place, note well,
    May make too great an act. For learn this, Silius:
    Better to leave undone than by our deed
    Acquire too high a fame when him we serve's away.   15
    Caesar and Antony have ever won
    More in their officer than person. Sossius,
    One of my place in Syria, his lieutenant,
    For quick accumulation of renown,
    Which he achieved by th'minute, lost his favour.   20
    Who does i'th'wars more than his captain can
    Becomes his captain's captain; and ambition,
    The soldier's virtue, rather makes choice of loss
    Than gain which darkens him.
    I could do more to do Antonius good,   25
    But 'twould offend him, and in his offence
    Should my performance perish.
SILIUS Thou hast, Ventidius, that
    Without the which a soldier and his sword
    Grants scarce distinction. Thou wilt write to Antony?   30

Ventidius plans to inform Antony of the Parthian defeat, then join him. Enobarbus and Agrippa discuss Octavia and Caesar's sadness. They mock Lepidus's flattery of his fellow Triumvirs.

1 Soldierly contempt (in pairs)

'Green-sickness' (line 6) was a form of anaemia supposed to afflict love-sick girls. Enobarbus probably uses the phrase to describe Lepidus's enormous hangover after his drinking bout on Pompey's ship.

a ''Tis a noble Lepidus'

Agrippa's apparent praise (line 6) is also mockingly contemptuous ('it' was a pronoun used to address children). Enobarbus even makes fun of Lepidus's name, which in Latin means 'fine, elegant'. In lines 7–20, the two men mimic the ingratiating way in which Lepidus sings the praises of Antony and Caesar. For example, the 'Arabian bird' is the mythical Phoenix which was re-born in fire, and 'the nonpareil' means 'the incomparable one'.

Practise speaking lines 1–20 as sarcastically or mockingly as you can. Present your version to the class.

b 'They are his shards, and he their beetle'

Consider two possible meanings for Enobarbus's description (line 20) of the masters of the world: 'shards' are either pats of dung (the shard beetle is so named because it is commonly found in dung, which it feeds upon), or an insect's wings/wing cases.

Talk about the different pictures these two meanings create of the three leaders of the Triumvirate. Imagine you are a political cartoonist and draw two satirical 'shard beetle' cartoons of the three leaders.

---

signify point out, declare
ne'er-yet never before
horse cavalry
jaded driven (like worn-out horses)
haste ... permit speed our heavy
  equipment will allow
brothers brothers-in-law

parted departed
dispatched settled matters
sealing completing their agreement
figures figures of speech
cast count
number put into verse

VENTIDIUS I'll humbly signify what in his name,
That magical word of war, we have effected:
How with his banners and his well-paid ranks
The ne'er-yet-beaten horse of Parthia
We have jaded out o'th'field.
SILIUS   Where is he now?   35
VENTIDIUS He purposeth to Athens, whither, with what haste
The weight we must convey with's will permit,
We shall appear before him. – On, there; pass along!
                                                                    Exeunt

ACT 3   SCENE 2
Rome

Enter AGRIPPA at one door, ENOBARBUS at another

AGRIPPA What, are the brothers parted?
ENOBARBUS They have dispatched with Pompey; he is gone.
The other three are sealing. Octavia weeps
To part from Rome; Caesar is sad; and Lepidus
Since Pompey's feast, as Menas says, is troubled   5
With the green-sickness.
AGRIPPA   'Tis a noble Lepidus.
ENOBARBUS A very fine one. O, how he loves Caesar!
AGRIPPA Nay, but how dearly he adores Mark Antony!
ENOBARBUS Caesar? Why, he's the Jupiter of men.
AGRIPPA What's Antony? The god of Jupiter.   10
ENOBARBUS Spake you of Caesar? How, the nonpareil!
AGRIPPA O Antony, O thou Arabian bird!
ENOBARBUS Would you praise Caesar, say 'Caesar', go no further.
AGRIPPA Indeed, he plied them both with excellent praises.
ENOBARBUS But he loves Caesar best; yet he loves Antony: 15
Hoo! Hearts, tongues, figures, scribes, bards, poets, cannot
Think, speak, cast, write, sing, number, hoo!
His love to Antony. But as for Caesar,
Kneel down, kneel down, and wonder.
AGRIPPA   Both he loves.
ENOBARBUS They are his shards, and he their beetle.

97

Caesar asks Antony to treat Octavia well, or their newly-formed alliance will surely falter. Antony reassures him. Octavia weeps as she bids her brother farewell.

The marriage that will cement the alliance of Caesar and Antony has taken place. Are the two men at last reconciled? Study the expressions and body language of Caesar, Antony and Octavia in this 1972 Royal Shakespeare Company production.

No further you need accompany us no further
Use me well in't treat Octavia (and therefore me) well
as my farthest ... approof as I have promised you will prove to be
piece masterpiece (Octavia)

mean go-between (Octavia)
I have said I stand by what I have said
curious minutely inquiring, or touchy
elements heavens

[Trumpets within]

So;   20

This is to horse. Adieu, noble Agrippa.
AGRIPPA Good fortune, worthy soldier, and farewell.

Enter CAESAR, ANTONY, LEPIDUS, *and* OCTAVIA

ANTONY No further, sir.
CAESAR You take from me a great part of myself;
Use me well in't. – Sister, prove such a wife   25
As my thoughts make thee, and as my farthest bond
Shall pass on thy approof. – Most noble Antony,
Let not the piece of virtue which is set
Betwixt us as the cement of our love
To keep it builded, be the ram to batter   30
The fortress of it; for better might we
Have loved without this mean, if on both parts
This be not cherished.
ANTONY   Make me not offended
In your distrust.
CAESAR   I have said.
ANTONY   You shall not find,
Though you be therein curious, the least cause   35
For what you seem to fear. So the gods keep you,
And make the hearts of Romans serve your ends!
We will here part.
CAESAR Farewell, my dearest sister, fare thee well.
The elements be kind to thee, and make   40
Thy spirits all of comfort! Fare thee well.
OCTAVIA My noble brother! *[She weeps]*
ANTONY The April's in her eyes; it is love's spring,
And these the showers to bring it on. – Be cheerful.
OCTAVIA *[To Caesar]* Sir, look well to my husband's house; and –   45
CAESAR What, Octavia?
OCTAVIA   I'll tell you in your ear.
[She whispers to Caesar]

*Antony and Octavia take their leave of Caesar. All three seem moved,
but Enobarbus and Agrippa are dubious of their leaders' sincerity.
Antony had even wept at the death of Brutus, his great enemy.*

1 Octavia – 'the swansdown feather'?

Read Antony's description of Octavia's emotions (lines 47–50). Who
and what might be the powerful currents soon to pull her this way and
that?

Decide what Octavia might have said to her brother to prompt the
answer he gives in line 60.

2 A touching farewell? (in groups of six)

Enobarbus comments mockingly 'Will Caesar weep?' (line 51),
pretending to be surprised that the great man should show such a
human weakness. Just as a horse with 'a cloud' (with no white marking
on its face) is of inferior quality, so weeping is the sign of an inferior
man. He then says (lines 59–60) that he too had wept with Antony at
the death of Brutus. Is Enobarbus being cynical, emotional, or both?

a Rehearse lines 51–67. Show your version to the rest of the class.
 The class then questions each character about his/her motives
 and opinions. The actors must answer in role.

b To help you decide whether Enobarbus and Agrippa are right to
 be so cynical of their leaders' behaviour, read *Julius Caesar* Act 3
 Scene 1 and Act 5 Scene 5 to find out if Shakespeare's Antony
 really did weep at the death of Julius Caesar and of Brutus.

3 Final thoughts on Lepidus

This is the last time Lepidus appears. Is he the laughable nonentity
that so many characters think he is? Write six words to sum up your
view of him.

---

will not ... tongue cannot
 find words to express
 her conflicting emotions
stands ... tide floats in still water
 just before the tide turns
rheum a head cold
did confound destroyed

wailed wept over
still continually
the time ... you I shall think of
 you constantly
wrestle with you embrace you (in
 friendship or friendly rivalry)

ANTONY Her tongue will not obey her heart, nor can
      Her heart inform her tongue – the swansdown feather,
      That stands upon the swell at the full of tide,
      And neither way inclines.   50
ENOBARBUS [*Aside to Agrippa*] Will Caesar weep?
AGRIPPA [*Aside to Enobarbus*] He has a cloud in's face.
ENOBARBUS [*Aside to Agrippa*]
      He were the worse for that were he a horse,
      So is he being a man.
AGRIPPA [*Aside to Enobarbus*] Why, Enobarbus,
      When Antony found Julius Caesar dead,
      He cried almost to roaring; and he wept   55
      When at Philippi he found Brutus slain.
ENOBARBUS [*Aside to Agrippa*]
      That year, indeed, he was troubled with a rheum;
      What willingly he did confound, he wailed,
      Believe't, till I wept too.
CAESAR   No, sweet Octavia,   60
      You shall hear from me still; the time shall not
      Outgo my thinking on you.
ANTONY   Come, sir, come,
      I'll wrestle with you in my strength of love.
      Look, here I have you [*Embracing him*]; thus I let you go,
      And give you to the gods.
CAESAR   Adieu. Be happy!   65
LEPIDUS Let all the number of the stars give light
      To thy fair way!
CAESAR   Farewell, farewell!
      Kisses Octavia
ANTONY   Farewell!
      Trumpets sound. Exeunt [*in separate groups*]

Cleopatra recalls the Messenger and commands him to tell her about Octavia. Fearful of again arousing her anger, he quickly learns to report Octavia's appearance in unflattering terms.

1 Silent thoughts, silent messages (in groups of four)

Cleopatra and the Messenger remember their last meeting well. The Messenger still has the bruises! As he answers the queen's questions, he knows he must choose his words carefully to avoid another beating. Take parts and read through the scene.

a Silent thoughts

Before the Messenger answers each question, he must say what is going through his mind. After each response to his words, Cleopatra must say what she is thinking. Charmian must also say what is in her mind as she adds her comments.

b Silent messages

When Cleopatra asks the Messenger if Octavia is as tall as her, he says that she is not. How does he know that this is the right answer to give? In some productions Charmian secretly prompts him! Try out this scene with Charmian and Alexas standing behind Cleopatra, miming the answers that the Messenger must give.

c 'Dull of tongue, and dwarfish'

Every Cleopatra relishes line 16, trying to ensure a huge laugh or a significant moment. Rehearse lines 1–21, concentrating on the effect of line 16.

Go to, go to nonsense
Herod of Jewry King of the Jews, notorious for his fierceness (Antony did behead one Jewish king)
Isis Egyptian goddess of fertility, intelligence and motion
gait walk

If e'er ... majesty you have seen me so you know real majesty
her station the way she stands
She shows ... life she seems lifeless
than a breather rather than a living being

ACT 3 SCENE 3
Alexandria Cleopatra's palace

Enter CLEOPATRA, CHARMIAN, IRAS, *and* ALEXAS

CLEOPATRA Where is the fellow?
ALEXAS   Half afeard to come.
CLEOPATRA Go to, go to.

Enter the MESSENGER *as before*

                          Come hither, sir.
ALEXAS   Good majesty,
    Herod of Jewry dare not look upon you
    But when you are well pleased.
CLEOPATRA   That Herod's head
    I'll have; but how, when Antony is gone,   5
    Through whom I might command it? – Come thou near.
MESSENGER Most gracious majesty!
CLEOPATRA   Didst thou behold Octavia?
MESSENGER Ay, dread queen.
CLEOPATRA   Where?
MESSENGER   Madam, in Rome.
    I looked her in the face, and saw her led
    Between her brother and Mark Antony.   10
CLEOPATRA Is she as tall as me?
MESSENGER   She is not, madam.
CLEOPATRA Didst hear her speak? Is she shrill-tongued or low?
MESSENGER Madam, I heard her speak. She is low-voiced.
CLEOPATRA That's not so good. He cannot like her long.
CHARMIAN Like her? O Isis! 'Tis impossible.   15
CLEOPATRA I think so, Charmian. Dull of tongue, and dwarfish. –
    What majesty is in her gait? Remember
    If e'er thou look'st on majesty.
MESSENGER   She creeps:
    Her motion and her station are as one.
    She shows a body rather than a life,   20
    A statue than a breather.

The Messenger continues to tell Cleopatra what he hopes will please her. Charmian praises the Messenger and flatters Cleopatra. The queen seems reassured by what she hears.

1 More quick thinking (in groups of three)

Perhaps the Messenger gets a little over-confident as he gives Octavia's age as thirty, for Cleopatra was thirty-eight at this time! But he quickly continues to paint as unattractive a picture of Octavia as he can. He says, for example, that she has brown hair and a low forehead (fair hair and high foreheads were marks of beauty in Elizabethan times).

Compare the Messenger's description of Octavia with your impression of her in Act 3 Scene 2. Has he described her accurately?

2 Follow Cleopatra's changing moods (in small groups)

Charmian tries to keep Cleopatra from exploding by flattering her. For example, she instantly agrees with Cleopatra that the Messenger has 'excellent' judgement (line 25). Select key phrases from this scene which show the queen's fluctuating moods as she seeks to reassure herself that she is more attractive than Octavia. Record them by copying and continuing this diagram:

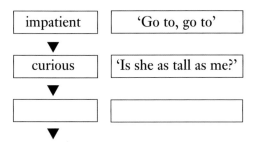

Is Cleopatra reassured in the end? What do you think might be the 'one thing more' she wanted to ask the Messenger (line 44)?

---

observance powers of observation
Three ... better note few in Egypt
 have better powers of observation
As low as she ... it extremely low
employ ... again send you back as
 my messenger
proper worthy, excellent

harried maltreated
by him according to his report
no such thing nothing much
Isis else defend may Isis forbid
serving ... long he being your
 servant for so long
I warrant you I'm sure it will

CLEOPATRA   Is this certain?
MESSENGER Or I have no observance.
CHARMIAN   Three in Egypt
    Cannot make better note.
CLEOPATRA   He's very knowing,
    I do perceive't. There's nothing in her yet.
    The fellow has good judgement.
CHARMIAN   Excellent.   25
CLEOPATRA Guess at her years, I prithee.
MESSENGER   Madam,
    She was a widow –
CLEOPATRA   Widow? Charmian, hark.
MESSENGER And I do think she's thirty.
CLEOPATRA Bear'st thou her face in mind? Is't long or round?
MESSENGER Round, even to faultiness.   30
CLEOPATRA For the most part, too, they are foolish that are so. –
    Her hair, what colour?
MESSENGER   Brown, madam, and her forehead
    As low as she would wish it.
CLEOPATRA   There's gold for thee.
    Thou must not take my former sharpness ill.
    I will employ thee back again; I find thee   35
    Most fit for business. Go make thee ready;
    Our letters are prepared.
                                        [Exit Messenger]
CHARMIAN   A proper man.
CLEOPATRA Indeed, he is so. I repent me much
    That so I harried him. Why, methinks, by him,
    This creature's no such thing.
CHARMIAN   Nothing, madam.   40
CLEOPATRA The man hath seen some majesty, and should know.
CHARMIAN Hath he seen majesty? Isis else defend,
    And serving you so long!
CLEOPATRA I have one thing more to ask him yet, good Charmian –
    But 'tis no matter; thou shalt bring him to me   45
    Where I will write. All may be well enough.
CHARMIAN I warrant you, madam.
                                        Exeunt

Antony makes several complaints against Caesar, who has declared war again on Pompey. Octavia begs him not to be angry with her brother. Antony agrees to Octavia's desire to act as mediator.

1 Husband and wife (in pairs)

Relations between Antony and Caesar are strained. In lines 5–10, Antony complains that Caesar in Rome has spoken insultingly ('scantly') about him. When forced to praise Antony ('pay me terms of honour'), Caesar gave him the least possible amount of credit ('most narrow measure lent me'). How is Antony and Octavia's marriage faring under this pressure?

a 'Led/Between her brother and Mark Antony'. So said the Messenger in the previous scene. Take a part each and have a chair for the absent Caesar. Octavia stands between the two men. As you speak lines 1–38, point or gesture to Antony, Caesar or Octavia. Show how Octavia is pulled one way and the other.

b 'If I lose mine honour,/I lose myself'. Antony is prepared to go to war to preserve his honour. Read lines 15–24 in different ways: sincerely, tenderly, uneasily and angrily. Each partner writes down why honour is so important to Antony. Compare your notes. Antony mentioned honour in Act 2 Scene 2, lines 87–105. What prompted him to speak of it then?

c Perform lines 24–38 in two ways:

• Antony is anxious to be rid of Octavia
• Antony takes a more concerned and fond farewell.

Decide which way is more convincing.

2 Splitting images

The 'arch of empire' held up by its triple pillars is breaking apart. Draw the picture that Octavia's simile (lines 30–2) brings to your mind.

---

semblable import similar
  seriousness
perforce of necessity
vented uttered
hint occasion (to praise Antony)
Stomach resent
Undo if I then undo

Let ... preserve it give your love to
  him who does most to preserve it
branchless pruned (of honour)
Shall stain which will eclipse
So ... yours if that is what you
  want
Should solder have to seal

ACT 3 SCENE 4
Antony's headquarters in Athens

Enter ANTONY *and* OCTAVIA

ANTONY Nay, nay, Octavia, not only that –
That were excusable, that and thousands more
Of semblable import – but he hath waged
New wars 'gainst Pompey, made his will and read it
To public ear, spoke scantly of me.   5
When perforce he could not
But pay me terms of honour, cold and sickly
He vented them, most narrow measure lent me;
When the best hint was given him, he not took't,
Or did it from his teeth.
OCTAVIA   O my good lord,   10
Believe not all, or, if you must believe,
Stomach not all. A more unhappy lady,
If this division chance, ne'er stood between,
Praying for both parts.
The good gods will mock me presently,   15
When I shall pray, 'O, bless my lord and husband!',
Undo that prayer by crying out as loud,
'O, bless my brother!' Husband win, win brother,
Prays and destroys the prayer; no midway
'Twixt these extremes at all.
ANTONY   Gentle Octavia,   20
Let your best love draw to that point which seeks
Best to preserve it. If I lose mine honour,
I lose myself; better I were not yours
Than yours so branchless. But, as you requested,
Yourself shall go between's. The meantime, lady,   25
I'll raise the preparation of a war
Shall stain your brother. Make your soonest haste;
So your desires are yours.
OCTAVIA   Thanks to my lord.
The Jove of power make me, most weak, most weak,
Your reconciler! Wars 'twixt you twain would be   30
As if the world should cleave, and that slain men
Should solder up the rift.

Antony allows Octavia to return to Rome. Eros reports that Caesar first used Lepidus in the war against Pompey, then arrested and imprisoned him. Enobarbus forecasts war between Caesar and Antony.

---

1 Observers of events (in pairs)

Caesar has moved fast to dispose of his rivals, Lepidus and Pompey. Enobarbus and Eros discuss the approaching political upheaval.

a 'World, thou hast a pair of chaps, no more' (line 11). How quick is Enobarbus to appreciate the importance of what he has heard? Speak lines 11–13 to each other several times. Describe the image created in your mind ('chaps' = jaws).

b 'He's walking in the garden – thus' (line 14). Eros imitates Antony's walk through the gardens and describes him angrily kicking aside the 'rush' (straw) on the ground. Read Scene 5 and use the information in it to write a short scene between Antony and the Messenger set in the garden. The Messenger is bringing news from Rome of Lepidus's impending execution and Pompey's murder by one of Antony's own officers. Will Antony treat the Messenger bringing this bad news as Cleopatra did in Act 2 Scene 5?

c ' 'Twill be naught,/But let it be', says Enobarbus (lines 20–1). 'Naught' could mean 'nothing important' or 'something ill-advised and disastrous'. What do you think Enobarbus has in mind?

2 Shakespeare and North's Plutarch

Plutarch writes that Lepidus was deposed by Caesar but not imprisoned and that it was Antony, not Caesar, who ordered him to be killed. Decide why Shakespeare changed the historical 'facts' in lines 6–10.

---

where this begins who started this conflict
Provide make arrangements for
success outcome
presently immediately
denied him rivality denied Lepidus equal partnership
his own appeal his own (Caesar's) accusation
the poor third Lepidus
is up is imprisoned
enlarge his confine sets him free
threats the throat threatens to cut the throat

ANTONY When it appears to you where this begins,
　　　　Turn your displeasure that way, for our faults
　　　　Can never be so equal that your love   35
　　　　Can equally move with them. Provide your going;
　　　　Choose your own company and command what cost
　　　　Your heart has mind to.

Exeunt

ACT 3 SCENE 5
Athens

Enter ENOBARBUS and EROS, meeting

ENOBARBUS How now, friend Eros?
EROS There's strange news come, sir.
ENOBARBUS What, man?
EROS Caesar and Lepidus have made wars upon Pompey.
ENOBARBUS This is old. What is the success?   5
EROS Caesar, having made use of him in the wars 'gainst Pompey,
　　presently denied him rivality, would not let him partake in the
　　glory of the action; and, not resting here, accuses him of letters
　　he had formerly wrote to Pompey; upon his own appeal seizes
　　him. So the poor third is up, till death enlarge his confine.   10
ENOBARBUS Then, world, thou hast a pair of chaps, no more;
　　　　And throw between them all the food thou hast,
　　　　They'll grind the one the other. Where's Antony?
EROS He's walking in the garden – thus – and spurns
　　　　The rush that lies before him; cries, 'Fool Lepidus!'   15
　　　　And threats the throat of that his officer
　　　　That murdered Pompey.
ENOBARBUS　　　　　　　　　Our great navy's rigged.
EROS For Italy and Caesar. More, Domitius:
　　　　My lord desires you presently. My news
　　　　I might have told hereafter.
ENOBARBUS　　　　　　　　　　　'Twill be naught,   20
　　　　But let it be. Bring me to Antony.
EROS　　　　　　　　　　　　　　　　Come, sir.

Exeunt

> *Caesar informs Maecenas and Agrippa that Antony has shared out Rome's eastern provinces between Cleopatra and their children. Antony has made several complaints about Caesar's own conduct.*

1 God-king and goddess-queen (in large groups)

Shakespeare does not show the famous scene in Alexandria where Antony and Cleopatra preside over the gift of kingdoms, provinces and islands to their children and to Caesarion (Julius Caesar's son by Cleopatra). But the 1992 Royal Shakespeare Company production did exactly that. As Caesar spoke lines 1–19, there appeared behind him a dumb-show of the two lovers enthroned in gold and surrounded by their children. Present your own silent version of the legendary 'donations' ceremony in Alexandria, with two of you speaking lines 1–19 as an accompanying commentary.

2 Syria, Cyprus, Lydia, Media, Parthia ... (in pairs)

Antony disposes of an impressive list of kingdoms and provinces. Locate the countries mentioned here on the map on page 3 to see just how much territory Antony has at his command.

3 Charges and counter-charges (in groups of three)

When men prepare to fight each other they need reasons and supporters. Draw two columns as shown and list Caesar's and Antony's complaints in lines 1–39. Decide how seriously they regard each complaint.

Caesar's complaints against Antony	Antony's complaints against Caesar
1 Antony has given Rome's eastern provinces to Antony's sons by Cleopatra	1 Caesar did not give him part of Pompey's territories in Sicily

Contemning contemptuous of
tribunal raised platform, dais
Caesarion ... son (see Activity1 above and page 241)
stablishment government
habiliments robes

Will their good thoughts call will withdraw their support and favour
spoiled overthrown
rated given
being being deposed
his revenue Lepidus's possessions

ACT 3   SCENE 6
Rome

Enter AGRIPPA, MAECENAS, and CAESAR

CAESAR Contemning Rome, he has done all this and more
In Alexandria. Here's the manner of't:
I'th'market-place, on a tribunal silvered,
Cleopatra and himself in chairs of gold
Were publicly enthroned; at the feet sat   5
Caesarion, whom they call my father's son,
And all the unlawful issue that their lust
Since then hath made between them. Unto her
He gave the stablishment of Egypt, made her
Of lower Syria, Cyprus, Lydia,   10
Absolute queen.
MAECENAS   This in the public eye?
CAESAR I'th'common show-place, where they exercise.
His sons he there proclaimed the kings of kings:
Great Media, Parthia, and Armenia
He gave to Alexander; to Ptolemy he assigned   15
Syria, Cilicia, and Phoenicia. She
In th'habiliments of the goddess Isis
That day appeared, and oft before gave audience –
As 'tis reported – so.
MAECENAS Let Rome be thus informed.   20
AGRIPPA Who, queasy with his insolence already,
Will their good thoughts call from him.
CAESAR The people knows it, and have now received
His accusations.
AGRIPPA   Who does he accuse?
CAESAR Caesar, and that having in Sicily   25
Sextus Pompeius spoiled, we had not rated him
His part o'th'isle. Then does he say he lent me
Some shipping, unrestored. Lastly, he frets
That Lepidus of the triumvirate
Should be deposed, and, being, that we detain   30
All his revenue.
AGRIPPA   Sir, this should be answered.
CAESAR 'Tis done already, and the messenger gone.

Caesar defends his arrest of Lepidus. He will give Antony a share of his conquests provided that Antony does likewise. Octavia arrives unannounced, without the ceremony that Caesar feels she deserves.

1 'That ever I should call thee castaway!'
(in small groups)

Caesar seems outraged that his sister has returned like a rejected 'castaway' without the royal ceremony ('ostentation') due to her. He expresses concern for Octavia, but might the political Caesar be secretly pleased? Decide whether Caesar is concerned or angry about his sister's return to Rome. To help you:

The use of 'I', 'me', 'my'/ 'thou', 'thee', 'thy' suggests closeness and intimacy. 'You', 'your' and the royal 'we', 'us' suggest distance and formality.

Which forms does Caesar use most to address his sister?

change removal
expectation those waiting
populous many
prevented forestalled
which ... unloved love which is
  not shown or spoken can die

constrained forced
pardon for permission to
Being an abstract because your
  departure removes the obstacle

I have told him Lepidus was grown too cruel,
That he his high authority abused
And did deserve his change. For what I have conquered,   35
I grant him part; but then in his Armenia
And other of his conquered kingdoms I
Demand the like.
MAECENAS   He'll never yield to that.
CAESAR Nor must not then be yielded to in this.

Enter OCTAVIA *with her train*

OCTAVIA Hail, Caesar, and my lord! Hail, most dear Caesar!   40
CAESAR That ever I should call thee castaway!
OCTAVIA You have not called me so, nor have you cause.
CAESAR Why have you stol'n upon us thus? You come not
          Like Caesar's sister. The wife of Antony
          Should have an army for an usher and   45
          The neighs of horse to tell of her approach
          Long ere she did appear. The trees by th'way
          Should have borne men, and expectation fainted,
          Longing for what it had not. Nay, the dust
          Should have ascended to the roof of heaven,   50
          Raised by your populous troops. But you are come
          A market maid to Rome, and have prevented
          The ostentation of our love, which, left unshown,
          Is often left unloved. We should have met you
          By sea and land, supplying every stage   55
          With an augmented greeting.
OCTAVIA   Good my lord,
          To come thus was I not constrained, but did it
          On my free will. My lord, Mark Antony,
          Hearing that you prepared for war, acquainted
          My grievèd ear withal, whereon I begged   60
          His pardon for return.
CAESAR   Which soon he granted,
          Being an abstract 'tween his lust and him.
OCTAVIA Do not say so, my lord.
CAESAR   I have eyes upon him,
          And his affairs come to me on the wind.
          Where is he now?   65

Caesar tells Octavia that Antony has returned to Cleopatra and is gathering support for war. Caesar tries to comfort Octavia and promises to punish Antony for his disgraceful treatment of her.

1 'Levying/The kings o'th'earth for war' (in small groups)

The monarchs and kingdoms under Antony's control (lines 70–8), together with those Caesar has already mentioned (lines 8–16), cover a vast range of territory (see map on page 3). Antony's military capability is enormous, and Caesar acknowledges this when he says that his concern for Octavia forced him to delay taking action against Antony (lines 82–4), thereby putting his own forces 'in negligent danger'.

Look back over Act 3 Scenes 4 and 5. Has Caesar really been so passive?

2 The language of propaganda?

Before going to war, it is common practice for a nation to abuse the enemy and give itself virtuous motives for fighting. List the abusive words the men use against Antony and Cleopatra, the words of sympathy they use towards Octavia, and the high moral words they use of themselves.

3 Destiny, chance or individual choice? (in small groups)

In lines 87–8, Caesar says that predestined events ('determined things') should be allowed to happen without complaint ('Hold unbewailed their way'). But how much of a helping hand has Caesar given destiny, and how much is due to chance?

Decide how much the following factors have contributed to the conflict between Antony and Octavius Caesar: destiny or fate; chance; the personalities of the two leaders; the differences between the Roman and Egyptian attitudes to life.

That does who do
withhold ... forth restrain my
  rapid advance (to battle)
drives/O'er your content
  tramples on your happiness
mark reach, range

To do you justice ... love you
  make me and your friends judges
  and soldiers in your cause
large unrestrained
abominations unnatural acts
turns you off rejects you
regiment government, control
trull whore, prostitute

OCTAVIA My lord, in Athens.
CAESAR No, my most wrongèd sister, Cleopatra
    Hath nodded him to her. He hath given his empire
    Up to a whore, who now are levying
    The kings o'th'earth for war. He hath assembled   70
    Bocchus, the King of Libya; Archelaus,
    Of Cappadocia; Philadelphos, King
    Of Paphlagonia; the Thracian king, Adallas;
    King Manchus of Arabia; King of Pont;
    Herod of Jewry; Mithridates, King   75
    Of Comagene; Polemon and Amyntas,
    The Kings of Mede and Lycaonia,
    With a more larger list of sceptres.
OCTAVIA Ay me most wretched,
    That have my heart parted betwixt two friends   80
    That does afflict each other!
CAESAR   Welcome hither.
    Your letters did withhold our breaking forth
    Till we perceived both how you were wrong led
    And we in negligent danger. Cheer your heart;
    Be you not troubled with the time, which drives   85
    O'er your content these strong necessities,
    But let determined things to destiny
    Hold unbewailed their way. Welcome to Rome,
    Nothing more dear to me. You are abused
    Beyond the mark of thought, and the high gods,   90
    To do you justice, makes his ministers
    Of us and those that love you. Best of comfort,
    And ever welcome to us.
AGRIPPA Welcome, lady.
MAECENAS Welcome, dear madam.   95
    Each heart in Rome does love and pity you;
    Only th'adulterous Antony, most large
    In his abominations, turns you off
    And gives his potent regiment to a trull
    That noises it against us.
OCTAVIA   Is it so, sir?   100
CAESAR Most certain. Sister, welcome. Pray you
    Be ever known to patience. My dear'st sister!

Exeunt

Enobarbus chides Cleopatra. Her presence on the battlefield will distract Antony. The queen insists she has the right to be present. Antony reveals that Caesar's forces are close.

'Well, is it, is it?'

1 Women at war (in pairs)

Cleopatra and Enobarbus enter in the middle of a heated argument. He believes the battlefield is no place for a woman. She disagrees. In his aside (lines 6–9), Enobarbus states very bluntly that to have stallions ('horse') and mares serving together in war is inviting disaster. Work out the sexual innuendoes in his remarks, then speak the lines to each other with gestures as if telling a dirty joke. To help you:

'serve' = either serve in war or copulate with

'bear' = either bear the weight of, or be mounted by, a stallion

'merely' = utterly (perhaps with a pun on 'marely').

forspoke spoken against	**charge** stake, responsibility for a man as a general
If not ... us even if the war had not been declared against me	**take in** conquer
puzzle distract	**Toryne** town near Actium
Traduced for levity criticised for frivolity	**Celerity** speed
	admired wondered at

116

ACT 3 SCENE 7
Actium

Enter CLEOPATRA and ENOBARBUS

CLEOPATRA I will be even with thee, doubt it not.
ENOBARBUS But why, why, why?
CLEOPATRA Thou hast forspoke my being in these wars,
    And say'st it is not fit.
ENOBARBUS   Well, is it, is it?
CLEOPATRA If not denounced against us, why should not we   5
    Be there in person?
ENOBARBUS [*Aside*]   Well, I could reply.
    If we should serve with horse and mares together,
    The horse were merely lost; the mares would bear
    A soldier and his horse.
CLEOPATRA   What is't you say?
ENOBARBUS Your presence needs must puzzle Antony,   10
    Take from his heart, take from his brain, from's time
    What should not then be spared. He is already
    Traduced for levity, and 'tis said in Rome
    That Photinus, an eunuch, and your maids
    Manage this war.
CLEOPATRA   Sink Rome, and their tongues rot   15
    That speak against us! A charge we bear i'th'war,
    And as the president of my kingdom will
    Appear there for a man. Speak not against it;
    I will not stay behind.

Enter ANTONY *and* CANIDIUS

ENOBARBUS   Nay, I have done.
    Here comes the emperor.
ANTONY   Is it not strange, Canidius,   20
    That from Tarentum and Brundusium
    He could so quickly cut the Ionian Sea
    And take in Toryne? – You have heard on't, sweet?
CLEOPATRA Celerity is never more admired
    Than by the negligent.

Antony decides to fight Caesar at sea, ignoring the advice of Enobarbus and Canidius. Cleopatra supports Antony's decision. A Messenger confirms Caesar's capture of nearby Toryne.

1 Antony's council of war (in groups of five)

How impressed are you by Antony's generalship and decision-making?

a Sit around a table and speak lines 20–59. Enobarbus and Canidius must attempt to get Antony to change his mind. Read the lines again, perhaps striking the table for emphasis, or standing up to emphasise your point of view. Antony can turn or walk away whenever Enobarbus and Canidius give their views.

b List the reasons Enobarbus and Canidius give for engaging Caesar on land. If Antony has such formidable land forces, why does he insist on fighting at sea?

2 'At Pharsalia, / Where Caesar fought with Pompey'

Pharsalus (see map page 3) was the site of Julius Caesar's decisive battle against Pompey the Great in 48 BC, which gave Caesar sole control of the Roman world. Why should Antony challenge Octavius Caesar to single combat at that particular place?

---

well becomed fittingly been spoken by
For that because
Ingrossed by swift impress hastily conscripted
yare light and manoeuvrable
fall you befall you
Distract divide, disrupt

footmen infantry
leave unexecuted prevent you using
merely completely
Our overplus ... burn we'll burn our surplus ships
head headland
descried sighted

ANTONY   A good rebuke,   25
    Which might have well becomed the best of men,
    To taunt at slackness. Canidius, we will fight
    With him by sea.
CLEOPATRA   By sea, what else?
CANIDIUS   Why will
    My lord do so?
ANTONY   For that he dares us to't.
ENOBARBUS So hath my lord dared him to single fight.   30
CANIDIUS Ay, and to wage this battle at Pharsalia,
    Where Caesar fought with Pompey. But these offers,
    Which serve not for his vantage, he shakes off,
    And so should you.
ENOBARBUS   Your ships are not well manned.
    Your mariners are muleteers, reapers, people   35
    Ingrossed by swift impress; in Caesar's fleet
    Are those that often have 'gainst Pompey fought.
    Their ships are yare, yours heavy. No disgrace
    Shall fall you for refusing him at sea,
    Being prepared for land.
ANTONY   By sea, by sea.   40
ENOBARBUS Most worthy sir, you therein throw away
    The absolute soldiership you have by land,
    Distract your army, which doth most consist
    Of war-marked footmen, leave unexecuted
    Your own renownèd knowledge, quite forgo   45
    The way which promises assurance, and
    Give up yourself merely to chance and hazard
    From firm security.
ANTONY   I'll fight at sea.
CLEOPATRA I have sixty sails, Caesar none better.
ANTONY Our overplus of shipping will we burn,   50
    And with the rest full-manned, from th'head of Actium
    Beat th'approaching Caesar. But if we fail,
    We then can do't at land.

Enter a MESSENGER

                Thy business?
MESSENGER The news is true, my lord; he is descried.
    Caesar has taken Toryne.   55

Antony is surprised by Caesar's swift move against him. A veteran soldier begs him not to fight Caesar at sea. Canidius blames Antony's unwise military strategy on Cleopatra's influence.

1 The common soldier (in groups of seven)

Enobarbus and Canidius have tried to reason with Antony but to no effect. Will the ordinary soldier be more successful?

One of you plays Antony. The rest of the group play the soldier and memorise a section each of lines 60–8. As Antony prepares to leave, detain him, keep him encircled and plead with him. Argue powerfully and echo each other's words to hammer home your views. Keep Antony encircled and make him listen to you. At the end, ask Antony why he still refuses to listen.

2 'This speed of Caesar's/Carries beyond belief'

Count the number of times the speed of Caesar and his army has been mentioned in this scene. Then work out how, according to the soldier, Caesar fooled Antony's spies about his military intentions. Write four words or phrases to describe Caesar's qualities as a general.

3 'With news the time's in labour'

Canidius says time 'throws forth' (gives birth) to fresh news each minute (lines 81–2). Talk with another student about the image this creates in your mind.

4 An edited Shakespeare (in groups of six)

Create and perform an edited one-minute version of this scene. Include Cleopatra and Enobarbus's argument, the council of war, the Messenger's news and the soldier's pleading.

---

his power Caesar's army
Thetis sea nymph
Have used to are accustomed to
Hercules Greek hero and warrior
his whole ... on't his plans are shaped without regard for where his real strength lies

horse whole cavalry undivided
Carries sweeps him forward
distractions detachments, separate groups

ANTONY Can he be there in person? 'Tis impossible;
          Strange that his power should be. Canidius,
          Our nineteen legions thou shalt hold by land,
          And our twelve thousand horse. We'll to our ship.
          Away, my Thetis!

                    Enter a SOLDIER

                    How now, worthy soldier?   60
SOLDIER O noble emperor, do not fight by sea;
          Trust not to rotten planks. Do you misdoubt
          This sword and these my wounds? Let th'Egyptians
          And the Phoenicians go a-ducking; we
          Have used to conquer standing on the earth   65
          And fighting foot to foot.
ANTONY   Well, well, away!
                    Exeunt Antony, Cleopatra, and Enobarbus
SOLDIER By Hercules, I think I am i'th'right.
CANIDIUS Soldier, thou art; but his whole action grows
          Not in the power on't. So our leader's led,
          And we are women's men.
SOLDIER   You keep by land   70
          The legions and the horse whole, do you not?
CANIDIUS Marcus Octavius, Marcus Justeius,
          Publicola, and Caelius are for sea,
          But we keep whole by land. This speed of Caesar's
          Carries beyond belief.   75
SOLDIER While he was yet in Rome,
          His power went out in such distractions as
          Beguiled all spies.
CANIDIUS   Who's his lieutenant, hear you?
SOLDIER They say, one Taurus.
CANIDIUS   Well I know the man.

                    Enter a MESSENGER

MESSENGER The emperor calls Canidius.   80
CANIDIUS With news the time's in labour, and throws forth
          Each minute some.
                                                 Exeunt

121

*Caesar and Antony with their armies await the outcome of the naval
battle near Actium. Enobarbus is horrified to see the whole of the
Egyptian fleet turn and sail away from the battle.*

1 The Battle of Actium (in small groups)

The Battle of Pharsalia decided the fate of Pompey the Great; the
Battle of Philippi decided the fate of Brutus and Cassius (see pages
241–2). Now the fortunes of Antony and Caesar are to be determined
on the waters off the coast of Actium. Caesar gives his officers precise
written instructions (Scene 8), while Antony waits to see the size of the
enemy fleet before deciding his strategy (Scene 9).

a The battle on an Elizabethan stage

Shakespeare's company would have had no lighting and little
scenery. They would, however, have had such props as armour,
spears, shields, banners, drums, pipes and trumpets. They could
also create off-stage sound effects – even real cannons (the Globe
theatre burnt down as the result of a fire caused by a cannon
during a performance of Shakespeare's *King Henry VIII*). Talk
about how you would stage Scenes 8, 9 and 10 in an open-air
Elizabethan theatre (see page 248 for an artist's reconstruction).
How could you create two vast armies and a naval battle?

b The battle on a twentieth-century stage

One lavish nineteenth-century production had the crews of
contending galleys firing arrows at each other. Modern
productions often opt for a more symbolic and stylised
presentation. Work out how you would stage Scenes 8, 9 and 10
for a production at your school or college.

c A radio play

Make a recording of Scenes 8, 9 and 10 using music and other
sound effects.

---

keep whole remain united	**admiral** flagship
prescript written instructions	**sixty** sixty ships
jump moment of chance	**synod** assembly
In eye of where we can observe	**What's thy passion?** why so
battle battle line (of ships)	angry?
Naught ruin, disaster	

ACT 3 SCENE 8 The coast near Actium

Enter CAESAR *and* TAURUS *with his army, marching*

CAESAR Taurus!
TAURUS My lord?
CAESAR Strike not by land; keep whole. Provoke not battle
Till we have done at sea. Do not exceed
The prescript of this scroll.
[He gives a scroll]
       Our fortune lies   5
Upon this jump.   *Exeunt*

ACT 3 SCENE 9 Near Actium

Enter ANTONY *and* ENOBARBUS

ANTONY Set we our squadrons on yond side o'th'hill,
In eye of Caesar's battle, from which place
We may the number of the ships behold
And so proceed accordingly.   *Exeunt*

ACT 3 SCENE 10 Near Actium

CANIDIUS *marches with his land army one way over the stage, and*
TAURUS *the lieutenant of Caesar the other way. After their going in is*
heard the noise of a sea fight. Alarum. Enter ENOBARBUS

ENOBARBUS Naught, naught, all naught! I can behold no longer.
Th'Antoniad, the Egyptian admiral,
With all their sixty, fly and turn the rudder.
To see't mine eyes are blasted.

Enter SCARUS

SCARUS   Gods and goddesses,
All the whole synod of them!
ENOBARBUS   What's thy passion? 5

123

Scarus reports Cleopatra and Antony's flight and plans to join them, but Canidius resolves to surrender to Caesar. Against his better judgement, Enobarbus decides to stay with Antony.

1 Vivid images

Scarus's anger, disappointment and disgust at his leader's dishonourable flight from the battle can be seen in the powerful images he uses. He says their situation is 'like the tokened pestilence' (line 9). For those dying of the plague, the sign ('token') of imminent death was the appearance of dark reddish spots.

a **'We have kissed away / Kingdoms and provinces'**
What picture does this description bring to your mind?

b **Animal images**
Cleopatra is a 'ribaudred nag', a foul useless horse or perhaps whore. She flees the battle like a cow with 'The breeze upon her', which suggests either the sails of her ship, or the gadfly (or 'breeze') whose stings would set the cows suddenly charging across the meadows. Antony follows her 'like a doting mallard' (lovesick drake) after its mate.

Imagine you are the political cartoonist for the *Actium Daily News*. Draw a cartoon of Cleopatra and Antony's flight using the animal images above.

2 Desperate choices (in groups of three)

Antony's defeat at Actium is decisive and his officers must now make decisions. Do they remain loyal, or desert and follow Caesar? Prepare a presentation of lines 24–36 to show the qualities each soldier has in defeat and the choice each makes. Block your moves and memorise your lines. How does each man leave the stage?

---

cantle section or segment
very ignorance utter stupidity
vantage the fortunes of battle
loofed puffed (turned into the wind preparing to change direction)
Claps ... sea wing sets his sails for flight

Been ... himself been true to himself
thereabouts considering desertion
good night indeed it's all over
to't to get to it
attend await
reason ... against me reason tells me I should do otherwise

SCARUS The greater cantle of the world is lost
            With very ignorance. We have kissed away
            Kingdoms and provinces.
ENOBARBUS   How appears the fight?
SCARUS On our side like the tokened pestilence,
            Where death is sure. Yon ribaudred nag of Egypt –   10
            Whom leprosy o'ertake! – i'th'midst o'th'fight,
            When vantage like a pair of twins appeared
            Both as the same, or rather ours the elder,
            The breeze upon her, like a cow in June,
            Hoists sail and flies.
ENOBARBUS   That I beheld.   15
            Mine eyes did sicken at the sight, and could not
            Endure a further view.
SCARUS   She once being loofed,
            The noble ruin of her magic, Antony,
            Claps on his sea wing, and, like a doting mallard,
            Leaving the fight in height, flies after her.   20
            I never saw an action of such shame.
            Experience, manhood, honour, ne'er before
            Did violate so itself.
ENOBARBUS   Alack, alack!

            Enter CANIDIUS

CANIDIUS Our fortune on the sea is out of breath,
            And sinks most lamentably. Had our general   25
            Been what he knew himself, it had gone well.
            O, he has given example for our flight
            Most grossly by his own!
ENOBARBUS Ay, are you thereabouts? Why then good night indeed.
CANIDIUS Toward Peloponnesus are they fled.   30
SCARUS 'Tis easy to't, and there I will attend
            What further comes.
CANIDIUS   To Caesar will I render
            My legions and my horse. Six kings already
            Show me the way of yielding.
ENOBARBUS   I'll yet follow
            The wounded chance of Antony, though my reason   35
            Sits in the wind against me.
                              [*Exeunt separately*]

Antony, ashamed of his dishonourable actions, offers his treasure ship to his followers, urging them to make their peace with Caesar. He promises to write letters to help his followers.

1 'I have lost command' (in groups of six)

Antony has not merely been defeated in battle, he has behaved shamefully in front of his troops. He has therefore 'lost command' of both himself and his troops. Use one or more of the following activities to explore Antony's state of mind in lines 1–24.

a Sit in a circle and read the lines, taking a sentence each. Do this several times, trying different ways of speaking to your followers: for example, despairingly, full of self-loathing.

b 'I am so lated in the world' (line 3). Antony uses the image of a traveller who is late reaching his destination. Night has fallen and he has lost his way. What other phrases does he use to express his sense of complete loss and failure?

c 'I have myself resolved upon a course/Which has no need of you' (lines 9–10). Talk about what this course of action might be.

d Find the paradoxical image of brown–white, youth–age which Antony uses to acknowledge that he has shown the foolishness of both the young man and the old man.

e Some actors like to think that Shakespeare wrote the opening lines of this scene because the actor playing Antony was having problems with the noise of his entrance across the creaking stage! Block the moves for lines 1–24 using the 'internal stage directions' (the clues in the lines themselves), then rehearse your version. Make this a sad and moving moment as Antony pleads with his followers to leave him, but they are very reluctant to go.

---

instructed taught by example
show their shoulders turn their backs (on the enemy)
followed that I followed that which I
they them the brown hairs also reprove the white

Sweep your way help clear your path (to Caesar)
loathness unwillingness
hint opportunity
Let ... leaves itself leave Antony whose senses have left him

ACT 3 SCENE 11
The coast of Egypt

Enter ANTONY *with* ATTENDANTS

ANTONY Hark! The land bids me tread no more upon't;
    It is ashamed to bear me. Friends, come hither.
    I am so lated in the world that I
    Have lost my way for ever. I have a ship
    Laden with gold. Take that, divide it; fly, 5
    And make your peace with Caesar.
ALL   Fly? Not we.
ANTONY I have fled myself, and have instructed cowards
    To run and show their shoulders. Friends, begone.
    I have myself resolved upon a course
    Which has no need of you. Begone. 10
    My treasure's in the harbour. Take it. O,
    I followed that I blush to look upon!
    My very hairs do mutiny, for the white
    Reprove the brown for rashness, and they them
    For fear and doting. Friends, begone. You shall 15
    Have letters from me to some friends that will
    Sweep your way for you. Pray you, look not sad,
    Nor make replies of loathness. Take the hint
    Which my despair proclaims. Let that be left
    Which leaves itself. To the seaside straightway! 20
    I will possess you of that ship and treasure.
    Leave me, I pray, a little. Pray you now,
    Nay, do so, for indeed I have lost command.
    Therefore I pray you. I'll see you by and by.
                 [Exeunt Attendants. Antony] sits down

Antony sits lost in a world of defeat and dishonour. Cleopatra's women urge her to comfort him. Eros attempts to rouse his master. At length Antony responds, chiding Cleopatra. She asks for forgiveness.

1 A painful reunion (in groups of five)

Actors say they can often find in Shakespeare's script the stage pictures, movements and gestures that are required. Lines 25–55 are a good example. To find the 'internal stage directions', draw a large plan of your stage and place Antony, seated in defeat and shame, downstage right. Have Cleopatra and the others enter upstage left. Work out the movements that lines 25–55 require. Consider the following points:

- 'Nay, gentle madam, to him.' Eros's first words suggest that Cleopatra does not go immediately to Antony. What does she do, and when does she finally pluck up courage to cross to him?
- Which line suggests that Antony cannot even look at Cleopatra? Decide when he finally breaks out of his cloud of despair.
- Work out Eros's movements and Charmian and Iras's promptings.
- Where do Antony and Cleopatra finally meet?

Using the movements you have decided on, play the scene with despair, pity, shame, compassion and love. Decide how Antony speaks his first words to Cleopatra and how she replies. Is Cleopatra behaving sincerely or is she play-acting?

2 'He at Philippi kept / His sword e'en like a dancer'

In *Julius Caesar*, Octavius is young and inexperienced in battle. Lines 35–40 recall the Battle of Philippi (see page 241). In Shakespeare's day, a dancing sword was an ornamental sword worn while dancing and was not used but 'kept' in its sheath. Write down what you think Antony was about to say at line 40 about Octavius.

Dealt on lieutenantry let his subordinates do his fighting
squares battle formations
stand by help me (I feel faint)
He's unqualitied he has lost his self-respect

sustain me hold me up
but/Your unless your
reputation honour
swerving error, offence
looking back looking back at
'Stroyed destroyed

Enter CLEOPATRA *led by* CHARMIAN, [IRAS], *and* EROS

EROS Nay, gentle madam, to him, comfort him.   25
IRAS Do, most dear queen.
CHARMIAN Do. Why, what else?
CLEOPATRA Let me sit down. O Juno!
ANTONY No, no, no, no, no.
EROS See you here, sir?   30
ANTONY O fie, fie, fie!
CHARMIAN Madam!
IRAS Madam, O good empress!
EROS Sir, sir!
ANTONY Yes, my lord, yes. He at Philippi kept   35
    His sword e'en like a dancer, while I struck
    The lean and wrinkled Cassius, and 'twas I
    That the mad Brutus ended. He alone
    Dealt on lieutenantry, and no practice had
    In the brave squares of war. Yet now – no matter.   40
CLEOPATRA Ah, stand by.
EROS   The queen, my lord, the queen.
IRAS Go to him, madam, speak to him.
    He's unqualitied with very shame.
CLEOPATRA Well then, sustain me. O!
EROS Most noble sir, arise. The queen approaches.   45
    Her head's declined, and death will seize her but
    Your comfort makes the rescue.
ANTONY I have offended reputation,
    A most unnoble swerving.
EROS   Sir, the queen.
ANTONY O, whither hast thou led me, Egypt? See   50
    How I convey my shame out of thine eyes
    By looking back what I have left behind
    'Stroyed in dishonour.
CLEOPATRA   O my lord, my lord,
    Forgive my fearful sails! I little thought
    You would have followed.

Antony tells Cleopatra that she knew his love for her would make him flee the battle. She begs his pardon and he forgives her. Caesar is informed that Antony's ambassador is a humble schoolmaster.

1 'O, whither hast thou led me, Egypt?'

Antony is compared to Mars in Act 1 Scene 1, line 4, and Cleopatra to Venus in Act 2 Scene 2, line 210. Renaissance painters often depicted Venus, the goddess of love, ensnaring Mars, the god of war, causing him to lay down his sword and remove his armour. Which images in lines 55–73 suggest that Cleopatra has 'led' Antony, much as Venus did Mars?

Thy beck an order from you
young man Octavius Caesar
treaties terms for negotiation
dodge ... lowness shuffle and cheat as failures must do
played ... pleased did exactly as I wanted

affection passion
on all cause whatever was at stake
rates equals, is worth
Even this this by itself
Is a is he
argument indication
pinion feather (a falconry image)

ANTONY   Egypt, thou knew'st too well   55
    My heart was to thy rudder tied by th'strings,
    And thou shouldst tow me after. O'er my spirit
    Thy full supremacy thou knew'st, and that
    Thy beck might from the bidding of the gods
    Command me.
CLEOPATRA   O, my pardon!
ANTONY   Now I must   60
    To the young man send humble treaties, dodge
    And palter in the shifts of lowness, who
    With half the bulk o'th'world played as I pleased,
    Making and marring fortunes. You did know
    How much you were my conqueror, and that   65
    My sword, made weak by my affection, would
    Obey it on all cause.
CLEOPATRA   Pardon, pardon!
ANTONY Fall not a tear, I say; one of them rates
    All that is won and lost. Give me a kiss.
           [*They kiss*]
    Even this repays me. – We sent our schoolmaster;   70
    Is a come back? – Love, I am full of lead. –
    Some wine within there, and our viands! Fortune knows
    We scorn her most when most she offers blows.
                  Exeunt

ACT 3   SCENE 12
Egypt   Caesar's camp

Enter CAESAR, AGRIPPA, THIDIAS, *and* DOLABELLA, *with others*

CAESAR Let him appear that's come from Antony.
    Know you him?
DOLABELLA   Caesar, 'tis his schoolmaster –
    An argument that he is plucked, when hither
    He sends so poor a pinion of his wing,
    Which had superfluous kings for messengers   5
    Not many moons gone by.

Caesar refuses Antony's requests but says he will agree to Cleopatra's terms provided that she either exiles or kills Antony. Thidias is sent to try to win her from Antony and to spy on Antony's activities.

1 The Schoolmaster as ambassador (in groups of four)

The Schoolmaster is one of many cameo roles in the play. How does this ordinary man react to being given such an important mission? Is he frightened, humble, pompous, confident or dignified? In lines 8–10, he describes his importance as being like a drop of dew on a leaf compared to the vast sea. One critic called these lines 'a pompous display of schoolmasterly rhetoric'. Another said they were 'a beautiful modest simile'.

Write brief director's notes on how you want this role to be played.

2 Caesar in victory

Caesar has followed Antony to Egypt, just as Julius Caesar followed Pompey the Great (see page 240), and he is closing in for the kill. Talk about Caesar's behaviour in victory and his plan for separating Antony from Cleopatra. What does it suggest about Caesar's personality?

3 'Women are not / In their best fortunes strong'

Women are weak creatures even in the happiest of circumstances, says Caesar (lines 26–33), and 'want' (times of difficulty) will corrupt even a Roman virgin priestess ('The ne'er-touched vestal').

Imagine that Caesar's words have been reported to Cleopatra. Write her response to his remarks and present it to the class. The class should then question you about your loyalty to Antony.

---

circle crown
hazarded ... grace dependent on your favour
Of ... fail, so will be heard and her wishes granted, provided
Bring him ... bands escort him through the troops

add ... offers offer anything you think
Make ... law decide your own reward: I will honour it
becomes his flaw copes with his broken condition
In ... moves in all he does

Enter AMBASSADOR *from Antony*

CAESAR   Approach and speak.
AMBASSADOR Such as I am, I come from Antony.
    I was of late as petty to his ends
    As is the morn-dew on the myrtle leaf
    To his grand sea.
CAESAR   Be't so. Declare thine office.   10
AMBASSADOR Lord of his fortunes he salutes thee, and
    Requires to live in Egypt; which not granted,
    He lessens his requests, and to thee sues
    To let him breathe between the heavens and earth
    A private man in Athens. This for him.   15
    Next, Cleopatra does confess thy greatness,
    Submits her to thy might, and of thee craves
    The circle of the Ptolemies for her heirs,
    Now hazarded to thy grace.
CAESAR   For Antony,
    I have no ears to his request. The queen   20
    Of audience nor desire shall fail, so she
    From Egypt drive her all-disgracèd friend
    Or take his life there. This if she perform
    She shall not sue unheard. So to them both.
AMBASSADOR Fortune pursue thee!
CAESAR   Bring him through the bands.   25
    [Exit Ambassador, attended]
    [To Thidias] To try thy eloquence now 'tis time. Dispatch.
    From Antony win Cleopatra. Promise,
    And in our name, what she requires; add more,
    From thine invention, offers. Women are not
    In their best fortunes strong, but want will perjure   30
    The ne'er-touched vestal. Try thy cunning, Thidias.
    Make thine own edict for thy pains, which we
    Will answer as a law.
THIDIAS   Caesar, I go.
CAESAR Observe how Antony becomes his flaw,
    And what thou think'st his very action speaks   35
    In every power that moves.
THIDIAS   Caesar, I shall.
    Exeunt

Cleopatra asks if she is to blame for the defeat. Enobarbus blames Antony for allowing his emotion to override his reason. Antony tells Cleopatra of Caesar's answer to her requests.

1 Who is more to blame? (in pairs)

Enobarbus says that 'Antony only' was to blame for their defeat because he allowed his 'will' (passion) and 'affection' (sexual desire) to 'nick' (get the better of) his reason and military judgement. Take it in turns to be Enobarbus and speak lines 1–12 to Cleopatra. Do you blame her as well?

Compare the way Cleopatra reacts to Enobarbus's home truths with the way she has reacted to unpleasant news in earlier scenes.

2 Divide and conquer (in groups of four)

The offer of generous terms to Cleopatra, provided she hands over Antony, is designed to drive a wedge between Caesar's two enemies. Does Antony test Cleopatra or trust her?

Read lines 13–28 several times and decide what is in Antony's mind as he tells Cleopatra of Caesar's offer. Present this section to the class with one of you as Antony's *alter ego* speaking his inner thoughts. What might be in Cleopatra's mind as she speaks line 19?

3 Heading for challenge (in small groups)

Antony challenges the youthful Caesar to prove his courage and fitness for command by meeting him in single combat (lines 20–8). Turn back to Scene 11 to find an image that echoes Antony's description of his own 'grizzled head' ('grizzled' = grey-haired). Then talk together about what you think has provoked Antony's challenge and how Caesar will respond.

Think, and die brood and die of depression
face show, appearance
ranges lines of warships
point moment of crisis
merèd question sole reason for the dispute

course pursue, follow
so she provided that she
note ... particular expect something exceptional
ministers servants, officers
prevail be victorious
gay caparisons impressive finery

ACT 3   SCENE 13
Alexandria   Cleopatra's palace

Enter CLEOPATRA, ENOBARBUS, *and* IRAS

CLEOPATRA What shall we do, Enobarbus?
ENOBARBUS   Think, and die.
CLEOPATRA Is Antony or we in fault for this?
ENOBARBUS Antony only, that would make his will
    Lord of his reason. What though you fled
    From that great face of war, whose several ranges   5
    Frighted each other? Why should he follow?
    The itch of his affection should not then
    Have nicked his captainship, at such a point,
    When half to half the world opposed, he being
    The merèd question. 'Twas a shame no less   10
    Than was his loss, to course your flying flags
    And leave his navy gazing.
CLEOPATRA   Prithee, peace.

Enter the AMBASSADOR, *with* ANTONY

ANTONY Is that his answer?
AMBASSADOR Ay, my lord.
ANTONY The queen shall then have courtesy, so she   15
    Will yield us up.
AMBASSADOR   He says so.
ANTONY   Let her know't. –
    To the boy Caesar send this grizzled head,
    And he will fill thy wishes to the brim
    With principalities.
CLEOPATRA   That head, my lord?
ANTONY To him again. Tell him he wears the rose   20
    Of youth upon him, from which the world should note
    Something particular. His coin, ships, legions,
    May be a coward's, whose ministers would prevail
    Under the service of a child as soon
    As i'th'command of Caesar. I dare him therefore   25
    To lay his gay caparisons apart

Enobarbus regards Antony's single-combat challenge to Caesar as a sign of failing judgement. He begins to question the wisdom of his own loyalty. Thidias brings Caesar's message: Cleopatra should trust him.

1 How loyal is Enobarbus? (in groups of three)

Six kings, as well as Canidius, have already deserted Antony (Act 3 Scene 10, lines 30–6). Will his closest friend do likewise? Prepare a presentation which shows honour and self-interest struggling for control of Enobarbus. One of you is self-interest, pushing Enobarbus to leave Antony. One of you is honour and loyalty, arguing for him to remain. The remaining person is Enobarbus. Listen to the arguments, question your 'two halves', then make your decision. The following will help your preparation:

- Self-interest. In lines 29–31, Enobarbus scorns the idea that Caesar, with great armies under his control ('high-battled Caesar'), would forego his good fortune ('Unstate his happiness') by fighting with a practised swordsman ('be staged to th'show/ Against a sworder').

- Honour and loyalty. 'Mine honesty (sense of honour) and I begin to square (quarrel)', says Enobarbus, wondering where the honour can be in remaining loyal to a fool. What reason does he give in lines 43–6 to believe there is still honour in following his 'fall'n lord'?

2 Why does Thidias pause? (in groups of three)

Line 53 has the single word 'So'. A short line in Shakespeare usually suggests a pause and is a hint to the actor. Work out what Thidias might do in that pause to show what he is thinking.

---

declined weak as I am
A parcel of closely linked to
things ... alike external events will affect a man's inner judgement
Knowing all measures experienced as he is
blown past its prime

i'th'story in history
apart privately
haply perhaps
Whose ... are whoever Antony belongs to, so do we
Caesar ... Caesar Caesar says don't worry, just trust him

136

And answer me declined, sword against sword,
Ourselves alone. I'll write it. Follow me.
                    [*Exeunt Antony and Ambassador*]
ENOBARBUS [*Aside*] Yes, like enough, high-battled Caesar will
          Unstate his happiness and be staged to th'show   30
          Against a sworder! I see men's judgements are
          A parcel of their fortunes, and things outward
          Do draw the inward quality after them
          To suffer all alike. That he should dream,
          Knowing all measures, the full Caesar will   35
          Answer his emptiness! Caesar, thou hast subdued
          His judgement too.

                        Enter a SERVANT

SERVANT   A messenger from Caesar.
CLEOPATRA What, no more ceremony? See, my women,
          Against the blown rose may they stop their nose
          That kneeled unto the buds. – Admit him, sir.   40
                                        [*Exit Servant*]
ENOBARBUS [*Aside*] Mine honesty and I begin to square.
          The loyalty well held to fools does make
          Our faith mere folly; yet he that can endure
          To follow with allegiance a fall'n lord
          Does conquer him that did his master conquer   45
          And earns a place i'th'story.

                        Enter THIDIAS

CLEOPATRA   Caesar's will?
THIDIAS Hear it apart.
CLEOPATRA   None but friends. Say boldly.
THIDIAS So haply are they friends to Antony.
ENOBARBUS He needs as many, sir, as Caesar has,
          Or needs not us. If Caesar please, our master   50
          Will leap to be his friend. For us, you know
          Whose he is we are, and that is Caesar's.
THIDIAS So.
          Thus then, thou most renowned: Caesar entreats
          Not to consider in what case thou stand'st   55
          Further than he is Caesar.

Thidias tells Cleopatra that Caesar knows she acted only out of fear of Antony. She agrees with him. Enobarbus leaves to inform Antony of Cleopatra's words. Thidias kisses the queen's hand.

1 Will Cleopatra betray Antony? (in groups of three)

Enobarbus certainly thinks so (lines 63–6). Play the scene from the entrance of Thidias to line 83 in two ways to help you decide. First, play Cleopatra as genuinely determined to leave Antony and yield herself up to Caesar in the hope of saving her kingdom. Second, play her as only pretending to yield to Caesar. What reasons might she have?

Is Cleopatra's 'O!' (line 58) genuine or ironic? Ask your Thidias if he believes Cleopatra is telling the truth or not.

2 More talk of honour

Antony and Enobarbus have already spoken of honour in this scene. What do Thidias and Cleopatra have to say about the queen's 'honour' in lines 59–63 ('constrainèd blemishes' means 'faults which you were forced to commit')?

Write a sentence each for Antony and Cleopatra which states what is at the heart of their notion of honour.

3 Rats leaving a sinking ship (in pairs)

The image Enobarbus uses in lines 63–6 is rather similar to the saying 'rats deserting a sinking ship'. Decide whether he is referring only to Cleopatra, or to himself as well.

---

most right most true
merely utterly
partly begs begs as far as a man of his great dignity can
shroud protection (but with ominous overtones)

landlord ruler, owner
in deputation on my behalf
doom of Egypt fate of Cleopatra
Wisdom ... shake it accept wisely the limits of what you can do and all will be well

CLEOPATRA   Go on: right royal.

THIDIAS He knows that you embrace not Antony
         As you did love, but as you feared him.

CLEOPATRA   O!

THIDIAS The scars upon your honour therefore he
         Does pity as constrainèd blemishes,   60
         Not as deserved.

CLEOPATRA   He is a god and knows
         What is most right. Mine honour was not yielded,
         But conquered merely.

ENOBARBUS [*Aside*]   To be sure of that,
         I will ask Antony. Sir, sir, thou art so leaky
         That we must leave thee to thy sinking, for   65
         Thy dearest quit thee.   *Exit Enobarbus*

THIDIAS   Shall I say to Caesar
         What you require of him? For he partly begs
         To be desired to give. It much would please him
         That of his fortunes you should make a staff
         To lean upon. But it would warm his spirits   70
         To hear from me you had left Antony
         And put yourself under his shroud,
         The universal landlord.

CLEOPATRA   What's your name?

THIDIAS My name is Thidias.

CLEOPATRA   Most kind messenger,
         Say to great Caesar this in deputation: 75
         I kiss his conqu'ring hand. Tell him I am prompt
         To lay my crown at's feet, and there to kneel.
         Tell him, from his all-obeying breath I hear
         The doom of Egypt.

THIDIAS   'Tis your noblest course.
         Wisdom and fortune combating together,   80
         If that the former dare but what it can,
         No chance may shake it. Give me grace to lay
         My duty on your hand.
                    [*He kisses her hand*]

Antony is enraged to find Cleopatra allowing Thidias to kiss her hand.
He orders Thidias to be taken out and whipped, then he turns angrily
on Cleopatra.

1 A dying lion rages

Three things make Antony explode with anger: Thidias's presumption,
Cleopatra's apparent faithlessness and the slow response of his servants.
Speak everything Antony says from where Thidias kisses Cleopatra's
hand to line 111. Antony must direct his anger in three directions: at
his servants, at Thidias and at Cleopatra. Emphasise the abuse he hurls
at Cleopatra and decide how violently he treats her.

'Take hence this jack and whip him.'

Your Caesar's father Julius
  Caesar (see page 241)
taking ... in conquering
As it as if it
fullest best and most fortunate
kite scavenging bird of prey

unto a muss in a scramble for
  goodies
jack fellow
lion's whelp young lion
tributaries dependent kings
blasted withered, blighted
feeders servants (Thidias)

CLEOPATRA Your Caesar's father oft,
　　　　When he hath mused of taking kingdoms in,　　　　85
　　　　Bestowed his lips on that unworthy place,
　　　　As it rained kisses.

Enter ANTONY *and* ENOBARBUS

ANTONY　　　　　　　　Favours? By Jove that thunders!
　　　　What art thou, fellow?
THIDIAS　　　　　　　　One that but performs
　　　　The bidding of the fullest man, and worthiest
　　　　To have command obeyed.
ENOBARBUS [*Aside*]　　　　You will be whipped.　　　　90
ANTONY [*Calling for Servants*]
　　　　Approach, there! – Ah, you kite! – Now, gods and devils,
　　　　Authority melts from me. Of late, when I cried 'Ho!',
　　　　Like boys unto a muss kings would start forth
　　　　And cry 'Your will?' – Have you no ears? – I am
　　　　Antony yet.

Enter Servants

　　　　Take hence this jack and whip him.　　　　95
ENOBARBUS [*Aside*] 'Tis better playing with a lion's whelp
　　　　Than with an old one dying.
ANTONY　　　　　　　　Moon and stars!
　　　　Whip him. Were't twenty of the greatest tributaries
　　　　That do acknowledge Caesar, should I find them
　　　　So saucy with the hand of she here – what's her name　　　　100
　　　　Since she was Cleopatra? Whip him, fellows,
　　　　Till like a boy you see him cringe his face
　　　　And whine aloud for mercy. Take him hence.
THIDIAS Mark Antony –
ANTONY　　　　　　　　Tug him away! Being whipped,
　　　　Bring him again; this jack of Caesar's shall　　　　105
　　　　Bear us an errand to him.

Exeunt [Servants] with Thidias

[*To Cleopatra*] You were half blasted ere I knew you. Ha?
　　　　Have I my pillow left unpressed in Rome,
　　　　Forborne the getting of a lawful race,
　　　　And by a gem of women, to be abused　　　　110
　　　　By one that looks on feeders?

*Antony accuses Cleopatra of being a faithless strumpet, and curses
himself for not seeing the truth earlier. How could she allow a mere
servant to kiss the hand that had pledged love to him?*

1 Echoes of the Bible (in pairs)

'O, that I were/Upon the hill of Basan, to outroar/The hornèd herd!'
Antony's cry (lines 129–31) would have struck home to an Elizabethan
audience for two reasons. They would recognise the reference to the
horns of the cuckold (a married man whose wife was unfaithful). They
would also hear the anguished words of the Old Testament psalmist,
who fears that God Himself has deserted him:

> My God, my God, why hast thou forsaken me?
> Why art thou so far from helping me, and from the words
> of my roaring? ...
> I am a worm and no man;
> A reproach of men, and despised of the people ...
> Many bulls have compassed me:
> Strong bulls of Bashan have beset me round.
> They gaped upon me with their mouths,
> As a ravening and a roaring lion.
> I am poured out like water,
> And all my bones are out of joint:
> My heart is like wax;
> It is melted in the midst of my bowels.   Psalm 22

Sit close together, face to face. Take it in turns to be Antony and speak
lines 107–34 to Cleopatra. In what ways is Antony's anguish like the
psalmist's? How anguished is Cleopatra?

2 Food and sex

Cleopatra, Antony's 'Egyptian dish', is again likened to food in lines
119–20. A 'trencher' is a wooden plate and a 'fragment' is a leftover.
Draw a picture of what these lines suggest to you.

---

boggler waverer, shifty one (hence 'adulterer, strumpet')
seel close up
at's at us
confusion ruin
Caesar/Pompey (see page 240)
vulgar fame common gossip

Luxuriously picked out chosen for your own lewd pleasures
'God quit you!' 'may God reward you'
this ... hearts Cleopatra's hand
haltered neck condemned man
yare nimble, quick

CLEOPATRA Good my lord –
ANTONY You have been a boggler ever.
    But when we in our viciousness grow hard –
    O, misery on't! – the wise gods seel our eyes,   115
    In our own filth drop our clear judgements, make us
    Adore our errors, laugh at's while we strut
    To our confusion.
CLEOPATRA   O, is't come to this?
ANTONY I found you as a morsel cold upon
    Dead Caesar's trencher; nay, you were a fragment 120
    Of Cneius Pompey's, besides what hotter hours,
    Unregistered in vulgar fame, you have
    Luxuriously picked out. For I am sure,
    Though you can guess what temperance should be,
    You know not what it is.
CLEOPATRA   Wherefore is this?   125
ANTONY To let a fellow that will take rewards
    And say 'God quit you!' be familiar with
    My playfellow, your hand, this kingly seal
    And plighter of high hearts! O, that I were
    Upon the hill of Basan, to outroar   130
    The hornèd herd! For I have savage cause,
    And to proclaim it civilly were like
    A haltered neck which does the hangman thank
    For being yare about him.

    Enter a SERVANT *with* THIDIAS

      Is he whipped?
SERVANT Soundly, my lord.   135
ANTONY Cried he? And begged a pardon?
SERVANT He did ask favour.

Antony humiliates the whipped Thidias then sends him back to inform Caesar of his anger. Antony predicts his own downfall. Cleopatra asks heaven to punish her if she is false to Antony.

1 Antony's cruelty (in groups of six)

One person is Thidias. The others, as Antony, take a section each of lines 138–56. Hurl your words at Thidias to show just how angry you are. Afterwards talk together about these two points:

a In lines 151–5, Antony gives Caesar leave to 'whip, or hang, or torture' Hipparchus, his freed slave ('my enfranchèd bondman'). Decide whether this is an example of Antony's cruelty or an appropriate tit-for-tat.

b Antony's savage treatment of Thidias echoes Cleopatra's savage treatment of the blameless Messenger in Act 2 Scene 5. Is Thidias also a blameless victim, or does he get what he deserves?

2 Cleopatra's declaration of love (in pairs)

If she is cold-hearted, says Cleopatra in lines 162–71, may heaven send down poisoned hailstones which will in melting ('By the discandying of this pelleted storm') kill her, her children and all of Egypt. What other hyperbolic (extravagant, larger-than-life) image of destruction does Cleopatra use to describe what she wishes to happen if she is proved false?

This is a make-or-break moment. Read lines 157–71. Start with Antony turned away from Cleopatra and decide when he turns to face her. When you have spoken lines 157–71 several times, ask Antony if he believes Cleopatra. Then read on and see if Shakespeare's Antony does.

---

fever thee give you the shivers
Look thou see to it that you
orbs orbits
As ... like whatever he wishes
quit repay, get even with
stripes marks made by the whip
terrene moon earthly goddess
  (Cleopatra)

stay his time wait (till he recovers)
one ... points Caesar's servant (who ties the laces or 'points' on his clothes)
determines comes to an end, melts
memory memorials, offspring

ANTONY [*To Thidias*] If that thy father live, let him repent
      Thou wast not made his daughter; and be thou sorry
      To follow Caesar in his triumph, since   140
      Thou hast been whipped for following him. Henceforth
      The white hand of a lady fever thee;
      Shake thou to look on't. Get thee back to Caesar.
      Tell him thy entertainment. Look thou say
      He makes me angry with him; for he seems   145
      Proud and disdainful, harping on what I am,
      Not what he knew I was. He makes me angry,
      And at this time most easy 'tis to do it,
      When my good stars that were my former guides
      Have empty left their orbs and shot their fires   150
      Into th'abysm of hell. If he mislike
      My speech and what is done, tell him he has
      Hipparchus, my enfranchèd bondman, whom
      He may at pleasure whip, or hang, or torture,
      As he shall like to quit me. Urge it thou.   155
      Hence with thy stripes, begone!
                          Exeunt [Servant and] Thidias
CLEOPATRA   Have you done yet?
ANTONY Alack, our terrene moon is now eclipsed,
      And it portends alone the fall of Antony.
CLEOPATRA I must stay his time.
ANTONY To flatter Caesar would you mingle eyes   160
      With one that ties his points?
CLEOPATRA   Not know me yet?
ANTONY Cold-hearted toward me?
CLEOPATRA   Ah, dear, if I be so,
      From my cold heart let heaven engender hail,
      And poison it in the source, and the first stone
      Drop in my neck; as it determines, so   165
      Dissolve my life! The next Caesarion smite,
      Till by degrees the memory of my womb,
      Together with my brave Egyptians all,
      By the discandying of this pelleted storm
      Lie graveless till the flies and gnats of Nile   170
      Have buried them for prey!

Antony accepts Cleopatra's faithfulness and prepares to fight once more against Caesar. He calls for one more night of revelry. Enobarbus thinks Antony has lost all judgement. He plans to desert.

1 The final moments (in small groups)

In the last minutes of this scene, Antony's confidence returns. As two of you read lines 171–98, the rest echo Antony's cheering, brave, bold, dare-devil words.

2 The ebb and flow of emotion (in small groups)

Scene 13 is full of surges of jealousy, despair, fear, fury and bravado. The graph below traces Antony and Enobarbus's movement between despair and confidence. Copy it and add further quotations.
Draw similar graphs for Antony's fury and calm; Antony's jealousy and love; Cleopatra's fear and reassurance.

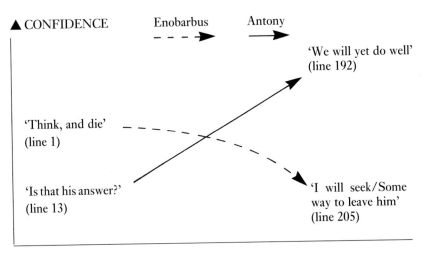

sits down in lays siege to
oppose his fate resist his destiny
fleet are afloat
chronicle place in history
treble ... breathed full of strength, courage and energy

maliciously fiercely, savagely
For when ... jests when fortune favoured me, I readily spared men's lives as if it were a game
gaudy festive, feasting
estridge goshawk (bird of prey)

ANTONY   I am satisfied.
        Caesar sits down in Alexandria, where
        I will oppose his fate. Our force by land
        Hath nobly held; our severed navy too
        Have knit again, and fleet, threat'ning most sea-like.   175
        Where hast thou been, my heart? Dost thou hear, lady?
        If from the field I shall return once more
        To kiss these lips, I will appear in blood;
        I and my sword will earn our chronicle.
        There's hope in't yet.   180
CLEOPATRA That's my brave lord!
ANTONY I will be treble-sinewed, hearted, breathed,
        And fight maliciously. For when mine hours
        Were nice and lucky, men did ransom lives
        Of me for jests; but now I'll set my teeth   185
        And send to darkness all that stop me. Come,
        Let's have one other gaudy night. Call to me
        All my sad captains. Fill our bowls once more;
        Let's mock the midnight bell.
CLEOPATRA   It is my birthday.
        I had thought t'have held it poor; but since my lord   190
        Is Antony again, I will be Cleopatra.
ANTONY We will yet do well.
CLEOPATRA [To Attendants] Call all his noble captains to my lord.
ANTONY Do so; we'll speak to them, and tonight I'll force
        The wine peep through their scars. Come on, my queen,   195
        There's sap in't yet. The next time I do fight
        I'll make Death love me, for I will contend
        Even with his pestilent scythe.
                                      Exeunt [all but Enobarbus]
ENOBARBUS Now he'll outstare the lightning. To be furious
        Is to be frighted out of fear, and in that mood   200
        The dove will peck the estridge; and I see still
        A diminution in our captain's brain
        Restores his heart. When valour preys on reason,
        It eats the sword it fights with. I will seek
        Some way to leave him.   Exit   205

Looking back at Act 3

Activities for groups or individuals

1 Fax machines in action

The action throughout Act 3 switches rapidly from one place to another: Parthia, Rome, Athens, Egypt and Actium. Messengers provide the necessary links between people and places. Had the fax machine been invented then, some messengers might well have escaped a beating!

In pairs, devise the fax message, or messages, that would have been sent at the end of every scene. Name the sender, place, recipient and his or her location. Keep the message short and clear. You might add a question or a request that requires a reply. Exchange your faxes one by one with another pair. See what replies you receive.

2 A lightning tour

Samuel Johnson, writing in 1765, said that what he enjoyed about the play was 'the continual hurry of the action, the variety of incidents and the quick succession of one person after another'. Devise your own 'lightning tour' of the thirteen scenes of Act 3. Announce the events of each scene in turn, followed by a ten-second mime or dialogue showing those events. How quickly can you take your audience through Act 3?

3 The many faces of Cleopatra

Cleopatra copes with many crises: Antony's marriage to Octavia, his defeat at Actium, Caesar's blandishments sent via Thidias, and Antony's despair, anger and desperation. In pairs, list the different situations Cleopatra encounters in Act 3 and the mood she assumes for each. Use your list to present 'the many faces of Cleopatra' in which one of you mimes her mood and the other explains it.

4 Sexism?

Cleopatra is often referred to as food for the male palate ('dish', 'morsel'). List the derogatory references to Cleopatra in Act 3 (Scenes 10, 12 and 13 especially). Talk about whether you find these descriptions sexist.

5 Canidius and Enobarbus

Make notes on why Canidius decides to defect to Caesar (Act 3 Scenes 7 and 10). Make notes on why Enobarbus decides to remain loyal (Act 3 Scenes 7, 10 and 13). Use this information to write an extra scene at the end of Act 3 in which Enobarbus meets Canidius.

6 Loving brother and sister?

Octavia, like Lepidus and Pompey before her, disappears from the story. Make notes on what Octavia and Caesar might think of each other. Use these notes as a basis for an improvised conversation between Octavia and Caesar after his victory at Actium.

7 Antony in defeat

Antony is often talked of as a tragic hero, a great and admirable man, but fatally flawed. Decide what you think of him as he struggles to cope with failure and dishonour.

Collect descriptions of Antony from Act 3, spoken by others and by himself. What images of melting, stripping, plucking can you find? Then list the flaws in Antony that you think have brought him down and the virtues that he shows in defeat.

Caesar scorns Antony's challenge to personal combat. Maecenas says Antony's anger will be his downfall. Caesar intends the next battle to be decisive. Antony learns of Caesar's refusal to fight.

1 Compare the two generals (in large groups)

The armies of the Roman world are preparing for 'the last of many battles' (line 12). Divide into two groups:

Group 1 (four students): prepare a presentation of Scene 1. Remember that you are at war. Talk about Caesar's attitude to Antony, especially when Caesar says his final two words. Is he controlled, scornful, angry or sympathetic? Use the letter and Caesar's military plans and maps as props. Finish your presentation by freezing into a tableau when Caesar says 'Poor Antony!'. Show clearly your character's reactions.

Group 2 (eight students): present Scene 2, lines 1–24. Make notes on Antony's tone of voice at each stage so that you convey his state of mind. There is much action in these lines, so block all your moves. Note also the reactions of Antony's followers. Finish your presentation by freezing into a tableau at line 24.

Show your presentations to each other. Then compare the two generals. Consider in particular the following questions:

a 'When one so great begins to rage, he's hunted/Even to falling', says Maecenas of Antony (lines 8–9). Do you think Antony rages, raves or behaves like a hunted animal in Scene 2?

b Different worlds. Both Caesar (lines 15–17) and Antony (in Scene 2) give orders for a feast that night. How do their words show that they live in very different worlds?

c Who is going to win this battle? Whom do you want to win?

---

as he had as if he had
Make boot of his distraction
 take advantage of his mad rage
best heads commanding officers
files ranks
but late until very recently

fetch him in defeat him
store abundant supply
waste expense
He thinks ... one he thinks luck
 and numbers are on his side

ACT 4   SCENE 1
Caesar's camp near Alexandria

Enter CAESAR, AGRIPPA, *and* MAECENAS, *with his army, Caesar reading a letter*

CAESAR   He calls me boy, and chides as he had power
To beat me out of Egypt. My messenger
He hath whipped with rods, dares me to personal combat,
Caesar to Antony. Let the old ruffian know
I have many other ways to die, meantime
Laugh at his challenge.   5
MAECENAS   Caesar must think,
When one so great begins to rage, he's hunted
Even to falling. Give him no breath, but now
Make boot of his distraction. Never anger   10
Made good guard for itself.
CAESAR   Let our best heads
Know that tomorrow the last of many battles
We mean to fight. Within our files there are,
Of those that served Mark Antony but late,
Enough to fetch him in. See it done,   15
And feast the army; we have store to do't,
And they have earned the waste. Poor Antony!   *Exeunt*

ACT 4   SCENE 2
Alexandria   Cleopatra's palace

Enter ANTONY, CLEOPATRA, ENOBARBUS, CHARMIAN, IRAS, ALEXAS, *with others*

ANTONY   He will not fight with me, Domitius?
ENOBARBUS   No.
ANTONY   Why should he not?
ENOBARBUS   He thinks, being twenty times of better fortune,
He is twenty men to one.

151

*Antony is determined to fight to the death. He summons his servants,
thanks them for their loyal service and bids them farewell. His words
puzzle Cleopatra.*

1 Enobarbus the cynic?

Enobarbus has never been easily swayed by blustering words. He
replies ambiguously when Antony asks him if he will fight well. 'Strike'
(line 9) could mean to 'attack', but also to 'furl sails' (implying surrender).
Decide which meaning Enobarbus intends and which meaning Antony
assumes.

2 'What means this?' (in groups of eight)

Cleopatra seems puzzled by Antony's behaviour (lines 14 and 24).
Cleopatra, as queen and leader, may have political and military matters
in mind. Cleopatra the woman may be more concerned for her lover's
personal well-being. Divide into two groups:

Group 1: list reasons why, as queen, she should be concerned.
Group 2: list reasons why, as a woman, she should be concerned.

Join together, compare notes, and talk about why Cleopatra asks this
question *twice.*

3 What do Antony's servants think?
(in groups of three or four)

The servants enter at line 10. Write, or present, a conversation later
that evening between one of the servants and his family, based on what
has been overheard in lines 10–46.

4 The Last Supper?

Some people have found echoes in this scene of Christ's Last Supper.
Read the New Testament (John: 13–17) and list any points of similarity
and dissimilarity.

---

bathe ... again (an old belief that
  bathing in blood restored youth)
Woo't thou will you
honest honourable, true
made so many men divided into
  as many men as are here
clapped up combined

Scant not don't neglect (to fill)
suffered acknowledged
period end
or if or if you do
like ... death like a devoted
  master, stay with you until death
yield reward

ANTONY   Tomorrow, soldier,   5
By sea and land I'll fight. Or I will live
Or bathe my dying honour in the blood
Shall make it live again. Woo't thou fight well?
ENOBARBUS I'll strike, and cry 'Take all.'
ANTONY   Well said. Come on!
Call forth my household servants. Let's tonight   10

Enter three or four SERVITORS

Be bounteous at our meal. – Give me thy hand,
Thou hast been rightly honest – so hast thou –
Thou – and thou – and thou. You have served me well,
And kings have been your fellows.
CLEOPATRA [*Aside to Enobarbus*]   What means this?
ENOBARBUS [*Aside to Cleopatra*]
'Tis one of those odd tricks which sorrow shoots   15
Out of the mind.
ANTONY   And thou art honest too.
I wish I could be made so many men,
And all of you clapped up together in
An Antony, that I might do you service
So good as you have done.
ALL   The gods forbid!   20
ANTONY Well, my good fellows, wait on me tonight:
Scant not my cups, and make as much of me
As when mine empire was your fellow too,
And suffered my command.
CLEOPATRA [*Aside to Enobarbus*]   What does he mean?
ENOBARBUS [*Aside to Cleopatra*]
To make his followers weep.
ANTONY   Tend me tonight;   25
May be it is the period of your duty.
Haply you shall not see me more, or if,
A mangled shadow. Perchance tomorrow
You'll serve another master. I look on you
As one that takes his leave. Mine honest friends,   30
I turn you not away, but, like a master
Married to your good service, stay till death.
Tend me tonight two hours, I ask no more,
And the gods yield you for't!

Enobarbus says Antony's words are distressing his followers, making them weep. Antony assures them he hopes for victory. Antony's palace guards begin their night watch. They hear strange music.

1 Shifting fortunes
(in groups of four)

Antony's guards are optimistic that if their navy succeeds in the coming battle, then the army too 'will stand up'. Their confidence is quickly shaken.

Prepare a presentation of Scene 3 showing the change in confidence. Block the moves as the soldiers come on guard and take up their positions (perhaps one in each corner of the room). Speak like soldiers, and show your reactions to the strange sounds. If you memorise your lines and use music and sound effects, you can maximise the dramatic effect.

At the end, tell the class your thoughts about your leader, Antony, and about the approaching battle.

discomfort distress
onion-eyed weeping
Grace goodness, or rue, the herb of grace
hearty kind-hearted
comfort encouragement
burn ... torches enjoy this night

consideration brooding thoughts
determine one way be decided one way or the other
Belike very probably
Here we this is our place
hautboys oboes
List listen

ENOBARBUS   What mean you, sir,
To give them this discomfort? Look, they weep,   35
And I, an ass, am onion-eyed. For shame,
Transform us not to women.
ANTONY   Ho, ho, ho!
Now the witch take me if I meant it thus!
Grace grow where those drops fall! My hearty friends,
You take me in too dolorous a sense,   40
For I spake to you for your comfort, did desire you
To burn this night with torches. Know, my hearts,
I hope well of tomorrow, and will lead you
Where rather I'll expect victorious life
Than death and honour. Let's to supper, come,   45
And drown consideration.

Exeunt

ACT 4   SCENE 3
Alexandria   Antony's camp

Enter a Company of SOLDIERS

1 SOLDIER Brother, good night. Tomorrow is the day.
2 SOLDIER It will determine one way. Fare you well.
         Heard you of nothing strange about the streets?
1 SOLDIER Nothing. What news?
2 SOLDIER Belike 'tis but a rumour. Good night to you.   5
1 SOLDIER Well, sir, good night.

They meet other SOLDIERS

2 SOLDIER Soldiers, have careful watch.
3 SOLDIER And you. Good night, good night.
         They place themselves in every corner of the stage
2 SOLDIER Here we; and if tomorrow
         Our navy thrive, I have an absolute hope   10
         Our landmen will stand up.
1 SOLDIER 'Tis a brave army, and full of purpose.
         Music of the hautboys is under the stage
2 SOLDIER Peace, what noise?
1 SOLDIER List, list!
2 SOLDIER Hark!   15

155

One soldier thinks the music is a good omen. Another fears it is a sign that the god Hercules, Antony's patron, is abandoning him. In Scene 4, Eros and Cleopatra help to arm Antony for battle.

1 'It signs well, does it not?'

Mark Antony claimed Hercules as his ancestor (a fact which Cleopatra sarcastically referred to in Act 1 Scene 3). Look at lines 20–2. What do the soldiers fear the mysterious noises might mean?

2 'Thou art/The armourer of my heart'
   (in groups of three)

Cleopatra attempts to help with Antony's armour but she doesn't know how the pieces are supposed to fit. Two of you are Antony and Cleopatra, the third is the director. Work out what might be happening as the actors speak lines 5–10. Also try speaking lines 6–7 in different ways. How do they reveal, visually and verbally, the dilemma that has faced Antony throughout the play?

   Finally, write director's notes on how the comedy and the seriousness of this moment might be conveyed.

---

signs well is a good omen
Hercules (see also pages 24 and 176)
so far ... quarter as far as our area of guard extends
give off come to an end, finish

Content agreed
chuck dearest
thine iron on my armour on me
brave defy
False you have put it on wrong
Sooth in truth

1 SOLDIER Music i'th'air.

3 SOLDIER Under the earth.

4 SOLDIER It signs well, does it not?

3 SOLDIER No.

1 SOLDIER Peace, I say! What should this mean?   20

2 SOLDIER 'Tis the god Hercules, whom Antony loved,
    Now leaves him.

1 SOLDIER   Walk. Let's see if other watchmen
    Do hear what we do.

2 SOLDIER How now, masters?

                [They] speak together

ALL How now? How now? Do you hear this?

1 SOLDIER Ay, is't not strange?   25

3 SOLDIER Do you hear, masters? Do you hear?

1 SOLDIER Follow the noise so far as we have quarter.
    Let's see how it will give off.

ALL Content. 'Tis strange.   30

                  Exeunt

ACT 4   SCENE 4
Alexandria   Cleopatra's palace

Enter ANTONY *and* CLEOPATRA *with* CHARMIAN *and others attending*

ANTONY Eros! Mine armour, Eros!

CLEOPATRA   Sleep a little.

ANTONY No, my chuck. Eros, come, mine armour, Eros!

        Enter EROS *[with armour]*

    Come, good fellow, put thine iron on.
    If fortune be not ours today, it is
    Because we brave her. Come.

CLEOPATRA   Nay, I'll help too.   5
    What's this for?

        [She tries to help arm him]

ANTONY   Ah, let be, let be! Thou art
    The armourer of my heart. False, false; this, this.

CLEOPATRA Sooth, la, I'll help. Thus it must be.

157

As Cleopatra and Eros help to arm Antony, he vows to fight like a true soldier. He is informed that his army awaits him. Before he leaves to do battle, he bids a soldierly farewell to Cleopatra.

1 Bindings and buckles (in groups of six)

For actors this is a very practical scene, full of stage business and props. The whole scene must be performed with 'dispatch' (speed).

a Breastplate, arm and leg guards, helmet, sword – this is what one production's prompt book showed was needed for this scene. Decide where and how each piece of equipment might be used.

b Images of binding and buckling. In lines 12–13, Antony vows that he will allow no one to 'doff' (unbuckle) his armour until he chooses. The armed and plated Antony is almost the first image in the play (see Philo's angry remarks in Act 1 Scene 1, lines 1–10). Compare your picture of Antony then and now.

2 The old Antony? (in small groups)

a The voice of command? Some people see a crisp decisiveness to Antony's speech in this scene. List three sections or lines where Antony seems at his most confident, giving each a descriptive title (for example, 'infectious enthusiasm' or 'businesslike commands') and saying why you chose it. Mention particular words, images or actions, or talk about the rhythm and syntax (sentence structure). Compare your notes with other groups.

b A military farewell. Present lines 24–38. Think about the soldiers' entrance, Antony's behaviour and the women's reactions.

Rarely excellently
squire knight's attendant
tight deft, skilful
Dispatch get on with it
royal occupation warfare
charge duty, responsibility
betime/betimes early

riveted trim armour
port city gate
dame my lady
check reproof
stand ... mechanic compliment
insist on any further ceremony

ANTONY   Well, well,
　　We shall thrive now. Seest thou, my good fellow?
　　Go, put on thy defences.
EROS   Briefly, sir.   10
CLEOPATRA Is not this buckled well?
ANTONY   Rarely, rarely.
　　He that unbuckles this, till we do please
　　To doff't for our repose, shall hear a storm.
　　Thou fumblest, Eros, and my queen's a squire
　　More tight at this than thou. Dispatch. O love,   15
　　That thou couldst see my wars today, and knew'st
　　The royal occupation, thou shouldst see
　　A workman in't.

　　　　　　　　Enter an armed SOLDIER

　　　　　　　　Good morrow to thee; welcome.
　　Thou look'st like him that knows a warlike charge.
　　To business that we love we rise betime   20
　　And go to't with delight.
SOLDIER   A thousand, sir,
　　Early though't be, have on their riveted trim
　　And at the port expect you.
　　　　　　　　Shout. Trumpets flourish

　　　　　　Enter CAPTAINS *and* SOLDIERS

CAPTAIN The morn is fair. Good morrow, general.
ALL Good morrow, general.
ANTONY   'Tis well blown, lads.   25
　　This morning, like the spirit of a youth
　　That means to be of note, begins betimes.
　　So, so. Come, give me that. This way. Well said.
　　Fare thee well, dame. Whate'er becomes of me,
　　This is a soldier's kiss.
　　　　　　　　[*He kisses her*]
　　　　　　　　Rebukable,   30
　　And worthy shameful check it were, to stand
　　On more mechanic compliment. I'll leave thee
　　Now like a man of steel. – You that will fight,
　　Follow me close. I'll bring you to't. Adieu.
　　　　　　Exeunt [*Antony, Eros, Captains, and Soldiers*]

Cleopatra goes to her room to wait. Antony admits his fault in not taking the soldier's advice to fight on land. He learns of Enobarbus's desertion and orders his friend's treasure to be sent after him.

1 The women who are left behind (in groups of five)

Imagine you are Cleopatra and her women, left behind to wait for news. Talk together about what you wish would happen and fear might happen. Present your conversation to the class.

2 'O, my fortunes have/Corrupted honest men' (in small groups)

Antony's immediate reaction is to blame himself for Enobarbus's desertion. Decide which man you think is more to blame.

3 Antony's magnanimity

There are many flaws in Antony's character, but also many strengths. How does he demonstrate his magnanimity (literally 'greatness of spirit') in Scene 5?

4 Write to Enobarbus

In lines 13–16, Antony orders Eros to write a letter to Enobarbus saying that he will sign ('subscribe') it. Write the letter that you think Antony might have sent.

5 Antony and Enobarbus (in groups of four)

Prepare a presentation of Scene 5. Include in your version the ghostly figure of Enobarbus, who comments on and reacts to what he sees. Make the soldier's words cut deep into Antony, and show how Antony's words affect the ghostly Enobarbus.

---

gallantly bravely
happy lucky
once formerly (when Antony spoke with him at Actium)

Detain no jot keep nothing back
Dispatch see to it quickly

CHARMIAN Please you retire to your chamber?
CLEOPATRA   Lead me.   35
　　　He goes forth gallantly. That he and Caesar might
　　　Determine this great war in single fight!
　　　Then Antony – but now – Well, on.   *Exeunt*

ACT 4   SCENE 5
Alexandria   Antony's camp

Trumpets sound. Enter ANTONY *and* EROS, *a* SOLDIER *meeting them*

SOLDIER The gods make this a happy day to Antony!
ANTONY Would thou and those thy scars had once prevailed
　　　To make me fight at land!
SOLDIER   Hadst thou done so,
　　　The kings that have revolted, and the soldier
　　　That has this morning left thee, would have still   5
　　　Followed thy heels.
ANTONY   Who's gone this morning?
SOLDIER   Who?
　　　One ever near thee. Call for Enobarbus,
　　　He shall not hear thee, or from Caesar's camp
　　　Say 'I am none of thine.'
ANTONY   What sayest thou?
SOLDIER   Sir,
　　　He is with Caesar.
EROS   Sir, his chests and treasure   10
　　　He has not with him.
ANTONY   Is he gone?
SOLDIER   Most certain.
ANTONY Go, Eros, send his treasure after. Do it.
　　　Detain no jot, I charge thee. Write to him –
　　　I will subscribe – gentle adieus and greetings;
　　　Say that I wish he never find more cause   15
　　　To change a master. O, my fortunes have
　　　Corrupted honest men. Dispatch. – Enobarbus!
　　　　　　　　　　　　　　　　　　　　　Exeunt

Caesar orders the deserters from Antony to be placed in the front line of battle. Enobarbus reflects on the fate of other deserters. He learns that his possessions have been sent over and added to by Antony.

---

1 Caesar the general (in groups of six)

Antony went into battle like a medieval knight, armed by his squire and fighting for honour and the love of his lady (Act 4 Scene 4). Caesar is a very different kind of leader. He orders Agrippa to place those who have deserted Antony in the front ranks for the coming battle ('Plant those that have revolted in the van'). Enobarbus tells of the fate of other deserters like Alexas and Canidius (lines 12–18). Do you admire or despise Caesar's actions?

2 Battle plans (in small groups)

Present to the class your idea of how Caesar might have planned and briefed his officers and men for this battle. You will need maps, battle plans and military orders.

3 'I will go seek / Some ditch wherein to die'

Everything that happens in this scene convinces Enobarbus that he has made a tragic mistake and must die (lines 38–9). What kind of blow does each piece of news inflict on Enobarbus?

4 'The time of universal peace is near'

Many in Shakespeare's audience would know that Octavius Caesar became Caesar Augustus, the first Roman emperor, whose rule was in many ways a 'time of universal peace' (line 5). What kind of 'universal peace' do you think would be enjoyed under Shakespeare's Caesar?

Prove this if this proves to be
three-nooked three-sectored
  (Europe, Asia, Africa)
bear the olive live at peace
charge Agrippa order Agrippa to
Jewry kingdom of the Jews
dissuade persuade

incline himself ally himself
fell away deserted
have entertainment are taken into
  service
His bounty overplus additional
  gifts
on my guard while I was on guard

ACT 4   SCENE 6
Caesar's camp near Alexandria

Flourish. Enter AGRIPPA, CAESAR, *with* ENOBARBUS, *and* DOLABELLA

CAESAR Go forth, Agrippa, and begin the fight.
     Our will is Antony be took alive;
     Make it so known.
AGRIPPA Caesar, I shall.   *[Exit]*
CAESAR The time of universal peace is near.   5
     Prove this a prosp'rous day, the three-nooked world
     Shall bear the olive freely.

Enter a MESSENGER

MESSENGER   Antony
     Is come into the field.
CAESAR   Go charge Agrippa
     Plant those that have revolted in the van,
     That Antony may seem to spend his fury   10
     Upon himself.

Exeunt [all but Enobarbus]

ENOBARBUS Alexas did revolt and went to Jewry on
     Affairs of Antony, there did dissuade
     Great Herod to incline himself to Caesar
     And leave his master Antony. For this pains,
     Caesar hath hanged him. Canidius and the rest   15
     That fell away have entertainment but
     No honourable trust. I have done ill,
     Of which I do accuse myself so sorely
     That I will joy no more.

Enter a SOLDIER *of Caesar's*

SOLDIER   Enobarbus, Antony   20
     Hath after thee sent all thy treasure, with
     His bounty overplus. The messenger
     Came on my guard, and at thy tent is now
     Unloading of his mules.
ENOBARBUS I give it you.   25

Antony's generosity leaves Enobarbus guilt-stricken. He is determined to live no longer, but to die in a ditch. Caesar's forces retreat before Antony's fierce attacks.

1 Can 'thoughts' kill? (in pairs)

Enobarbus certainly thinks so (lines 35–7). In Shakespeare's day, to be 'full of thoughts' was to be full of distress, grief and despair. Such 'thoughts' were believed capable of actually bursting the heart. 'This blows my heart', cries Enobarbus in line 35.

Take turns to play Enobarbus and tell each other your thoughts (lines 31–40). Decide which lines most powerfully convey Enobarbus's desperately tired despair.

'I am alone the villain of the earth.'

safed provided safe conduct for
host army
Jove king of the gods
feel ... most no one feels it as
bitterly as I
turpitude shameful disgrace
a swifter mean my suicide

thought will do't grief alone will
break it
has work is in trouble
our oppression the enemy attack
clouts blows (or bandages)
bench-holes latrines
scotches gashes

SOLDIER Mock not, Enobarbus,
    I tell you true. Best you safed the bringer
    Out of the host; I must attend mine office,
    Or would have done't myself. Your emperor
    Continues still a Jove.   *Exit*   30
ENOBARBUS I am alone the villain of the earth,
    And feel I am so most. O Antony,
    Thou mine of bounty, how wouldst thou have paid
    My better service when my turpitude
    Thou dost so crown with gold! This blows my heart.   35
    If swift thought break it not, a swifter mean
    Shall outstrike thought; but thought will do't, I feel.
    I fight against thee? No, I will go seek
    Some ditch wherein to die. The foul'st best fits
    My latter part of life.   *Exit*   40

ACT 4   SCENE 7
Alexandria   The battlefield

Alarum. Drums and Trumpets. Enter AGRIPPA *and others*

AGRIPPA Retire! We have engaged ourselves too far.
    Caesar himself has work, and our oppression
    Exceeds what we expected.

                    Exeunt

Alarums. Enter ANTONY, *and* SCARUS *wounded*

SCARUS O my brave emperor, this is fought indeed!
    Had we done so at first, we had droven them home   5
    With clouts about their heads.
ANTONY   Thou bleed'st apace.
SCARUS I had a wound here that was like a T,
    But now 'tis made an H.
            [Sound retreat] far off
ANTONY   They do retire.
SCARUS We'll beat 'em into bench-holes. I have yet
    Room for six scotches more.   10

Antony's army pursues Caesar's retreating forces. Antony praises the efforts of his men, especially Scarus, who has been outstandingly brave. Antony greets Cleopatra as the conqueror of his heart.

1 A moment of glory (the whole class)

Enobarbus's dark solitary despair in Scene 6 is suddenly eclipsed by sounds of war. Surprisingly, Caesar's forces are in disarray. Turn Scene 7 and the opening of Scene 8 into a grand spectacle of battle and victory. You will need a large space. Make the two scenes flow into one another with scarcely a pause. Show:

a The retreat of Agrippa and his men.

b The excitement of Antony, Scarus and Eros – the comradeship, the exhaustion and pain. Work on conveying the grim joking and word-play. The badly-wounded Scarus, for example, jokes about turning his T-shaped wound into an H-shaped one ('H' and 'ache' were pronounced the same). He also talks of beating the enemy back to their latrines ('bench-holes') and is still joking about his wounds as he exits: 'I'll halt (that is, limp) after'.

c The army's triumphant return to Cleopatra and her attendants at the start of Scene 8.

2 Scarus returns home (in pairs)

In Scene 8, Antony orders his men to 'clip' (embrace) their wives and tell them of the great deeds they have done (lines 8–9). Improvise the conversation when Scarus returns to his wife and tells her of his deeds, his wounds, what his general said to him and how he met with Cleopatra. Base his story on Scenes 7 and 8. Mention, for example, how Antony's men chase the enemy and 'snatch 'em up' from behind as hounds catch hares (Scene 7, line 13).

---

serves ... victory gives us the chance of a complete victory
runner runaway
sprightly cheerful
gests deeds
doughty-handed brave fighters
as't ... like mine as if it had been your own personal battle

Hector Greek warrior hero
fairy enchantress, possessor of magical powers
attire and all dressed as you are
proof of harness my impenetrable armour
the pants my panting chest

Enter EROS

EROS They are beaten, sir, and our advantage serves
    For a fair victory.
SCARUS   Let us score their backs
    And snatch 'em up as we take hares, behind!
    'Tis sport to maul a runner.
ANTONY   I will reward thee
    Once for thy sprightly comfort and tenfold   15
    For thy good valour. Come thee on.
SCARUS I'll halt after.
                                     Exeunt

ACT 4   SCENE 8
Alexandria   The battlefield

Alarum. *Enter* ANTONY *again in a march;* SCARUS, *with others*

ANTONY We have beat him to his camp. Run one before,
    And let the queen know of our gests.
                             [*Exit a Soldier*]
                        Tomorrow,
    Before the sun shall see's, we'll spill the blood
    That has today escaped. I thank you all,
    For doughty-handed are you, and have fought   5
    Not as you served the cause, but as't had been
    Each man's like mine; you have shown all Hectors.
    Enter the city, clip your wives, your friends,
    Tell them your feats, whilst they with joyful tears
    Wash the congealment from your wounds and kiss   10
    The honoured gashes whole.

    Enter CLEOPATRA, [*with Attendants*]

          [*To Scarus*] Give me thy hand;
    To this great fairy I'll commend thy acts,
    Make her thanks bless thee. [*To Cleopatra*] O thou day
      o'th'world,
    Chain mine armed neck; leap thou, attire and all,
    Through proof of harness to my heart, and there   15
    Ride on the pants triumphing!   [*They embrace*]

Cleopatra welcomes Antony's safe return. Antony praises Scarus's bravery and Cleopatra promises him a gift of gold armour. They leave to march triumphantly through Alexandria.

1 Triumphant celebrations (in small groups)

Present lines 16–39 as a chorus. Speak lines and phrases together and echo keywords (for example, ones linked to battle) so that you shout out Antony's triumph and Cleopatra's excited delight.

2 The older man's boast

Antony has beaten the 'boy' Caesar. He may be getting old, but Antony believes he still has enough strength of mind to match his physical powers ('nerves') against any younger man's (lines 19–22). Are you convinced? Find evidence from Scenes 7, 8 and 9 to suggest that this victory is by no means decisive.

3 An underlying irony?

Antony makes much of Cleopatra's hand. What is ironic about this, in view of what happened to Thidias in Act 3 Scene 13?

4 From triumph to death (in large groups)

As the shouts of triumph die away, Scene 9 turns to Enobarbus's last despairing moments. Present Scene 8, line 35 to Scene 9, line 33. Create the celebratory music and noise which close Scene 8, followed by the silence and darkness of the night as the sentries observe Enobarbus. Think about the tone of Enobarbus's final speech. Use the sound of the distant drums as an ironic funeral salute.

---

virtue courage
great snare perils of war
something somewhat
carbuncled studded with jewels
Phoebus' car sun god's chariot
hacked targets battered shields
owe own

camp this host house this army
carouses toasts
taborins small drums
court of guard guardroom
shiny bright with moonlight
embattle arm, prepare for battle
shrewd cursed, disastrous

CLEOPATRA   Lord of lords,
    O infinite virtue, com'st thou smiling from
    The world's great snare uncaught?
ANTONY   My nightingale,
    We have beat them to their beds. What, girl, though grey
    Do something mingle with our younger brown, yet ha' we   20
    A brain that nourishes our nerves and can
    Get goal for goal of youth. Behold this man;
    Commend unto his lips thy favouring hand. –
    Kiss it, my warrior.
           [Scarus kisses Cleopatra's hand]
              He hath fought today
    As if a god in hate of mankind had
    Destroyed in such a shape.   25
CLEOPATRA   I'll give thee, friend,
    An armour all of gold; it was a king's.
ANTONY He has deserved it, were it carbuncled
    Like holy Phoebus' car. Give me thy hand.
    Through Alexandria make a jolly march;   30
    Bear our hacked targets, like the men that owe them.
    Had our great palace the capacity
    To camp this host, we all would sup together
    And drink carouses to the next day's fate,
    Which promises royal peril. Trumpeters,   35
    With brazen din blast you the city's ear;
    Make mingle with our rattling taborins,
    That heaven and earth may strike their sounds together,
    Applauding our approach.
              [Trumpets sound.] Exeunt

ACT 4   SCENE 9   Caesar's camp near Alexandria

Enter a SENTRY *and* WATCHMEN. ENOBARBUS *follows*

SENTRY If we be not relieved within this hour,
    We must return to th'court of guard. The night
    Is shiny, and they say we shall embattle
    By th'second hour i'th'morn.
I WATCH   This last day was
    A shrewd one to's.

The sentries on night guard overhear Enobarbus praying to the moon to break his heart for his cruel treachery. Before he dies, he begs Antony to forgive his disloyalty. The sentries bear him away.

'True melancholy.' For Shakespeare's audience, 'melancholy' (line 12) was not merely sadness. It was a deep and black despair that could 'blow the heart'. They also believed that night air and moonlight caused illness, depression and even madness.

1 Hear Enobarbus's despair (in small groups)

As one of you reads lines 7–23, the others echo all words of darkness, dankness, sorrow and self-accusation.

close concealed
list listen to
revolted who have deserted
upon record in recorded history
sovereign mistress the moon
disponge drop (as from a squeezed sponge)

Which ... powder (grief was thought to drain blood from the heart)
in ... particular yourself
rank ... register mark me down as
raught reached
demurely softly, quietly
of note a person of rank

ENOBARBUS   O, bear me witness, night –   5
2 WATCH What man is this?
I WATCH   Stand close and list him.
                    [*They stand aside*]
ENOBARBUS Be witness to me, O thou blessèd moon,
        When men revolted shall upon record
        Bear hateful memory: poor Enobarbus did
        Before thy face repent.
SENTRY   Enobarbus?   10
2 WATCH Peace! Hark further.
ENOBARBUS O sovereign mistress of true melancholy,
        The poisonous damp of night dispunge upon me,
        That life, a very rebel to my will,
        May hang no longer on me. Throw my heart   15
        Against the flint and hardness of my fault,
        Which, being dried with grief, will break to powder
        And finish all foul thoughts. O Antony,
        Nobler than my revolt is infamous,
        Forgive me in thine own particular,   20
        But let the world rank me in register
        A master-leaver and a fugitive.
        O Antony! O Antony!   [*He dies*]
I WATCH   Let's speak to him.
SENTRY Let's hear him, for the things he speaks
        May concern Caesar.
2 WATCH   Let's do so. But he sleeps.   25
SENTRY Swoons rather, for so bad a prayer as his
        Was never yet for sleep.
I WATCH   Go we to him.
                    [*They approach Enobarbus*]
2 WATCH Awake, sir, awake. Speak to us.
I WATCH Hear you, sir?
SENTRY   The hand of death hath raught him.
                    Drums afar off
        Hark, the drums demurely wake the sleepers.   30
        Let us bear him to th'court of guard;
        He is of note. Our hour is fully out.
2 WATCH Come on, then. He may recover yet.
                    Exeunt [*with the body*]

171

Antony learns that Caesar's navy has put to sea and decides to do likewise. Caesar orders his land army to maintain a defensive position. Antony leaves to observe the sea battle. Scarus awaits the outcome.

1 The final battle (in groups of three)

As at Actium, Antony and Caesar's forces meet at sea. Scenes 10, 11 and 12 give brief flashes of the preparations and the reactions of the generals as they watch from the shore.

Read aloud the page of script opposite, but do not turn over to see what happens next. Decide who you think will be victorious and gather as much evidence as you can to support your view. Then turn over to see if you are correct.

2 Write your historical account

Shakespeare took many details for his battle scenes from the Greek historian Plutarch (for example, the ill-omen of swallows nesting in Cleopatra's ships). Using Shakespeare's play as your 'source', write your historical account of the land battle near Alexandria (Scenes 2 to 8) and the final sea battle (Scenes 10 to 12). Record the military tactics, the generals' states of mind, the sequence of events and the omens and prophecies.

3 Earth, air, fire and water

Many Elizabethans believed that the entire world was made up of these four elements. Antony has fought with Caesar on land and at sea and now would even 'fight i'th'fire or i'th'air' (Scene 10, line 3). What frame of mind does he appear to be in?

---

foot foot soldiers (infantry)
They have ... haven Antony's ships have left harbour
Where from which hills
appointment battle dispositions
But being charged unless we are attacked

still quiet, inactive
vales low ground
hold ... advantage take up our strongest position
Yet ... joined they have not begun
augurers soothsayers
fretted eaten away, chequered

ACT 4　SCENE 10　The battlefield

Enter ANTONY and SCARUS, with their army

ANTONY Their preparation is today by sea;
　　　We please them not by land.
SCARUS 　　　　　　　　　　For both, my lord.
ANTONY I would they'd fight i'th'fire or i'th'air;
　　　We'd fight there too. But this it is: our foot
　　　Upon the hills adjoining to the city　　　　　　　5
　　　Shall stay with us – order for sea is given;
　　　They have put forth the haven –
　　　Where their appointment we may best discover
　　　And look on their endeavour.　　　　　　*Exeunt*

ACT 4　SCENE 11　The battlefield

Enter CAESAR and his army

CAESAR But being charged, we will be still by land –
　　　Which, as I take't, we shall, for his best force
　　　Is forth to man his galleys. To the vales,
　　　And hold our best advantage.　　　　　　*Exeunt*

ACT 4　SCENE 12　The battlefield

Enter ANTONY and SCARUS

ANTONY Yet they are not joined. Where yond pine does stand
　　　I shall discover all. I'll bring thee word
　　　Straight how 'tis like to go.　　　　　　*Exit*
　　　　　Alarum afar off, as at a sea fight
SCARUS 　　　　　　　　　　Swallows have built
　　　In Cleopatra's sails their nests. The augurers
　　　Say they know not, they cannot tell, look grimly,　　　5
　　　And dare not speak their knowledge. Antony
　　　Is valiant, and dejected, and by starts
　　　His fretted fortunes give him hope and fear
　　　Of what he has and has not.

173

Antony tells of the sudden surrender of the Egyptian fleet. He is enraged that Cleopatra has betrayed him. When Cleopatra appears, he threatens and taunts her with what will happen to her in Rome.

1 Antony's rage (in large groups)

Antony's anger is titanic and directed largely at Cleopatra, whom he thinks is responsible. Form a circle with Cleopatra outside. As one of the group speaks Antony's words (lines 9–49), the rest echo loudly and angrily all words of abuse (for example, 'foul Egyptian', 'my charm'). When Cleopatra enters the circle at line 30, the whole group shouts lines 32–9 at her, while advancing on her menacingly. On her exit, the group resumes its echoing of Antony's words. Take turns as Cleopatra. Talk together about how she feels at facing such language and decide what evidence there is to justify Antony's accusations.

2 Cleopatra's fear (in large groups)

Antony knows that Cleopatra will be exhibited like a freak-show in Rome for the amusement of poor weak fools ('diminutives' and 'dolts'). Create your own moving pictures of what awaits her (lines 33–9). Then talk together about what Cleopatra finds most frightening in Antony's words.

3 Images of melting and dissolving

Antony feels his power and support dwindling. His former followers now 'do discandy' (melt away) and 'melt their sweets' (lavish their flattery) on Caesar. He feels like a dying pine tree stripped of its bark. What might have suggested this image to Antony?

Draw a picture or make a collage of Antony as he now sees himself. Illustrate it with images from lines 18–24 (see also pages 178 and 192).

Triple-turned three-times faithless (to Julius Caesar, Pompey and himself)
charm witch, enchantress
spanieled followed devotedly
grave charm deadly enchantress
becked forth summoned me out to
crownet crown

right proper
fast and loose (a con trick using false knots)
Avaunt! (a word used to get rid of supernatural beings)
spot blemish, disgrace
visage face

Enter ANTONY

ANTONY   All is lost!
This foul Egyptian hath betrayèd me.   10
My fleet hath yielded to the foe, and yonder
They cast their caps up and carouse together
Like friends long lost. Triple-turned whore! 'Tis thou
Hast sold me to this novice, and my heart
Makes only wars on thee. Bid them all fly;   15
For when I am revenged upon my charm,
I have done all. Bid them all fly. Begone!

                                        [*Exit Scarus*]

O sun, thy uprise shall I see no more.
Fortune and Antony part here; even here
Do we shake hands. All come to this? The hearts   20
That spanieled me at heels, to whom I gave
Their wishes, do discandy, melt their sweets
On blossoming Caesar; and this pine is barked
That overtopped them all. Betrayed I am.
O, this false soul of Egypt! This grave charm,   25
Whose eye becked forth my wars and called them home,
Whose bosom was my crownet, my chief end,
Like a right gipsy hath at fast and loose
Beguiled me to the very heart of loss.
What, Eros, Eros!

Enter CLEOPATRA

                          Ah, thou spell! Avaunt!   30
CLEOPATRA Why is my lord enraged against his love?
ANTONY Vanish, or I shall give thee thy deserving
And blemish Caesar's triumph. Let him take thee
And hoist thee up to the shouting plebeians!
Follow his chariot, like the greatest spot   35
Of all thy sex; most monster-like be shown
For poor'st diminutives, for dolts, and let
Patient Octavia plough thy visage up
With her preparèd nails!

                                        Exit Cleopatra

Antony is convinced that Cleopatra has betrayed him and vows to kill her. Back at her palace, Cleopatra decides to lock herself in her monument and send word to Antony that she has killed herself.

1 Hercules and the shirt of Nessus

In lines 42–7, Antony likens himself to Hercules (Alcides), from whom he claimed to be descended. Nessus the Centaur, mortally wounded by Hercules's poisoned arrow, gave a shirt soaked with his poisoned blood to Hercules's wife, Deianira, saying it would act as a love charm to win back Hercules's affections. She sent Lichas to give the shirt to Hercules. When Hercules put it on, the poison fatally maddened him and he hurled the innocent Lichas into the sea. Deianira killed herself, horrified at what she had done.

Watch for other echoes of Hercules's death in the next two scenes, and see page 24 for a contrasting earlier image of Hercules and Antony.

Hercules with 'the heaviest club'.

Thou fell'st into you were a victim of
Subdue ... self destroy myself
Telamon Ajax (Greek hero who raged at not being given the shield of the dead Achilles)

boar of Thessaly savage boar (in Greek mythology)
embossed enraged, exhausted
rive not more ... going off do not tear apart more destructively than when great persons die

'Tis well thou'rt gone,
If it be well to live. But better 'twere   40
Thou fell'st into my fury, for one death
Might have prevented many. Eros, ho!
The shirt of Nessus is upon me. Teach me,
Alcides, thou mine ancestor, thy rage.
Let me lodge Lichas on the horns o'th'moon,   45
And with those hands that grasped the heaviest club
Subdue my worthiest self. The witch shall die.
To the young Roman boy she hath sold me, and I fall
Under this plot. She dies for't. Eros, ho!   *Exit*

ACT 4   SCENE 13
Alexandria   Cleopatra's palace

Enter CLEOPATRA, IRAS, and MARDIAN

CLEOPATRA Help me, my women! O, he's more mad
        Than Telamon for his shield; the boar of Thessaly
        Was never so embossed.
CHARMIAN   To th'monument!
        There lock yourself and send him word you are dead.
        The soul and body rive not more in parting   5
        Than greatness going off.
CLEOPATRA   To th'monument!
        Mardian, go tell him I have slain myself.
        Say that the last I spoke was 'Antony',
        And word it, prithee, piteously. Hence, Mardian,
        And bring me how he takes my death. To th'monument!   10
                                              Exeunt

*Antony feels his whole identity dissolving like the evening clouds.
Cleopatra's betrayal has been the final reversal of his fortunes. All that
remains is suicide. Mardian arrives from Cleopatra.*

1 Does Antony die like a god? (in groups of eight or more)

The previous scenes have switched quickly from palace to camp, and
from one part of the battlefield to another. Scenes 14 and 15 focus
closely on the death of Antony. Read Scenes 14 and 15 (there are eight
major speaking parts). Then talk together about your first impressions
of Antony's death. Is it a dignified, heroic and moving moment, or a
grotesquely comic bungled suicide attempt?

2 Melting and dissolving again (in pairs)

Antony is reeling from the double blow of defeat by Caesar and
betrayal by Cleopatra. So powerful is Antony's sense of personal
dissolution that he asks (in line 1) if Eros can still see him.

a Take turns to speak Antony's lines 1–22. Decide where you might
look away into the distance and where you turn to face Eros.

b Talk about how Antony uses images of clouds, water and sunset
to express his inner dissolution (lines 1–14).

c Make a list of the objects that Antony sees in the sunset clouds
(lines 2–11). Say how each imagined object reflects Antony's
nature and personality.

3 'She has robbed me of my sword'

Compare Antony's outburst in line 23 with Act 2 Scene 2, line 237, Act
2 Scene 5, lines 21–3, Act 3 Scene 11, lines 65–7 and Act 3 Scene 13,
lines 177–80. Identify what you think is the nature of Cleopatra's
'disarming' power.

---

pendent overhanging
black vesper's pageants signs of
the coming of evening
even with a thought quick as
thought
rack dislimns the cloud mass
changes shape

knave boy
annexed unto't joined
Packed ... triumph (Antony uses
images of card cheats – 'trump' is
derived from 'triumph')
Ourselves ... ourselves suicide

ACT 4 SCENE 14
Alexandria Cleopatra's palace

Enter ANTONY *and* EROS

ANTONY Eros, thou yet behold'st me?
EROS   Ay, noble lord.
ANTONY Sometime we see a cloud that's dragonish,
    A vapour sometime like a bear or lion,
    A towered citadel, a pendent rock,
    A forkèd mountain, or blue promontory   5
    With trees upon't that nod unto the world
    And mock our eyes with air. Thou hast seen these signs;
    They are black vesper's pageants.
EROS   Ay, my lord.
ANTONY That which is now a horse, even with a thought
    The rack dislimns and makes it indistinct   10
    As water is in water.
EROS   It does, my lord.
ANTONY My good knave Eros, now thy captain is
    Even such a body. Here I am Antony,
    Yet cannot hold this visible shape, my knave.
    I made these wars for Egypt, and the queen,   15
    Whose heart I thought I had, for she had mine –
    Which whilst it was mine had annexed unto't
    A million more, now lost – she, Eros, has
    Packed cards with Caesar and false-played my glory
    Unto an enemy's triumph.   20
    Nay, weep not, gentle Eros; there is left us
    Ourselves to end ourselves.

Enter MARDIAN

               O, thy vile lady!
    She has robbed me of my sword.
MARDIAN   No, Antony,
    My mistress loved thee, and her fortunes mingled
    With thine entirely.
ANTONY   Hence, saucy eunuch, peace!   25
    She hath betrayed me and shall die the death.

Mardian falsely reports Cleopatra's suicide. Antony instantly determines to join her in death. Eros unbuckles Antony's armour. Antony calls on Cleopatra to wait beyond death for him to join her.

1 'Unarm, Eros. The long day's task is done'
(in small groups)

Throughout the play, Antony's sword and armour symbolise the power and authority of a great Roman statesman and general. Now all that great power is ending.

a 'No more a soldier. Bruisèd pieces, go' (line 42). Draw two pictures of Antony, one armed and one unarmed. Around each picture write key words to describe Antony. For example, the armed Antony might have 'public figure, soldier, man of duty'.

b Violent disintegration. One person reads what Antony says as Eros unarms him (lines 38–43). The others echo all 'violence' or 'breaking' words. Find similar words that Mardian uses to describe Cleopatra's death (lines 29–34). Identify the irony in the two sets of lines.

c 'The sevenfold shield of Ajax' (line 38). Ajax (the Greek hero mentioned as Telamon in Scene 13, line 2) carried a mighty shield made of seven thicknesses of ox hide. How does this image reflect Antony's growing sense of vulnerability?

2 'Dido and her Aeneas'

In lines 44–54, Antony has a vision of himself and Cleopatra walking as lovers in the Underworld, outshining even Dido, Queen of Carthage, and her lover Aeneas, the founder of Rome. But, according to legend, Dido killed herself when Aeneas deserted her to follow his Roman duty. When Aeneas later encountered her in the Underworld, Dido scornfully refused to acknowledge him.

unto thy hand just as you wanted	**Bruisèd** battered
She rendered ... her she died speaking your name	**length** prolonging of life
	Mars ... does is a waste of effort
The battery the pounding blows	**Seal** finish the business
once ... continent for once be stronger than my body	**couch** lie
	port bearing, manner
Apace hurry	**want troops** lack admirers

MARDIAN Death of one person can be paid but once,
        And that she has discharged. What thou wouldst do
        Is done unto thy hand. The last she spake
        Was 'Antony, most noble Antony!'   30
        Then in the midst a tearing groan did break
        The name of Antony; it was divided
        Between her heart and lips. She rendered life
        Thy name so buried in her.
ANTONY   Dead, then?
MARDIAN   Dead.
ANTONY Unarm, Eros. The long day's task is done,   35
        And we must sleep. [*To Mardian*] That thou depart'st hence
        safe
        Does pay thy labour richly; go.
                                        Exit Mardian
                                Off, pluck off!
        [*Eros unarms him*]
        The sevenfold shield of Ajax cannot keep
        The battery from my heart. O, cleave, my sides!
        Heart, once be stronger than thy continent;   40
        Crack thy frail case! Apace, Eros, apace!
        No more a soldier. Bruisèd pieces, go;
        You have been nobly borne. – From me awhile.
                                        Exit Eros
        I will o'ertake thee, Cleopatra, and
        Weep for my pardon. So it must be, for now   45
        All length is torture; since the torch is out,
        Lie down and stray no farther. Now all labour
        Mars what it does; yea, very force entangles
        Itself with strength. Seal then, and all is done.
        Eros! – I come, my queen. – Eros! – Stay for me.   50
        Where souls do couch on flowers, we'll hand in hand,
        And with our sprightly port make the ghosts gaze.
        Dido and her Aeneas shall want troops,
        And all the haunt be ours. – Come, Eros, Eros!

                        Enter EROS

EROS What would my lord?

181

Antony tells Eros that the time has come when he must keep his promise to kill his master. Eros protests, but Antony insists. Eros asks Antony to turn his face away.

1 'The time is come' (in small groups)

Antony is ashamed that he still lives when Cleopatra's brave death has shown him how to die. He, who had 'Quartered (divided and conquered) the world' and assembled vast fleets of ships, like cities (lines 57–9), must now be Caesar's captive, led bound behind his chariot.

The faithful Eros must kill his master. The pictures here and on page 184 show how two productions presented this moment. Rehearse your version of lines 78–97.

to lack for lacking	**corrigible** submissive
which ... Caesar tells who by her death tells Caesar	**subdued ... shame** overcome by deep shame
exigent extreme need	**wheeled seat** chariot
prosecution infliction	**branded ... ensued** humiliates your master who must follow like a slave
darts arrows (see page 94)	
windowed placed in a window	
pleached bound together	**precedent** former

ANTONY   Since Cleopatra died   55
        I have lived in such dishonour that the gods
        Detest my baseness. I, that with my sword
        Quartered the world, and o'er green Neptune's back
        With ships made cities, condemn myself to lack
        The courage of a woman – less noble mind   60
        Than she which by her death our Caesar tells
        'I am conqueror of myself.' Thou art sworn, Eros,
        That when the exigent should come – which now
        Is come indeed – when I should see behind me
        Th'inevitable prosecution of   65
        Disgrace and horror, that on my command
        Thou then wouldst kill me. Do't. The time is come.
        Thou strik'st not me, 'tis Caesar thou defeat'st.
        Put colour in thy cheek.

EROS   The gods withhold me!
        Shall I do that which all the Parthian darts,   70
        Though enemy, lost aim and could not?

ANTONY   Eros,
        Wouldst thou be windowed in great Rome and see
        Thy master thus with pleached arms, bending down
        His corrigible neck, his face subdued
        To penetrative shame, whilst the wheeled seat   75
        Of fortunate Caesar, drawn before him, branded
        His baseness that ensued?

EROS   I would not see't.

ANTONY Come, then, for with a wound I must be cured.
        Draw that thy honest sword, which thou hast worn
        Most useful for thy country.

EROS   O, sir, pardon me!   80

ANTONY When I did make thee free, swor'st thou not then
        To do this when I bade thee? Do it at once,
        Or thy precedent services are all
        But accidents unpurposed. Draw, and come.

EROS Turn from me then that noble countenance   85
        Wherein the worship of the whole world lies.

ANTONY Lo thee! [*He turns from him*]

Eros kills himself. Antony attempts suicide but his wound is not immediately fatal. The guards ignore Antony's pleas to kill him. Dercetus takes Antony's sword, hoping to win favour with Caesar.

1 Cosmic and apocalyptic images (in groups of seven)

The guards' words on seeing the wounded Antony (lines 108–10) echo Saint John's vision of the end of the world (Revelation 8:11–13): 'And there fell a great star from heaven ... and I heard one angel saying ... "Woe, woe, woe to the inhabitants of the earth"...'.

Rehearse lines 90–120. Decide how Dercetus, Diomedes and the guards react to the wounded and helpless Antony.

Present your version to the class. Freeze the action at key moments (such as lines 93–4), showing your picture of Antony's attempted suicide. In your final freeze at the end of line 120, show your image of a 'great star' falling.

Antony awaits
the final blow.

got upon ... record gained a far
  more noble place in history than I
dies thy scholar learns from your
  example
dispatch me kill me quickly

ill badly
at his period at its end
Shall enter ... him get me into his
  favour

EROS My sword is drawn.

ANTONY   Then let it do at once
The thing why thou hast drawn it.

EROS   My dear master,
My captain, and my emperor, let me say   90
Before I strike this bloody stroke, farewell.

ANTONY 'Tis said, man, and farewell.

EROS Farewell, great chief. Shall I strike now?

ANTONY   Now, Eros.

EROS (*Kills himself*)
Why, there then! Thus I do escape the sorrow
Of Antony's death.

ANTONY   Thrice nobler than myself!   95
Thou teachest me, O valiant Eros, what
I should, and thou couldst not. My queen and Eros
Have by their brave instruction got upon me
A nobleness in record. But I will be
A bridegroom in my death and run into't   100
As to a lover's bed. Come then, and Eros,
Thy master dies thy scholar. To do thus
I learned of thee.
                    [*He falls on his sword*]
                    How, not dead? Not dead?
The guard, ho! O, dispatch me!

Enter a [Company of the] GUARD, [*one of them* DERCETUS]

1 GUARD What's the noise?   105

ANTONY I have done my work ill, friends.
O, make an end of what I have begun!

2 GUARD The star is fall'n.

1 GUARD And time is at his period.

ALL Alas, and woe!   110

ANTONY Let him that loves me strike me dead.

1 GUARD Not I.

2 GUARD Nor I.

3 GUARD Nor anyone.

                    Exeunt [all the Guard but Dercetus]

DERCETUS Thy death and fortunes bid thy followers fly.   115
This sword but shown to Caesar with this tidings
Shall enter me with him.
                    [*He takes up Antony's sword*]

185

Diomedes reports that Cleopatra had a premonition that Antony might take his life and sent him to tell Antony that she still lives. Antony calls for his guards and asks them to carry him to her.

1 True nobility? (in groups of three)

In Scene 12, Antony raged at Cleopatra's apparent deception when her fleet suddenly surrendered to Caesar. Now, in his agony, Antony learns of yet another of the queen's deceptions (line 124). He speaks no words of anger or reproach. He simply asks to be taken to her.

a Take parts and read lines 118–45. Describe Antony's manner towards Diomedes and the guards. How do you think he should speak line 124?

b Write two soliloquies for Antony. The first expresses how he felt immediately after the battle in Scene 12. The second explains how and why he feels as he does now. When you have spoken your soliloquies to each other, talk together about Antony. Is he truly noble?

2 'Carry me now, good friends' (in groups of six)

Memorise and rehearse lines 136–45. Show the pain of the mortally wounded Antony as he is lifted and carried off stage.

3 Antony and Hercules

Read again the account of Hercules's death on page 176. How similar are the deaths of Antony and his legendary ancestor?

Sufficing sufficient
found found true
disposed with come to terms with
purged expelled, got rid of
bides is to be found

may not live ... out may not outlive those who serve you
To grace by gracing or honouring
Bid that ... lightly if we appear to welcome what is sent to punish us, then it is we who punish it

Enter DIOMEDES

DIOMEDES Where's Antony?

DERCETUS There, Diomed, there.

DIOMEDES Lives he? Wilt thou not answer, man?   120

[Exit Dercetus]

ANTONY Art thou there, Diomed? Draw thy sword and give me
    Sufficing strokes for death.

DIOMEDES   Most absolute lord,
    My mistress Cleopatra sent me to thee.

ANTONY When did she send thee?

DIOMEDES   Now, my lord.

ANTONY   Where is she?

DIOMEDES Locked in her monument. She had a prophesying fear   125
    Of what hath come to pass. For when she saw –
    Which never shall be found – you did suspect
    She had disposed with Caesar, and that your rage
    Would not be purged, she sent you word she was dead;
    But fearing since how it might work, hath sent   130
    Me to proclaim the truth, and I am come,
    I dread, too late.

ANTONY Too late, good Diomed. Call my guard, I prithee.

DIOMEDES What ho, the emperor's guard! The guard, what ho!
    Come, your lord calls.   135

Enter four or five of the GUARD *of Antony*

ANTONY Bear me, good friends, where Cleopatra bides.
    'Tis the last service that I shall command you.

1 GUARD Woe, woe are we, sir, you may not live to wear
    All your true followers out.

ALL   Most heavy day!

ANTONY Nay, good my fellows, do not please sharp fate   140
    To grace it with your sorrows. Bid that welcome
    Which comes to punish us, and we punish it,
    Seeming to bear it lightly. Take me up.
    I have led you oft; carry me now, good friends,
    And have my thanks for all.   145

Exeunt, bearing Antony [and Eros]

Cleopatra vows never to leave her monument. She refuses to be comforted and grieves over the mortally wounded Antony. He pleads for death to wait and allow him one last kiss.

Apocalyptic images. Like the guards' words in the previous scene, Cleopatra's words on seeing the dying Antony (lines 10–12) echo the biblical visions of the end of the world (see Revelation 8:12).

Our size ... makes it our sorrow must be as great as the events which have caused it
darkling in darkness

varying ever changing
importune death awhile beg death not to come too quickly

ACT 4   SCENE 15
Cleopatra's monument

Enter CLEOPATRA *and her Maids aloft, with* CHARMIAN *and* IRAS

CLEOPATRA O Charmian, I will never go from hence.
CHARMIAN Be comforted, dear madam.
CLEOPATRA   No, I will not.
    All strange and terrible events are welcome,
    But comforts we despise. Our size of sorrow,
    Proportioned to our cause, must be as great   5
    As that which makes it.

Enter [below] DIOMEDES

               How now? Is he dead?
DIOMEDES His death's upon him, but not dead.
    Look out o'th'other side your monument;
    His guard have brought him thither.

Enter [below] ANTONY, *and the* GUARD *[bearing him]*

CLEOPATRA O sun,   10
    Burn the great sphere thou mov'st in; darkling stand
    The varying shore o'th'world! O Antony,
    Antony, Antony! Help, Charmian, help, Iras, help!
    Help friends below! Let's draw him hither.
ANTONY   Peace!
    Not Caesar's valour hath o'erthrown Antony,   15
    But Antony's hath triumphed on itself.
CLEOPATRA So it should be, that none but Antony
    Should conquer Antony, but woe 'tis so!
ANTONY I am dying, Egypt, dying; only
    I here importune death awhile, until
    Of many thousand kisses the poor last   20
    I lay upon thy lips.

Cleopatra fears capture. She and her ladies lift Antony up into the monument. Antony advises Cleopatra to seek safety from Caesar and to trust only Proculeius. She vows to trust only in her own will.

Staging the raising of Antony. Cleopatra draws Antony to her, even in death. Talk together about how you would stage lines 30–41.

imperious show imperial triumph
brooched ornamented (as with a brooch)
still conclusion silent judgement
Demuring upon looking smugly at
heaviness sorrow, or weight
Juno/Jove queen/king of the gods

Mercury winged messenger of the gods
huswife hussy, worthless woman
Fortune (personified as a blind goddess turning a wheel)
offence insulting language

CLEOPATRA   I dare not, dear –
Dear my lord, pardon – I dare not,
Lest I be taken. Not th'imperious show
Of the full-fortuned Caesar ever shall   25
Be brooched with me. If knife, drugs, serpents, have
Edge, sting, or operation, I am safe.
Your wife Octavia, with her modest eyes
And still conclusion, shall acquire no honour
Demuring upon me. But come, come, Antony –   30
Help me, my women – we must draw thee up.
Assist, good friends.
ANTONY   O, quick, or I am gone.
                              [*They begin lifting*]
CLEOPATRA Here's sport indeed! How heavy weighs my lord!
Our strength is all gone into heaviness,
That makes the weight. Had I great Juno's power,   35
The strong-winged Mercury should fetch thee up
And set thee by Jove's side. Yet come a little;
Wishers were ever fools. O, come, come, come!
            They heave Antony aloft to Cleopatra
And welcome, welcome! Die when thou hast lived;
Quicken with kissing. Had my lips that power,   40
Thus would I wear them out.
                              [*She kisses him*]
ALL A heavy sight!
ANTONY I am dying, Egypt, dying.
Give me some wine, and let me speak a little.
CLEOPATRA No, let me speak, and let me rail so high   45
That the false huswife Fortune break her wheel,
Provoked by my offence.
ANTONY   One word, sweet queen:
Of Caesar seek your honour, with your safety. O!
CLEOPATRA They do not go together.
ANTONY   Gentle, hear me.
None about Caesar trust but Proculeius.   50
CLEOPATRA My resolution and my hands I'll trust,
None about Caesar.

Antony urges Cleopatra not to grieve, but to remember his former glory and rejoice that he has chosen a noble death. When he dies, Cleopatra faints from the sudden shock of emptiness and loss.

'O see, my women: The crown o'th'earth doth melt.' Talk together about lines 64–5, and gather together all the images and associations it brings to your mind. Which other words and images from lines 61–70 echo Cleopatra's sense of loss, decay and emptiness?

basely dishonourably
put off my helmet surrender
woo't will you
garland victory wreath of flowers
soldier's pole possible meanings: military standard, spear, polestar, phallus, maypole (echoing 'garlands')

the odds is gone there is no difference between great and small
remarkable splendidly conspicuous

ANTONY The miserable change now at my end
        Lament nor sorrow at, but please your thoughts
        In feeding them with those my former fortunes,   55
        Wherein I lived the greatest prince o'th'world,
        The noblest; and do now not basely die,
        Not cowardly put off my helmet to
        My countryman – a Roman by a Roman
        Valiantly vanquished. Now my spirit is going;   60
        I can no more.
CLEOPATRA   Noblest of men, woo't die?
        Hast thou no care of me? Shall I abide
        In this dull world, which in thy absence is
        No better than a sty? O see, my women:

                                        [*Antony dies*]

        The crown o'th'earth doth melt. My lord!   65
        O, withered is the garland of the war;
        The soldier's pole is fall'n! Young boys and girls
        Are level now with men; the odds is gone,
        And there is nothing left remarkable
        Beneath the visiting moon. [*She starts to faint*]   70
CHARMIAN O, quietness, lady!
IRAS She's dead too, our sovereign.
CHARMIAN Lady!
IRAS Madam!
CHARMIAN O madam, madam, madam!   75
IRAS Royal Egypt! Empress!

Cleopatra realises that she is just a woman with a woman's feelings. Nothing matters now Antony is dead. She vows to bury him and then to follow his example in the 'high Roman fashion'.

1 Royalty, humanity, finality (in large groups)

To Iras, Cleopatra is 'Royal Egypt' and 'Empress'. But the queen, in her grief, realises that she is merely human and moved by the same emotions as the poorest milkmaid who does the most menial of 'chares' or tasks (lines 78–80). Without Antony, 'All's but naught'.

Create a presentation of lines 61–96 which highlights Cleopatra's royalty, her common humanity, and her sense of death and finality.

Place Cleopatra's followers in three groups at different levels around her – perhaps close to, kneeling and standing. As Cleopatra faints, recovers and prepares to bury Antony, each group echoes her words. One group echoes the 'royalty' words (for example, 'sceptre'), one the 'humanity' words (for example, 'woman') and one the 'finality' words (for example, 'naught'). To help you prepare, work out:

- how you will place Cleopatra and the dead Antony
- whether Cleopatra remains static or moves
- which of her lines are spoken to Antony and which to her women (women were sometimes addressed as 'sirs' in Shakespeare's day, see line 90)
- how to stage the final stage direction ('*Exeunt*' = everyone leaves the stage).

Show your version to the rest of the class and decide whether this Cleopatra is different from the Cleopatra of earlier scenes. Do you believe her when she vows to kill herself?

It were it would be fitting
injurious wilfully inflicting injury
  or harm
our jewel Antony
is sottish is for fools

does/Become ... mad is only
  suitable for madmen
lamp Antony
brave fine
case body
briefest swiftest

194

[Cleopatra stirs]
CHARMIAN Peace, peace, Iras.
CLEOPATRA No more but e'en a woman, and commanded
    By such poor passion as the maid that milks
    And does the meanest chares. It were for me   80
    To throw my sceptre at the injurious gods,
    To tell them that this world did equal theirs
    Till they had stol'n our jewel. All's but naught;
    Patience is sottish, and impatience does
    Become a dog that's mad. Then is it sin   85
    To rush into the secret house of death
    Ere death dare come to us? How do you, women?
    What, what, good cheer! Why, how now, Charmian?
    My noble girls! Ah, women, women! Look,
    Our lamp is spent, it's out. Good sirs, take heart.   90
    We'll bury him; and then, what's brave, what's noble,
    Let's do't after the high Roman fashion
    And make death proud to take us. Come, away.
    This case of that huge spirit now is cold.
    Ah, women, women! Come, we have no friend   95
    But resolution and the briefest end.
           Exeunt, [those above] bearing off Antony's body

Looking back at Act 4

Activities for groups or individuals

1 A reporter's eye

You are a reporter responsible for describing the events of Act 4. Write a headline plus your opening sentence for each of the fifteen scenes. A newspaper article usually begins with an eye-catching sentence to make the reader want to read on.

2 Loyalty and betrayal

Act 4 presents those, like Eros, who are loyal to Antony and those, like Dercetus, who merely follow the side most advantageous to their prospects. Divide into two groups:

Group 1 are the self-seekers, those determined to end up on the winning side. Trace the battle manoeuvres and tactics in Act 4, the ebb and flow of military strength, the omens and desertions. What reasons do you have for deserting Antony?

Group 2 are loyal to Antony. Review the events leading to Antony's defeat and suicide. What reasons do you have for remaining loyal?

Join together and argue your case.

3 A man armoured against his secret self?

Enobarbus has been the hard-bitten professional soldier, whose caustic comments are full of common-sense wisdom. Yet he dies of a broken heart. Trace the development of the insoluble dilemma that eventually kills him.

Study his comments, asides and Chorus-like remarks in Acts 1–4, especially his words in Act 3 Scene 13 and Act 4 Scenes 6 and 9 (it is the convention in soliloquies that a character always speaks frankly). Then write notes advising the actor playing Enobarbus on how he could show his decline. For example, are there incidents and remarks early in the play which hint at a more vulnerable side to Enobarbus's nature?

4 A love tested and not found wanting?

The critic Harley Granville-Barker wrote: 'Antony's death is inglorious, but he *has* loved Cleopatra, the worst and the best of her – and gives her the worst and the best of him.' Explore this claim in two ways:

- Look back at Acts 3 and 4 through Antony's eyes. Say what is the best and worst of Cleopatra.
- Look back at Acts 3 and 4 through Cleopatra's eyes. Say what is the best and worst of Antony.

5 Your thoughts on Antony

Just as the dilemma of being true to both reason and love destroyed Enobarbus, so the impossible dilemma of being true to both love and honour destroys Antony.

a Melting and dissolving images. In the extremities of his despair, Antony senses his very identity dissolving and scattering. Collect together the different melting, stripping and dissolving images from Act 4 Scenes 12, 14 and 15 and place them around your picture of Antony.

b 'Great hero', 'love's martyr', 'self-deluding fool'. How valid are each of these judgements of Antony?

c 'A tortured destruction.' What is the greatest torture for Antony – dishonour, failure, faithlessness, treachery or something else?

d Disintegration, yet realisation. Towards their end, all the great Shakespearian heroes (Hamlet, Lear, Macbeth, Othello) say something that seems to express a truth they have discovered in their tortured journey through the play. For Macbeth it is the realisation that 'life's but a walking shadow' (*Macbeth* Act 5 Scene 5, line 23). Find Antony's moments of realisation in Act 4 Scenes 14 and 15. Does life for him become as meaningless as it seems to have become for Macbeth?

Draw together your ideas by writing two obituaries of Antony: (1) for the people of Rome, stressing Antony's 'Roman' qualities like military skill, status, masculinity, leadership and power; and (2) for the people of Alexandria, praising Antony's 'Egyptian' virtues.

Caesar instructs Dolabella to go to Antony and insist that he surrenders.
Dercetus brings Antony's sword and informs Caesar of his rival's death.
Caesar says the news should shatter the world.

1 Sincerity or hypocrisy? (in groups of six)

Plutarch describes how Octavius Caesar, on hearing the news of Antony's death, withdrew into the privacy of his tent 'and there burst out with tears' lamenting the fate of his brother-in-law, equal in empire and companion in battle. Does Shakespeare's Caesar weep as much?

Read lines 1–51 with a sincere Caesar. Read again, but this time your Caesar utters forced, insincere compliments. Hot-seat the two Caesars and ask each to justify his style of speaking.

2 'What art thou that dar'st/Appear thus to us?' (in groups of seven)

To enter the king's presence with weapons drawn was a treasonable offence in Elizabethan England. Antony's sword and armour have symbolised his strength and power from the opening moments of the play. One of you direct the rest of the group in a performance of lines 4–26. Concentrate on finding ways of emphasising the dramatic and symbolic importance of Antony's sword.

3 'Shook lions into civil streets'

Octavius Caesar's words (lines 14–19) echo the strange and unnatural events that took place the night before Julius Caesar was murdered. Read *Julius Caesar* Act 1 Scene 3, lines 20–35 and Act 2 Scene 2, lines 13–37. What echoes do you detect?

---

frustrate helpless
he mocks ... makes he makes
  himself ridiculous by his delay in
  surrendering
spend upon fight against
breaking destruction, or bringing
  the news

crack explosion
civil city
a single doom just one man's
  death
moiety half
self self-same

ACT 5 SCENE I
Alexandria Caesar's camp

Enter CAESAR, AGRIPPA, DOLABELLA, MAECENAS, GALLUS,
PROCULEIUS, *with his council of war*

CAESAR Go to him, Dolabella, bid him yield;
    Being so frustrate, tell him, he mocks
    The pauses that he makes.
DOLABELLA   Caesar, I shall.   [*Exit*]

    Enter DERCETUS, *with the sword of Antony*

CAESAR Wherefore is that? And what art thou that dar'st
    Appear thus to us?
DERCETUS   I am called Dercetus.   5
    Mark Antony I served, who best was worthy
    Best to be served. Whilst he stood up and spoke
    He was my master, and I wore my life
    To spend upon his haters. If thou please
    To take me to thee, as I was to him   10
    I'll be to Caesar; if thou pleasest not,
    I yield thee up my life.
CAESAR   What is't thou say'st?
DERCETUS I say, O Caesar, Antony is dead.
CAESAR The breaking of so great a thing should make
    A greater crack. The round world   15
    Should have shook lions into civil streets
    And citizens to their dens. The death of Antony
    Is not a single doom; in the name lay
    A moiety of the world.
DERCETUS   He is dead, Caesar,
    Not by a public minister of justice,   20
    Nor by a hirèd knife; but that self hand
    Which writ his honour in the acts it did
    Hath, with the courage which the heart did lend it,
    Splitted the heart. This is his sword;
          [*He offers the sword*]
    I robbed his wound of it. Behold it stained   25
    With his most noble blood.

Agrippa and Maecenas pay tribute to the dead Antony. Caesar's lament for the loss of Antony is interrupted by the arrival of a messenger from Cleopatra asking Caesar what he requires of her.

1 A genuine tribute? (in groups of four)

Imagine that four servants have overheard everything Caesar, Maecenas and Agrippa have said in the play about Antony. Two servants are cynical and critical of their masters, the other two support them wholeheartedly. Work in pairs as follows:

Pair A (the cynics). Jot down the accusations Caesar, Maecenas and Agrippa made against Antony while he was alive (Act 1 Scene 4, Act 2 Scene 2, Act 3 Scene 2 and Act 3 Scene 6). Why might the tributes expressed in lines 26–48 opposite appear insincere? What cynical interpretation could you put on Caesar's use of disease imagery (lines 36–7)? Express your doubts about whether 'Caesar is (truly) touched' (line 33).

Pair B (the believers). Note your masters' earlier criticisms of Antony, which you believe to be true and accurate. Prepare a speech, in role, expressing the generous nature of your masters' tributes to Antony and the accuracy of their assessment of him (lines 30–40). The following will help you:

'do launch diseases' = must lance infections
'I must perforce ... thine' = I must of necessity have either lost all my power to you or watched you lose your power to me
'sovereign' = valuable, powerful
'competitor' = partner
'in top of all design' = in the loftiest enterprise
'the heart ... did kindle' = my heart was inspired by his
'divide our equalness to this' = tear apart our equal partnership

Pair A argue their case with pair B. Take a class vote on how sincere you believe Caesar, Maecenas and Agrippa to be.

---

persisted deeds deliberate actions
Waged ... him were equally
  matched in him
will give will insist on giving
meeter more suitable

looks out of him reveals its
  urgency in his eyes and expression
yet still (though likely soon to
  become a subject of Rome)
preparedly may frame herself
  may prepare to shape her course

CAESAR   Look you sad, friends?
    The gods rebuke me, but it is tidings
    To wash the eyes of kings.
AGRIPPA   And strange it is
    That nature must compel us to lament
    Our most persisted deeds.
MAECENAS   His taints and honours   30
    Waged equal with him.
AGRIPPA   A rarer spirit never
    Did steer humanity; but you gods will give us
    Some faults to make us men. Caesar is touched.
MAECENAS When such a spacious mirror's set before him,
    He needs must see himself.
CAESAR   O Antony,   35
    I have followed thee to this; but we do launch
    Diseases in our bodies. I must perforce
    Have shown to thee such a declining day,
    Or look on thine; we could not stall together
    In the whole world. But yet let me lament   40
    With tears as sovereign as the blood of hearts
    That thou, my brother, my competitor
    In top of all design, my mate in empire,
    Friend and companion in the front of war,
    The arm of mine own body, and the heart   45
    Where mine his thoughts did kindle – that our stars,
    Unreconciliable, should divide
    Our equalness to this. Hear me, good friends –

Enter an EGYPTIAN

    But I will tell you at some meeter season.
    The business of this man looks out of him;   50
    We'll hear him what he says. – Whence are you?
EGYPTIAN A poor Egyptian yet, the queen my mistress,
    Confined in all she has, her monument,
    Of thy intents desires instruction,
    That she preparedly may frame herself   55
    To th'way she's forced to.

Caesar sends a message assuring Cleopatra that she will be treated honourably and instructs Proculeius to ensure that she does not commit suicide. He wants to bring her back alive to Rome.

Caesar (right) with his council of war. Identify how the director's imagination has adapted lines 73–7.

1 Who is watching whom? (in pairs)

Caesar sends Proculeius then Gallus to guard Cleopatra. Later Dolabella is added to the watchers. What do these actions suggest to you about Caesar?

2 What are Cleopatra's true intentions?

If Cleopatra is really planning to take her own life, why does she now send a message to Caesar asking him what she should do?

---

some of ours my messengers
ungentle harsh
passion grief
mortal stroke suicide
her life having her alive
be eternal ... triumph give eternal fame to my triumph

with your speediest as quickly as you can
how you find of her what state of mind you find her in
second support
hardly reluctantly
still constantly
my writings letters to Antony

CAESAR   Bid her have good heart.
      She soon shall know of us, by some of ours,
      How honourable and how kindly we
      Determine for her; for Caesar cannot live
      To be ungentle.
EGYPTIAN   So the gods preserve thee!   *Exit*   60
CAESAR Come hither, Proculeius. Go and say
      We purpose her no shame. Give her what comforts
      The quality of her passion shall require,
      Lest, in her greatness, by some mortal stroke
      She do defeat us; for her life in Rome   65
      Would be eternal in our triumph. Go,
      And with your speediest bring us what she says
      And how you find of her.
PROCULEIUS   Caesar, I shall.   *Exit Proculeius*
CAESAR Gallus, go you along.
                                          [*Exit Gallus*]
                    Where's Dolabella,
      To second Proculeius?
ALL   Dolabella!   70
CAESAR Let him alone, for I remember now
      How he's employed. He shall in time be ready.
      Go with me to my tent, where you shall see
      How hardly I was drawn into this war,
      How calm and gentle I proceeded still   75
      In all my writings. Go with me and see
      What I can show in this.
                                          Exeunt

Cleopatra scorns Caesar and thinks of suicide. Proculeius asks what she wishes from Caesar. She asks that her son may be allowed to rule Egypt. Proculeius assures her of Caesar's generosity.

---

1 Cleopatra's final battle (in groups of ten)

Glenda Jackson, who played Cleopatra in the 1978 Royal Shakespeare Company production, said this of the final scene:

> You think you have seen the whole play, then suddenly there are twenty minutes at the end after Antony has died, when Cleopatra readies herself for her own death, which is absolutely extraordinary. When you begin to rehearse it, you think 'Well, I won't have any energy left!'.

> Events in Act 5 give Cleopatra no pause. Continuously new requirements are made of her. There is no moment when she can simply grieve, no moment when she can hide herself away, recover herself. Above all, she is facing something in herself that she has never had to face before. She is moving towards the realisation that she has *got* to die.

To help you gain a first impression of the final scene, take a part each (double up the parts of Clown/Seleucus, Mardian/First Guard). Sit in a circle and read it through.

2 Prisoners to Fortune (in pairs)

Cleopatra's opening lines suggest that she is beginning to realise the worthlessness of her former glory. Even Caesar is vulnerable to the whims of Fortune. He is merely its 'knave' or servant (line 3). Take turns as director and actor rehearsing lines 1–8. Advise the actor on the emotion you hear in Cleopatra's voice. Then talk together about the images Cleopatra uses to describe the power and attraction of death (lines 4–8), and how her words in line 7 echo Antony's in the opening scene (Act 1 Scene 1, line 37).

A better life a truer life
do that thing (commit suicide)
shackles ... change prevents the chances and changes of life
never palates ... Caesar's will never again taste the earth which gives life to all men

study ... demands consider what requests for favourable terms
keep decorum behave as a queen
your full reference all your requests
pray in aid for kindness ask you to help him be generous to you

204

ACT 5   SCENE 2
Alexandria   Cleopatra's monument

Enter CLEOPATRA, CHARMIAN, IRAS, *and* MARDIAN

CLEOPATRA My desolation does begin to make
    A better life. 'Tis paltry to be Caesar;
    Not being Fortune, he's but Fortune's knave,
    A minister of her will. And it is great
    To do that thing that ends all other deeds,   5
    Which shackles accidents and bolts up change,
    Which sleeps, and never palates more the dung,
    The beggar's nurse and Caesar's.

Enter [to the gates of the monument] PROCULEIUS

PROCULEIUS Caesar sends greeting to the Queen of Egypt,
    And bids thee study on what fair demands   10
    Thou mean'st to have him grant thee.
CLEOPATRA   What's thy name?
PROCULEIUS My name is Proculeius.
CLEOPATRA   Antony
    Did tell me of you, bade me trust you, but
    I do not greatly care to be deceived
    That have no use for trusting. If your master   15
    Would have a queen his beggar, you must tell him
    That majesty, to keep decorum, must
    No less beg than a kingdom. If he please
    To give me conquered Egypt for my son,
    He gives me so much of mine own as I   20
    Will kneel to him with thanks.
PROCULEIUS   Be of good cheer;
    You're fall'n into a princely hand. Fear nothing.
    Make your full reference freely to my lord,
    Who is so full of grace that it flows over
    On all that need. Let me report to him   25
    Your sweet dependency, and you shall find
    A conqueror that will pray in aid for kindness
    Where he for grace is kneeled to.

Proculeius assures Cleopatra of Caesar's good intentions, but soldiers break in and seize her. Proculeius prevents Cleopatra's attempt to stab herself. She vows to find some other way of killing herself.

1 Does she really mean it?

Do you think that Cleopatra really means what she says in lines 28–32?

2 Dramatic effect (in groups of eight)

Proculeius, the one man Antony said Cleopatra could trust, appears to be the first to deceive and betray her. However, the stage direction at line 34 is not Shakespeare's but a later addition. In the 1992 Royal Shakespeare Company production, Proculeius was as surprised as Cleopatra when the guards broke in. But in the BBC production (see photograph), Proculeius ordered the soldiers to take Cleopatra.

Rehearse different versions of lines 29–41. Is the soldiers' entry silent, or a sudden and violent break-in? Give reasons why your Proculeius is or is not surprised.

vassal slave	**come forth** be revealed
send him acknowledge	**If idle … necessary** if I have to
doctrine lesson	talk incessantly to do it
surprised captured	**mortal house** body
Relieved rescued	**pinioned** with clipped wings
languish lingering diseases	**varletry** mob, rabble
well acted admirably demonstrated	**censuring** harshly judging

CLEOPATRA   Pray you tell him
  I am his fortune's vassal, and I send him
  The greatness he has got. I hourly learn   30
  A doctrine of obedience, and would gladly
  Look him i'th'face.
PROCULEIUS   This I'll report, dear lady.
  Have comfort, for I know your plight is pitied
  Of him that caused it.

  [*Some of the Guard come behind Cleopatra and seize her*]

  You see how easily she may be surprised.   35
  Guard her till Caesar come.
IRAS   Royal queen!
CHARMIAN O Cleopatra! Thou art taken, queen.
CLEOPATRA Quick, quick, good hands. [*Drawing a dagger*]
PROCULEIUS   Hold, worthy lady, hold!
                      [*He seizes and disarms her*]
  Do not yourself such wrong, who are in this
  Relieved, but not betrayed.
CLEOPATRA   What, of death too,   40
  That rids our dogs of languish?
PROCULEIUS   Cleopatra,
  Do not abuse my master's bounty by
  Th'undoing of yourself. Let the world see
  His nobleness well acted, which your death
  Will never let come forth.
CLEOPATRA   Where art thou, Death?   45
  Come hither, come! Come, come, and take a queen
  Worth many babes and beggars.
PROCULEIUS   O, temperance, lady!
CLEOPATRA Sir, I will eat no meat, I'll not drink, sir;
  If idle talk will once be necessary
  I'll not sleep, neither. This mortal house I'll ruin,   50
  Do Caesar what he can. Know, sir, that I
  Will not wait pinioned at your master's court,
  Nor once be chastised with the sober eye
  Of dull Octavia. Shall they hoist me up
  And show me to the shouting varletry   55
  Of censuring Rome? Rather a ditch in Egypt

Cleopatra lists the deaths she would prefer to captivity. Dolabella takes over guard of Cleopatra from Proculeius. Cleopatra tells Dolabella of a dream she has had of Antony.

1 'Let the water-flies/Blow me into abhorring!'

This perhaps means 'let the flies deposit eggs in me and thus make me abhorrent' or 'let the flies cause me to swell abhorrently with maggots'.

Find the lines in Act 3 Scene 13 where, in an earlier moment of intense emotion, Cleopatra made a similar vow. Compare the two vows, noting what motivates Cleopatra to speak on each occasion. Which of these two images do you find more powerful, more touching, more sincere?

2 Whom does Cleopatra trust? (in groups of four)

Cleopatra reveals to Dolabella her dream of an Antony in whose 'bounty/There was no winter' (lines 85–6). Does this show that she trusts Dolabella more than Proculeius? To explore the possibilities, take parts as Cleopatra, Cleopatra's *alter ego*, Dolabella and Proculeius.

Rehearse lines 38–80 with Cleopatra's *alter ego* interjecting to comment on what she thinks of each man. The *alter ego* must make clear what it is that each man says or does to make Cleopatra react so differently. For example, consider Dolabella's first words to Cleopatra, 'Most noble empress, you have heard of me?' Would Cleopatra find them offensive or flattering?

Nilus' Nile
pyramides (pronounced as four
  syllables with stress on second
  syllable – pyrámides)

gibbet post from which the bodies
  of hanged criminals were
  suspended as a warning to others
extend exaggerate, magnify
trick way, custom
stuck were set

Be gentle grave unto me! Rather on Nilus' mud
Lay me stark nak'd and let the water-flies
Blow me into abhorring! Rather make
My country's high pyramides my gibbet   60
And hang me up in chains!
PROCULEIUS   You do extend
These thoughts of horror further than you shall
Find cause in Caesar.

Enter DOLABELLA

DOLABELLA   Proculeius,
What thou hast done thy master Caesar knows,
And he hath sent for thee. For the queen,   65
I'll take her to my guard.
PROCULEIUS   So, Dolabella,
It shall content me best. Be gentle to her.
[*To Cleopatra*] To Caesar I will speak what you shall please,
If you'll employ me to him.
CLEOPATRA   Say I would die.
                    Exit Proculeius [*with Soldiers*]
DOLABELLA Most noble empress, you have heard of me?   70
CLEOPATRA I cannot tell.
DOLABELLA   Assuredly you know me.
CLEOPATRA No matter, sir, what I have heard or known.
You laugh when boys or women tell their dreams;
Is't not your trick?
DOLABELLA   I understand not, madam.
CLEOPATRA I dreamt there was an emperor Antony.   75
O, such another sleep, that I might see
But such another man!
DOLABELLA   If it might please ye –
CLEOPATRA His face was as the heav'ns, and therein stuck
A sun and moon, which kept their course and lighted
The little O, the earth.
DOLABELLA   Most sovereign creature –   80

Cleopatra tells Dolabella her dream of a super-human Antony exceeding all comparison. Dolabella says he too feels grief. He confirms that Cleopatra will be led in triumph through Rome.

1 Cleopatra's vision (in small groups)

In her grief and desolation, Cleopatra imagines a god-like Antony surrounded by shimmering images of power, generosity, delight and careless extravagance. The following will help you with lines 75–99:

line 81 'His legs bestrid the ocean': the Colossus of Rhodes was one of the Seven Wonders of the ancient world. This giant bronze statue of the sun god was thought to stand astride the entry to Rhodes harbour. Write down the other images which create a huge god-like Antony.

lines 82–3 'His voice was propertied as all the tunèd spheres': the crystal spheres on which the planets were believed to be fixed were thought to emit mysterious music. How many other cosmic images are used to describe Antony?

lines 87–9 'His delights were dolphin-like': dolphins were the kings of the sea and famous for their playful antics. How does Cleopatra's image answer criticism of Antony's debauchery?

lines 89–91 'Realms and islands were as plates dropped from his pockets': Caesar was furious at Antony's disposal of Rome's eastern provinces (Act 3 Scene 6, lines 8–16 and 68–78). Cleopatra remembers only the careless extravagance. Talk about whether your memory of Antony is as approving as Cleopatra's.

lines 91–9 'Think you there was or might be such a man?': no dream can match Cleopatra's vision of Antony. Neither can imagination ('fancy') or nature. Cleopatra's memory of Antony is of nature perfected ('Nature's piece'). Antony was far greater than anything imagination could conceive.

---

was propertied/As all had all the qualities of
livery service, uniform
crowns/crownets kings/princes
plates silver coins
As ... weight equally heavily

Would I ... feel may I never succeed in my own desires if I do not feel
rebound of yours reflection of your (grief)

CLEOPATRA His legs bestrid the ocean; his reared arm
　　　　　Crested the world; his voice was propertied
　　　　　As all the tunèd spheres, and that to friends;
　　　　　But when he meant to quail and shake the orb,
　　　　　He was as rattling thunder. For his bounty,　　　　85
　　　　　There was no winter in't; an autumn 'twas
　　　　　That grew the more by reaping. His delights
　　　　　Were dolphin-like; they showed his back above
　　　　　The element they lived in. In his livery
　　　　　Walked crowns and crownets; realms and islands were　　90
　　　　　As plates dropped from his pocket.
DOLABELLA　　　　　　　　　　　　　Cleopatra –
CLEOPATRA Think you there was or might be such a man
　　　　　As this I dreamt of?
DOLABELLA　　　　　　　　Gentle madam, no.
CLEOPATRA You lie up to the hearing of the gods.
　　　　　But if there be nor ever were one such,　　　　　95
　　　　　It's past the size of dreaming. Nature wants stuff
　　　　　To vie strange forms with fancy; yet t'imagine
　　　　　An Antony were Nature's piece 'gainst fancy,
　　　　　Condemning shadows quite.
DOLABELLA　　　　　　　　　　　Hear me, good madam:
　　　　　Your loss is as yourself, great; and you bear it　　　100
　　　　　As answering to the weight. Would I might never
　　　　　O'ertake pursued success but I do feel,
　　　　　By the rebound of yours, a grief that smites
　　　　　My very heart at root.
CLEOPATRA　　　　　　　　I thank you, sir.
　　　　　Know you what Caesar means to do with me?　　　105
DOLABELLA I am loath to tell you what I would you knew.
CLEOPATRA Nay, pray you, sir.
DOLABELLA　　　　　　　Though he be honourable –
CLEOPATRA He'll lead me then in triumph.
DOLABELLA Madam, he will, I know't.

Cleopatra kneels in submission to Caesar. He promises no harm will come to her, but says her children will suffer if she attempts suicide. Cleopatra hands him an inventory of her personal wealth.

1 What kind of entrance? (in groups of six to twelve)

Talk about how this crucial meeting should be presented. Is Caesar stern, friendly, triumphant, or what? One story says that the historical Octavius was so afraid of Cleopatra's 'bewitching powers' that he dared not look at her. Is that how you think Shakespeare's Caesar would behave?

Try out lines 110–16 in several ways. Perform your preferred version to the class and justify the behaviour of your Caesar and Cleopatra.

2 Cleopatra and Caesar meet at last (in pairs)

For the first time in the play, Caesar and Cleopatra meet face to face. How honest are they with each other? Read lines 113–39 together, then make brief notes on:

a Cleopatra. She knows Caesar intends leading her in triumph through Rome. Has she submitted to her fate or is she only pretending to submit? Count the number of insincerities in her words.

b Caesar. Decide why he should use the royal 'we' in speaking to Cleopatra. Count the number of insincerities in his words. How many open or veiled threats does he make?

When you have worked on a and b above, join with another pair and compare notes. Then use your notes to present lines 110–49 using *alter egos* to speak Caesar and Cleopatra's secret thoughts as their meeting proceeds.

Take ... thoughts do not reproach yourself
project argue
clear free from blame
extenuate excuse
If ... intents if you carry out my plans for you

lay ... cruelty make me look cruel
scutcheons captured shields
all for Cleopatra everything that concerns you
brief list, inventory
Not ... admitted except for a few trivial things

212

Flourish. Enter PROCULEIUS, CAESAR, GALLUS, MAECENAS, *and others of his train*

ALL Make way there! Caesar!   110
CAESAR Which is the Queen of Egypt?
DOLABELLA It is the emperor, madam.
                      Cleopatra kneels
CAESAR Arise, you shall not kneel.
        I pray you, rise. Rise, Egypt.
CLEOPATRA [*Rising*]   Sir, the gods
        Will have it thus. My master and my lord   115
        I must obey.
CAESAR   Take to you no hard thoughts.
        The record of what injuries you did us,
        Though written in our flesh, we shall remember
        As things but done by chance.
CLEOPATRA   Sole sir o'th'world,
        I cannot project mine own cause so well   120
        To make it clear, but do confess I have
        Been laden with like frailties which before
        Have often shamed our sex.
CAESAR   Cleopatra, know
        We will extenuate rather than enforce.
        If you apply yourself to our intents,   125
        Which towards you are most gentle, you shall find
        A benefit in this change; but if you seek
        To lay on me a cruelty by taking
        Antony's course, you shall bereave yourself
        Of my good purposes and put your children   130
        To that destruction which I'll guard them from
        If thereon you rely. I'll take my leave.
CLEOPATRA And may through all the world! 'Tis yours, and we,
        Your scutcheons and your signs of conquest, shall
        Hang in what place you please. Here, my good lord.   135
                [She offers him a scroll]
CAESAR You shall advise me in all for Cleopatra.
CLEOPATRA This is the brief of money, plate, and jewels
        I am possessed of. 'Tis exactly valued,
        Not petty things admitted. Where's Seleucus?

Seleucus reveals that Cleopatra has kept back at least half her wealth. Cleopatra angrily rebukes Seleucus, saying that he has betrayed and shamed her. She apologises to Caesar for her attempt to deceive him.

1 A failed attempt or a double bluff? (in groups of six)

Plutarch's account states very clearly that Cleopatra was hoping to trick Caesar. Shakespeare's presentation is more ambiguous, as the following possibilities suggest:

a It could be a genuine attempt by Cleopatra to keep back her wealth, which Seleucus reveals. Her anger is therefore very real.

b Cleopatra has anticipated that Seleucus might betray her. Her anger is again very real, but she is prepared for the betrayal and therefore not entirely disconcerted.

c The whole thing was stage-managed by Cleopatra and Seleucus to give Caesar the impression that she intends to live, not commit suicide.

d It was arranged to make Cleopatra seem so pitiable that Caesar would feel compelled to allow her to keep at least some of her wealth.

Which of these versions (or any other) do you think is most likely? Look at the 'internal stage directions' in the script to help you decide how savage Cleopatra is in her attack on Seleucus (for example, 'Goest thou back? ... I'll catch thine eyes ...', lines 154–5).

2 'Some nobler token I have kept apart / For Livia'

Livia is Caesar's wife. How do you think Cleopatra says lines 163–70? Is she flattering Caesar, making it up as she goes along, or does she adopt some other manner?

Upon his peril at the risk of punishment if he lies
pomp is followed greatness is served
shift estates change places
hired paid for, bought
rarely exceptionally

Parcel add one more to
Immoment toys unimportant trifles
modern ordinary
unfolded / With ... bred exposed by my own servant
my chance my (fallen) fortune

[*Enter* SELEUCUS]

SELEUCUS Here, madam.   140

CLEOPATRA This is my treasurer. Let him speak, my lord,
    Upon his peril, that I have reserved
    To myself nothing. Speak the truth, Seleucus.

SELEUCUS Madam, I had rather seal my lips
    Than to my peril speak that which is not.   145

CLEOPATRA What have I kept back?

SELEUCUS Enough to purchase what you have made known.

CAESAR Nay, blush not, Cleopatra. I approve
    Your wisdom in the deed.

CLEOPATRA   See, Caesar! O, behold
    How pomp is followed! Mine will now be yours,   150
    And should we shift estates yours would be mine.
    The ingratitude of this Seleucus does
    Even make me wild. – O slave, of no more trust
    Than love that's hired! What, goest thou back? Thou shalt
    Go back, I warrant thee! But I'll catch thine eyes   155
    Though they had wings. Slave, soulless villain, dog!
    O rarely base!

CAESAR   Good queen, let us entreat you.

CLEOPATRA O Caesar, what a wounding shame is this,
    That thou vouchsafing here to visit me,
    Doing the honour of thy lordliness   160
    To one so meek, that mine own servant should
    Parcel the sum of my disgraces by
    Addition of his envy! Say, good Caesar,
    That I some lady trifles have reserved,
    Immoment toys, things of such dignity   165
    As we greet modern friends withal, and say
    Some nobler token I have kept apart
    For Livia and Octavia, to induce
    Their mediation, must I be unfolded
    With one that I have bred? The gods! It smites me   170
    Beneath the fall I have. [*To Seleucus*] Prithee, go hence,
    Or I shall show the cinders of my spirits
    Through th'ashes of my chance. Wert thou a man,
    Thou wouldst have mercy on me.

CAESAR   Forbear, Seleucus.
                 [*Seleucus withdraws*]

Caesar allows Cleopatra to retain her treasure. He departs with
reassuring words. Her fears about his deceit are confirmed when
Dolabella informs her that she and her children are to be sent to Rome.

1 'He words me, girls, he words me' (in small groups)

With Caesar gone, Cleopatra need pretend no longer. She knows that
Caesar has no intention of allowing her children to rule Egypt, and that
she will be led in triumph through Rome. Cleopatra 'is moving towards
the realisation that she has *got* to die' (see page 204).

Make a guess at what the 'it' refers to in lines 194–5. Is there a
connection with what Cleopatra whispers to Charmian in line 191?

2 'The bright day is done,/ And we are for the dark' (in pairs)

Speak Iras's words (lines 192–3)
to each other in different ways.
Antony used a similar image in
Act 4 Scene 14, lines 35–6. Talk
about the effect these echoing
'day/night' images have on you.

'We remain your friend.' Write the
thoughts of this Caesar and
Cleopatra.

---

misthought misjudged
We answer ... name we have to
  answer for our servants' errors
i'th'roll of conquest in the list of
  spoils of war
Bestow it use it
make prize haggle

Make not ... prisons don't
  imagine you are a prisoner
dispose you arrange your affairs
Hie thee again come back quickly
spoke given orders
makes religion compels me

CLEOPATRA Be it known that we, the greatest, are misthought   175
    For things that others do; and when we fall,
    We answer others' merits in our name,
    Are therefore to be pitied.
CAESAR   Cleopatra,
    Not what you have reserved nor what acknowledged
    Put we i'th'roll of conquest. Still be't yours;   180
    Bestow it at your pleasure, and believe
    Caesar's no merchant, to make prize with you
    Of things that merchants sold. Therefore be cheered.
    Make not your thoughts your prisons. No, dear queen,
    For we intend so to dispose you as   185
    Yourself shall give us counsel. Feed and sleep.
    Our care and pity is so much upon you
    That we remain your friend; and so adieu.
CLEOPATRA My master, and my lord!
CAESAR   Not so. Adieu.

Flourish. Exeunt Caesar and his train

CLEOPATRA He words me, girls, he words me, that I should not   190
    Be noble to myself. But hark thee, Charmian.

[She whispers to Charmian]

IRAS Finish, good lady. The bright day is done,
    And we are for the dark.
CLEOPATRA   Hie thee again.
    I have spoke already, and it is provided;
    Go put it to the haste.
CHARMIAN   Madam, I will.   195

Enter DOLABELLA

DOLABELLA Where's the queen?
CHARMIAN   Behold, sir.   *[Exit]*
CLEOPATRA   Dolabella!
DOLABELLA Madam, as thereto sworn by your command,
    Which my love makes religion to obey,
    I tell you this: Caesar through Syria
    Intends his journey, and within three days   200
    You with your children will he send before.
    Make your best use of this. I have performed
    Your pleasure and my promise.

Cleopatra describes the indignities she would suffer in Rome. Iras vows to tear out her eyes rather than witness such a sight. Cleopatra sends for her 'best attires' in which to meet Antony.

1 Cleopatra's nightmare (in large groups)

The historical Cleopatra knew what a Roman triumph was like, because she witnessed her sister led in chains before Julius Caesar's chariot. Shakespeare's Cleopatra foresees degradation and humiliation as 'Mechanic slaves' (workmen), 'Saucy lictors' (insolent Roman officials) and 'scald' (foul) ballad singers mock her.

In lines 215–20, Cleopatra describes how she and Antony will be the laughing stock and target of 'quick comedians' (quick-witted comic actors). Use the information above and lines 206–20 to create a play called *Cleopatra's Nightmare*. In your drama, Cleopatra sleeps, dreams and recreates every horror that Rome has in store for her.

2 '... I shall see
Some squeaking Cleopatra boy my greatness'

The word 'boy' (line 219) means 'to act on stage like a boy'. On Shakespeare's stage, all the female roles would have been played by boys. Here the boy actor deliberately draws attention to his own attempts at playing Cleopatra, as she scornfully foresees.

3 The ceremony that ends in death (in small groups)

Cleopatra sets her suicide plan in motion. How might the actors playing Cleopatra, Charmian and Iras portray their fear and resolution?

Choose three lines which suggest death from anywhere between lines 190–231. Write detailed director's notes on how you want the lines to be played.

---

rules measuring sticks, rulers
Uplift us to the view lift us up for all to see
Rank of gross diet stinking with bad food
strumpets prostitutes

Extemporally in improvised scenes
Cydnus (where she first met Antony – see 2.2.196–236)
Sirrah (address to servants)
dispatch hurry, or kill
chare task

CLEOPATRA   Dolabella,
    I shall remain your debtor.
DOLABELLA   I your servant.
    Adieu, good queen. I must attend on Caesar.   205
CLEOPATRA Farewell, and thanks.
                             Exit [Dolabella]
    Now, Iras, what think'st thou?
    Thou an Egyptian puppet shall be shown
    In Rome as well as I. Mechanic slaves
    With greasy aprons, rules, and hammers shall
    Uplift us to the view. In their thick breaths,   210
    Rank of gross diet, shall we be enclouded
    And forced to drink their vapour.
IRAS   The gods forbid!
CLEOPATRA Nay, 'tis most certain, Iras. Saucy lictors
    Will catch at us like strumpets, and scald rhymers
    Ballad us out o'tune. The quick comedians   215
    Extemporally will stage us and present
    Our Alexandrian revels; Antony
    Shall be brought drunken forth, and I shall see
    Some squeaking Cleopatra boy my greatness
    I'th'posture of a whore.
IRAS   O the good gods!   220
CLEOPATRA Nay, that's certain.
IRAS I'll never see't! For I am sure my nails
    Are stronger than mine eyes.
CLEOPATRA   Why, that's the way
    To fool their preparation and to conquer
    Their most absurd intents.

        Enter CHARMIAN

                 Now, Charmian!   225
    Show me, my women, like a queen. Go fetch
    My best attires. I am again for Cydnus,
    To meet Mark Antony. Sirrah Iras, go –
    Now, noble Charmian, we'll dispatch indeed –
    And when thou hast done this chare I'll give thee leave   230
    To play till Doomsday. Bring our crown and all.
                 [Exit Iras.] A noise within
    Wherefore's this noise?

A country man brings in a basket of figs. Cleopatra asks if he has brought the poisonous snake which kills without pain. The country man confirms the snake's deadly power.

---

1 The queen and the Clown (in pairs)

Desiring death, Cleopatra seeks help from the Clown (a simple country man).

The Clown seems to be making bawdy innuendoes. 'Honest' = chaste, 'lie' = go with men, 'die' = come to orgasm and 'worm' = penis. Some people find his strangely humorous words rather unnerving at this intense moment in the play. What effect do they have on you?

---

placed fixed
fleeting ever changing
Avoid depart
worm snake
immortal (a genuine or deliberate mistake?)
of one of them from one of them

no longer than as recently as
But he ... they do (this seems to be garbled nonsense; does the Clown mangle his language anywhere else?)
falliable (he means 'true, infallible')
do his kind act according to its nature

220

Enter a GUARDSMAN

GUARDSMAN   Here is a rural fellow
    That will not be denied your highness' presence.
    He brings you figs.
CLEOPATRA Let him come in.

Exit Guardsman
          What poor an instrument   235
    May do a noble deed! He brings me liberty.
    My resolution's placed, and I have nothing
    Of woman in me. Now from head to foot
    I am marble-constant; now the fleeting moon
    No planet is of mine.

Enter GUARDSMAN, *and* CLOWN [*bringing in a basket*]

GUARDSMAN   This is the man.   240
CLEOPATRA Avoid, and leave him.

Exit Guardsman
    Hast thou the pretty worm of Nilus there,
    That kills and pains not?
CLOWN Truly I have him, but I would not be the party that should
    desire you to touch him, for his biting is immortal. Those that   245
    do die of it do seldom or never recover.
CLEOPATRA Remember'st thou any that have died on't?
CLOWN Very many, men and women too. I heard of one of them no
    longer than yesterday – a very honest woman, but something
    given to lie, as a woman should not do but in the way of honesty   250
    – how she died of the biting of it, what pain she felt. Truly, she
    makes a very good report o'th'worm. But he that will believe all
    that they say shall never be saved by half that they do. But this is
    most falliable, the worm's an odd worm.
CLEOPATRA Get thee hence, farewell.   255
CLOWN I wish you all joy of the worm. [*Setting down his basket*]
CLEOPATRA Farewell.
CLOWN You must think this, look you, that the worm will do his
    kind.
CLEOPATRA Ay, ay, farewell.   260
CLOWN Look you, the worm is not to be trusted but in the keeping
    of wise people, for indeed there is no goodness in the worm.

Cleopatra tells her women to dress her in her royal robes. Elated at the thought of again meeting her 'husband', she kisses her servants farewell. Iras falls dead.

---

1 Your thoughts on the Clown (in small groups)

In the 1992 Royal Shakespeare Company production, the Soothsayer made several dramatic appearances at crucial moments in the play. He also played the part of the Clown. If you were directing the play, would you fuse the roles of Soothsayer and Clown in this way? Decide what advice you would give the Clown on how to play the part. For example, are his words cheekily rude, stupid, insinuating ... ?

2 Cleopatra prepares to die (in groups of three)

Cleopatra's women dress and prepare their queen for her final journey into death. In the theatre, lines 274–94 are usually played slowly to give every word and movement its full emotional impact. Rehearse and perform your 'majestic' version of these lines. Concentrate on the women's slow, measured movements, and try to deliver the imaginative and emotional intensity of the language.

3 Fire and air, cloud and rain

Fire and air were higher elements. The 'baser' elements of earth and water belonged to the lower regions of existence. On page 179, Antony speaks in a similar vein to Cleopatra's lines 283–4. To explore the richness and poetic intensity of the language of lines 274–94, play the Image Game:

> Write line 283 'I am fire and air' at the top of a sheet of paper. Each person in turn writes at the bottom the images/associations this line conjures up, folds over the paper to hide their words and passes the sheet on. At the end, unfold the sheet to reveal the different associations recorded.

Take thou no care don't worry
dress attire in seductive clothes, or prepare for cooking
whoreson rascally
Immortal longings longings for immortality
Yare quickly

excuse ... wrath justify the gods' subsequent anger at men's pride
Now ... title may my courage now prove my right to call you husband
aspic poison of the asp
nature life

222

CLEOPATRA Take thou no care; it shall be heeded.

CLOWN Very good. Give it nothing, I pray you, for it is not worth the
    feeding. 265

CLEOPATRA Will it eat me?

CLOWN You must not think I am so simple but I know the devil
    himself will not eat a woman. I know that a woman is a dish for
    the gods, if the devil dress her not. But truly, these same whore-
    son devils do the gods great harm in their women, for in every 270
    ten that they make, the devils mar five.

CLEOPATRA Well, get thee gone. Farewell.

CLOWN Yes, forsooth. I wish you joy o'th'worm. *Exit*

[*Enter* IRAS *with royal attire*]

CLEOPATRA Give me my robe. Put on my crown. I have
    Immortal longings in me. Now no more 275
    The juice of Egypt's grape shall moist this lip.
        [*The women dress her*]
    Yare, yare, good Iras; quick. Methinks I hear
    Antony call. I see him rouse himself
    To praise my noble act. I hear him mock
    The luck of Caesar, which the gods give men 280
    To excuse their after wrath. Husband, I come!
    Now to that name my courage prove my title!
    I am fire and air; my other elements
    I give to baser life. So, have you done?
    Come, then, and take the last warmth of my lips. 285
    Farewell, kind Charmian. Iras, long farewell.
        [*She kisses them. Iras falls and dies*]
    Have I the aspic in my lips? Dost fall?
    If thou and nature can so gently part,
    The stroke of death is as a lover's pinch,
    Which hurts, and is desired. Dost thou lie still? 290
    If thus thou vanishest, thou tell'st the world
    It is not worth leave-taking.

CHARMIAN Dissolve, thick cloud, and rain, that I may say
    The gods themselves do weep!

Cleopatra fears Iras will meet Antony first. She applies one asp to her breast and encourages another to bite her. She dies. The guards enter and Charmian takes another asp for herself.

'Poor venomous fool,/Be angry, and dispatch.' Perhaps Cleopatra's death is dignified and regal, as shown in this 1972 Royal Shakespeare Company production. Other productions have presented it as a soft and gentle death, a painful death, a death full of touching and kissing. How would you suggest that these final moments of Cleopatra's life should be played?

curlèd with curled hair (remember Enobarbus's remark in 2.2.234)
make demand of her make love to her
mortal wretch deadly creature
intrinsicate intricate, mysterious
dispatch end it quickly

Unpolicied outmanoeuvred
eastern star Venus, morning star
What should I why should I
Phoebus the sun god
mend straighten
rustling clattering
beguiled tricked, cheated

CLEOPATRA   This proves me base.
        If she first meet the curlèd Antony,   295
        He'll make demand of her, and spend that kiss
        Which is my heaven to have. Come, thou mortal wretch,
              [*She applies an asp*]
        With thy sharp teeth this knot intrinsicate
        Of life at once untie. Poor venomous fool,
        Be angry, and dispatch. O, couldst thou speak,   300
        That I might hear thee call great Caesar ass
        Unpolicied!
CHARMIAN   O eastern star!
CLEOPATRA   Peace, peace!
        Dost thou not see my baby at my breast,
        That sucks the nurse asleep?
CHARMIAN   O, break! O, break!
CLEOPATRA As sweet as balm, as soft as air, as gentle –   305
        O Antony! – Nay, I will take thee too.
              [*She applies another asp*]
        What should I stay –   *Dies*
CHARMIAN In this wild world? So, fare thee well.
        Now boast thee, Death, in thy possession lies
        A lass unparalleled. Downy windows, close;   310
        And golden Phoebus never be beheld
        Of eyes again so royal! Your crown's awry;
        I'll mend it, and then play –

              Enter the GUARD *rustling in*

I GUARD Where's the queen?
CHARMIAN   Speak softly. Wake her not.
I GUARD Caesar hath sent –
CHARMIAN   Too slow a messenger.   315
              [*She applies an asp*]
        O, come apace, dispatch! I partly feel thee.
I GUARD Approach, ho! All's not well. Caesar's beguiled.
2 GUARD There's Dolabella sent from Caesar. Call him.
                              [*Exit a Guardsman*]

Charmian declares that Cleopatra's death is appropriate for a queen.
Dolabella says Caesar's prophecy is fulfilled. Caesar pays tribute to
Cleopatra's courage. He seeks the cause of her death.

'It is well done, and fitting for a princess/
Descended of so many royal kings.' Cleopatra's Greek ancestors went back
300 years to the first Ptolemy, one of the generals of Alexander the Great.
Describe your final thoughts on Cleopatra at this moment. Is she truly 'a
princess/Descended of so many royal kings'?

thy thoughts ... this	**That you** what you
what you thought might happen	**levelled** guessed
has come true	**trimming up the diadem**
augurer prophet	straightening the crown

1 GUARD What work is here, Charmian? Is this well done?
CHARMIAN It is well done, and fitting for a princess   320
       Descended of so many royal kings.
       Ah, soldier!   *Charmian dies*

Enter DOLABELLA

DOLABELLA How goes it here?
2 GUARD   All dead.
DOLABELLA   Caesar, thy thoughts
       Touch their effects in this. Thyself art coming
       To see performed the dreaded act which thou   325
       So sought'st to hinder.

Enter CAESAR and all his train, marching

ALL A way there, a way for Caesar!
DOLABELLA O sir, you are too sure an augurer:
       That you did fear is done.
CAESAR   Bravest at the last,
       She levelled at our purposes and, being royal,   330
       Took her own way. The manner of their deaths?
       I do not see them bleed.
DOLABELLA   Who was last with them?
1 GUARD A simple countryman, that brought her figs.
       This was his basket.
CAESAR   Poisoned, then.
1 GUARD   O Caesar,
       This Charmian lived but now; she stood and spake.   335
       I found her trimming up the diadem
       On her dead mistress; tremblingly she stood,
       And on the sudden dropped.

Caesar and Dolabella deduce from the marks on the bodies and the slime on the fig leaves that Cleopatra died from the bite of an asp. Caesar orders Cleopatra to be buried with great ceremony by Antony's side.

1 Who has the final victory? (in pairs)

Many Elizabethans admired the historical Octavius Caesar. He was the strong ruler whose reign was 'The time of universal peace' (Act 4 Scene 6, line 5). On Antony's death, Octavius was indeed supreme ruler and 'Sole sir o'th'world' (Act 5 Scene 2, line 119).

In the play, however, it is open to argument as to who has the final victory. 'Caesar has the world, but Antony and Cleopatra had the living', is one critic's response to the dilemma. Who do you think triumphs at the end of the play – Caesar or Antony and Cleopatra?

2 The final tribute

Write the epitaph that you would inscribe on the tomb of Antony and Cleopatra to the 'pair so famous'. Write it in iambic pentameter (see page 246).

3 The final image (in large groups)

Decide on the final stage picture you would create for your production: a processional exit bearing the three bodies? Cleopatra's body left spotlit on stage? a tableau and slow fade?

Discuss, rehearse and show the final image the audience would see in your production of *Antony and Cleopatra*. Many modern productions do not obey the final stage direction (*'Exeunt omnes'* = everyone leaves the stage). They close with the dead bodies still on stage for dramatic effect. What would you do?

As she as if she
toil of grace net of beauty
vent discharge
blown swollen
conclusions infinite innumerable experiments
clip embrace

Strike ... make them touch with sorrow those who brought about these deeds
his glory the glory that Antony deserves, or Caesar's glory in bringing about their defeat
solemnity ceremony

CAESAR   O, noble weakness!
    If they had swallowed poison, 'twould appear
    By external swelling; but she looks like sleep,   340
    As she would catch another Antony
    In her strong toil of grace.
DOLABELLA   Here on her breast
    There is a vent of blood, and something blown;
    The like is on her arm.
1 GUARD This is an aspic's trail, and these fig-leaves   345
    Have slime upon them, such as th'aspic leaves
    Upon the caves of Nile.
CAESAR   Most probable
    That so she died; for her physician tells me
    She hath pursued conclusions infinite
    Of easy ways to die. Take up her bed,   350
    And bear her women from the monument.
    She shall be buried by her Antony.
    No grave upon the earth shall clip in it
    A pair so famous. High events as these
    Strike those that make them; and their story is   355
    No less in pity than his glory which
    Brought them to be lamented. Our army shall
    In solemn show attend this funeral,
    And then to Rome. Come, Dolabella, see
    High order in this great solemnity.   360
                Exeunt omnes, [bearing the dead bodies]

Looking back at the play
Activities for groups or individuals

1 Caesar demands an inquest

There have been three deaths. Despite his best efforts, Caesar has been cheated of his chance to parade Cleopatra through the streets of Rome. How did she learn of his intentions, and who gave her the means to kill herself?

Conduct the coroner's inquest. Call Dolabella, Proculeius, Seleucus, the guards, Mardian and the Clown to give evidence. As each witness steps down, he voices the private thoughts that he dared not speak in public.

2 First and last moments

The play opens in Alexandria with the Roman soldier, Philo, angrily expressing his disgust at Antony and Cleopatra's conduct. It ends in Alexandria with Caesar's final tribute to this 'pair so famous'. Perform edited versions of the opening forty and final sixty lines of the play.

3 Different ways of seeing

The story of Antony and Cleopatra has been viewed through many different eyes. Write headlines and opening paragraphs for the following publications. Each article must use information taken from the play.

The Rome Times *The Alexandria Tribune*	(both quality newspapers supporting their respective governments)
The Helios	(a Roman tabloid mass-circulation newspaper)
The Plebeian Daily Worker	(a Roman underground press publication)

A scandal magazine
A feminist magazine
A true love romance magazine
A combat magazine

Display these articles around the room and attempt to reach a consensus as to how your class 'sees' the story of Antony and Cleopatra.

4 A simple story?

For all its complex mingling of cultures, attitudes and viewpoints, the plot of *Antony and Cleopatra* can be very simply told. Tell the story in not more than fifty words.

5 Final thoughts on Cleopatra

Debate the following questions:

a What would your ideal Cleopatra look like? Compile your group's picture of the kind of woman that best embodies Shakespeare's words. Are there any specific clues in the script?

b Find evidence to support each opposition in these contrasting descriptions of Cleopatra: proud and humble, raging tigress and demure girl, regal and skittish, feminine and warlike, gentle and callously inhuman, very beautiful yet old and mysteriously evil.

c How sure are you of the constancy of Cleopatra's love for Antony? Do you believe her apparent transformation from fatal seductress to dedicated loving wife? Take sides and argue the case for and against.

d What is it about Shakespeare's Cleopatra that makes her one of the world's most famous dramatic creations?

Cleopatra and her women with the dead Antony. None of the four characters survive. Talk together about why you think the tragedy of *Antony and Cleopatra* has had such a strong and enduring appeal.

What is the play about?

'The play is a Janus'

The Roman god Janus possessed two faces, one on the front and one on the back of his head. *Antony and Cleopatra* provokes equally divided responses, which is not surprising considering the play's many shifting and contradictory viewpoints. One director said, 'I may see two sides to every issue, but Shakespeare sometimes sees three or four'. Cleopatra herself sees Antony as both the Gorgon and Mars (Act 2 Scene 5, lines 118–19).

There are sharp divisions of opinion even on what kind of play *Antony and Cleopatra* is. Is it tragedy, comedy, satire or romance? The sense of loss and waste that the deaths of both hero and heroine inspire suggest it is a tragedy. Yet the play is often comic as it moves from the exasperating moods of Cleopatra, to Antony's botched suicide or the Clown's *double entendres*. Some see the play as a bitter satire, where world leaders indulge in drunken singing, where Antony is a braggart soldier and Cleopatra a vain and inconstant whore. Others see it as 'the greatest love story ever told'.

A web of meanings

The play can be seen as containing many oppositions. Certain 'paired themes' recur throughout the play, linking together plot, characters and language. The following oppositions, for example, echo, reinforce and comment upon each other and the whole play.

Rome–Egypt	public duty–private happiness	loyalty–betrayal
male–female	fertility–corruption	past–present
love–lust	extravagance–discipline	change–stillness
fate–individual choice	measurable–immeasurable	time–timelessness

In pairs, explore this web of meanings. Each pair chooses one of the above oppositions and collects evidence (such as quotations, key words, actions) for their opposition. Draw a Janus head on a large sheet of paper. Each pair in turn writes their opposition plus evidence on each side of the Janus head. When everyone has made a contribution, draw arrows setting up *new* links between different oppositions. On each arrow write a phrase explaining why you have made the new link.

Love

The play is, without doubt, a famous love story. Place the following statements in rank order. Compare your opinions with those of other students, then write a sentence expressing your view of Antony and Cleopatra's love affair.

a 'It is the story of an ageing lecher and a shrewish strumpet, who threw away a kingdom for lust.'

b 'The most magnificent love affair the world has ever known, blazes like a fire in the night, but leaves sad ashes in the morning.'

c 'The play is about the fragility of human beings when they place themselves totally at risk.'

d 'The play asks the question, "What *value* is there in love?" '

e 'It isn't the greatest love story in the world. It isn't really about that. It's about betrayal, and about ageing and power.'

Politics and human frailties

Antony and Cleopatra's love affair is not a private matter. They move in a public, political world. Their actions are open to public criticism, their decisions affect whole nations. The play explores this world of power politics, showing people seeking power, the way power changes hands, the pressures and burdens on those who lead. The play shows also the human frailties of those who wield great power. Its great leaders are tense, ill-tempered, sensitive, ineffectual, cruel and selfish. They shed tears and get drunk.

Compile a check-list of five to ten points stating what makes a successful politician and leader. Illustrate your list from the play.

Fortune, destiny or individual choice?

The play is full of prophecies and omens. Characters are constantly aware of the power of both Fortune (chance) and destiny (the will of the gods). Pompey, for example, is certain that the gods will support his cause (Act 2 Scene 1), yet equally certain that harsh Fortune has tried to beat him down (Act 2 Scene 6).

Describe the following characters' differing attitudes to Fortune, Destiny and the gods: Menas (Act 2 Scenes 6 and 7), Antony (Act 2 Scene 3 and Act 4 Scenes 2 and 15), Octavius (Act 3 Scene 6 and Act 4 Scene 6), Octavia (Act 3 Scene 4) and Cleopatra (Act 4 Scene 15 and Act 5 Scene 2). How much belief does each have in the power of the individual to choose his or her own destiny?

Complex and contradictory characters

There are many ambiguities in the presentation of Antony and Cleopatra. Antony is a Mars and a Hercules, but also a 'strumpet's fool'. Cleopatra is a great and enchanting empress, but also the 'nag of Egypt'. They are equally contradictory in their actions. Antony flees the Battle of Actium, yet fights heroically outside Alexandria. Cleopatra hides fearfully in her monument, sending a deceitful message of her death, yet bravely faces death 'in the high Roman fashion'.

Cleopatra

Glenda Jackson, the Cleopatra of the 1978 Royal Shakespeare Company production, gives her thoughts on playing the Queen of Egypt:

> In building up the idea of this extraordinary woman, Shakespeare continually presents us with alternative viewpoints. Every time you think 'Oh, that's what she's like!' he presents you with an alternative view. It is like the most wonderful flickering fish all the time ...
>
> Everything that people say about Cleopatra always has a grain of truth in it. But the comments are always (as in life) much more indicative of those speaking than those of whom they speak ...
>
> Each time you come on, it is as a new facet to her character. It is like being in a new play. She lives in the moment ...
>
> Cleopatra moves with astonishing speed from emotion to emotion, from response to response, on a turning circle that is minute. But the essential paradox of Cleopatra's nature is that, for all her pretence, she can only be as enchanting as she is if her emotions are genuinely felt. She is not a superficial person. She doesn't ever delude herself. Even when she is pretending to delude herself, she doesn't ...
>
> She *is* a 'wonderful piece of work'. Throughout the entire play it never occurs to her that she is not the most desirable, wonderful, remarkable, beautiful, astonishing, intelligent woman that God ever created. She is also a woman of such incredible energy and appetite for life, that it is hard for her to kill herself. Everything about her fights it.

Talk together about the insights that Glenda Jackson's comments give you into the character of Cleopatra. Then choose a scene where Cleopatra's moods change at speed, and devise a presentation showing these changes.

Captions can complement pictures, adding an extra dimension to the visual image. Write captions for these pictures which encapsulate what each picture suggests to you about the nature of Antony and Cleopatra's relationship.

Judi Dench and Anthony Hopkins (National Theatre, 1987).

Glenda Jackson and Alan Howard (Royal Shakespeare Company, 1978).

Claire Higgins and Richard Johnson (Royal Shakespeare Company, 1992).

Mark Antony

John Caird, the director of the 1992 Royal Shakespeare Company production, gives his opinion of what attracts Antony to Cleopatra:

> In Egypt, everything is familial, warm and natural – even your servants are people you joke with. Money and time are things to be spent and enjoyed. For Antony, it's easy to see how he finds Egypt irresistible and the woman in charge of it even more irresistible …
>
> I think Antony should be a man who is past his prime, although he could hang on to power for another five to ten years if he chose to. There is a lot of evidence in the play to suggest that this is a relationship between an older man besotted by a younger woman who is desperately in need of a father figure to give her some sort of emotional anchor.

- List aspects of Cleopatra's behaviour that you think Antony finds irresistible.
- Find evidence to support John Caird's image of a 'besotted Antony'. Then find examples of Cleopatra behaving as if Antony is her 'emotional anchor'.

Antony the 'noble ruin'

Love strips Antony of everything he has previously valued: power, ambition, reputation, honour, integrity as a soldier and leader. Following his shameful defeat at Actium, his agonised sense of failure is such that he believes he has 'lost command', both of himself and of others. His only answer to Caesar's demands is a foolish challenge to single combat.

Yet there is nobility and greatness even in failure. Anthony does not forget his followers, and blames neither Enobarbus for his desertion, nor Cleopatra for her deception. Above all, he finds a new integrity in his realisation that he cares more for Cleopatra than he does for himself and that life without her is no life at all.

Is Antony a great hero?

In his tribute to the dead Antony (Act 5 Scene 1, lines 30–1), Maecenas says that 'his taints and honours waged equal with him', that is, Anthony possesses both distressing frailties and heroic virtues. To explore the contradictions and ambivalences in Antony's character, conduct your own inquiry. Your question is: 'Is Antony a great hero?' You will need a judging panel, hostile and supportive witnesses and scribes to record the evidence and the arguments presented.

'All for love'?

The epic love affair of Antony and Cleopatra challenges conventional and respectable morality. It is a great and powerful love shared by two people at the height of their fame and glory. When Antony rejects the messengers from Rome and declares 'here is my space', he is proclaiming a very special value in his relationship with Cleopatra. For Cleopatra, too, this is a deep and mature passion, unlike the loves of her youth, her 'salad days'. Although there may be many other motives for their suicides, the strength of their mutual love means that neither can live without the other.

The pendulum of love

Antony and Cleopatra's relationship is a constantly swinging pendulum of emotions. Look back at the scenes where the two are together. For each scene record the swings in their emotions on a chart like the one below. Write quotations for each key point in the swing (you may wish to add other emotions).

Some see Act 3 Scene 11, lines 55–73 as a pivotal moment in the play, when Antony and Cleopatra's entire world hangs in the balance. 'Love is at stake at this moment. If Cleopatra fails now, then love itself fails.' What other pivotal moments can you find in their relationship?

Collect the statements and proclamations of love that Antony and Cleopatra make to (or about) each other. Then collect examples of their acts of deceit and betrayal. At what moments are you convinced of the depth and sincerity of their love?

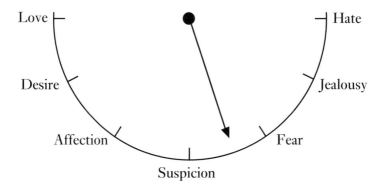

Octavius Caesar

Octavius is one of Shakespeare's successful men. But success in public life sometimes requires the exercise of qualities which in private life are very unattractive. Many people find Octavius deeply unattractive. They see him as the master of concealment, the clever politician whose words have a hidden political purpose. When Cleopatra wins her final 'victory' over this coldly ambitious man, they are delighted.

Others, however, see him as the man of destiny, the practical man who gets things done. For many Elizabethans, Octavius's victory marked the beginning of a golden age, a 'time of universal peace'.

Prepare a speech arguing that Octavius Caesar is the villain of the play. Then write a speech in his defence. Which view do you favour?

Enobarbus

Enobarbus is almost entirely Shakespeare's invention (see page 243). His story has been described as 'the tragedy of a cynical mind coupled with a soft heart'. He is a sardonic commentator on the behaviour of Caesar and Lepidus (Act 3 Scene 2), and is not afraid to speak his mind in the most powerful company (Act 2 Scene 2, lines 110–15). His blunt common sense tells him that Antony will never leave Cleopatra. He sees that the marriage to Octavia will 'strangle' the alliance between Antony and Caesar. At times, Enobarbus is very much a chorus figure observing the behaviour of those around him.

Reason urges Enobarbus to follow Canidius in deserting a doomed leader, because survival and dishonour are better than death. But this gruff military veteran's heart is governed by feelings of loyalty, love and friendship. In the end, Enobarbus ironically finds both dishonour *and* death.

Talk together about why some people believe that Enobarbus comes closest to being the moral centre of the play.

Octavia – an innocent and powerless figure?

Octavia speaks barely thirty lines spread over four scenes. Imagine that you have been cast to play this role, and your director describes to you her idea of Octavia's character: 'She is an innocent, abused by both Antony and Octavius, lost in a political world which first consumes and then ignores her. She is bewildered by her divided sympathies.' Look at the scenes where you appear, and decide how far you agree with your director's view of your character.

Lepidus and Pompey

In *Julius Caesar* (Act 4 Scene 1), Antony calls Lepidus 'a slight unmeritable man, meet (suitable) to be sent on errands'. In *Antony and Cleopatra,* he is a man out of his depth, mocked by allies, subordinates and servants alike, desperate to keep the peace between Antony and Octavius, if only to ensure his own survival.

Pompey begins full of confidence (Act 2 Scene 1), relishing his own success and scornful of his opponents, who obviously regard him as a serious threat. But he fails to take his opportunities. Once he has made peace and spurned the chance to assassinate the Triumvirate, he is no longer a force to be reckoned with.

Some people see Lepidus and Pompey as the real failures of the play. What redeeming features do they have?

Cleopatra's court

> Cleopatra is a dangerous person to be around. She wouldn't have anyone around her who was *boring*. She would only have people around her who were stimulating, outrageous, original. (Glenda Jackson)

Imagine you are preparing to play the role of either Alexas, Mardian, Charmian or Iras. Make notes on how you would behave in each scene, both when speaking and when watching. How would you avoid boring Cleopatra, while at the same time coping with her unpredictability?

Menas, Agrippa and Maecenas

Ventidius, victorious against the formidable Parthians, cynically comments that it is the underlings who do all the real work (Act 3 Scene 1, lines 16–17). Menas offers Pompey the world. Agrippa and Maecenas give Octavius unfailing support.

Write down your impressions of these three right-hand men. Compare your notes with those of other students. Are the relationships between each of these men and their masters different in any way?

'Relays of minor characters each with a life of their own'

Antony and Cleopatra has a huge list of characters. Actors must sometimes play as many as four different parts.

Productions have often doubled the following roles: Proculeius/ Soothsayer, Philo/Scarus, Thidias/Alexas, Ventidius/Dolabella, Demetrius/Maecenas. Choose one of these doublings and write the actor's notes showing how he will differentiate between the two roles.

The politics of the play

A divided society

For many decades before the conflict between Mark Antony and Octavius Caesar, the Roman Republic had been under considerable strain. Roman society was made up largely of an aristocracy of a few wealthy families (the patricians), a commercial class (the *equites*), a relatively poor city proletariat (the plebeians) and the slaves. The patricians monopolised the Senate and important positions of power, from which the plebeians were largely excluded.

Constant friction and struggles for power took place within and between these groups. Only by free handouts of money and corn, or by providing lavish and bloody entertainments at the Roman games, could the patricians hope to gain the support of the lower classes and keep them from rioting. The wealth that Rome gained through its overseas conquests widened these divisions. Most of the spoils of victory went to enrich the patrician senators and their families, leaving the plebeians even more impoverished and hostile.

Mark Antony, Octavius Caesar and Sextus Pompeius are all patricians. They give their views of the plebeians in Act 1 Scene 2, lines 178–87, Act 1 Scene 4, lines 40–7 and Act 2 Scene 1, lines 8–11. Cleopatra also speaks of the Roman people shortly before her death (Act 5 Scene 2, lines 54–6 and 206–20). Read these five sets of lines and decide whether the four characters share the same view of the ordinary people of Rome.

The first Triumvirate

It was inevitable that rival generals should emerge as the champions of either the Senate or the plebeians, hoping thereby to gain control of Rome and her provinces. Julius Caesar, although himself a patrician, was a champion of the plebeians, while Pompey the Great allied himself with the patricians.

In 60 BC, Julius Caesar, Pompey and Crassus formed an alliance (the first Triumvirate or 'rule by three') to share control of the Roman provinces. Crassus, however, was killed during an expedition to subdue the formidable Parthian empire. Soon after, Julius Caesar and Pompey clashed. Pompey was routed at the Battle of Pharsalia in 48 BC. He fled to Egypt, where Cleopatra was embroiled in a power struggle with her brother, King Ptolemy. Ptolemy's supporters killed Pompey in the hope of gaining favour with Julius Caesar, who arrived in pursuit of Pompey.

The young and intelligent Cleopatra quickly charmed Julius Caesar, who first defeated Ptolemy and then made Cleopatra Queen of Egypt. They had a son, Caesarion. When Caesar returned to Rome, Cleopatra accompanied him as his mistress.

Following the defeat of Pompey, Julius Caesar was virtually the sole master of the Roman Republic, a king in all but name. But the tensions and conflicts in Roman society were too strong to tolerate the rule of one man. Many in Republican Rome hated the idea of a king. In 44 BC, a group of senators led by Brutus and Cassius assassinated Caesar on the very day the Roman Senate was to proclaim him king. In *Julius Caesar*, Shakespeare gives his view of these events, ending with Mark Antony gaining power. In *Antony and Cleopatra*, Antony loses all that political power – and life itself.

The second Triumvirate

The Republicans under Brutus and Cassius were not successful for long. Mark Antony took over the leadership of Caesar's supporters, aided by Octavius Caesar, the great-nephew and adopted son of Julius Caesar. Octavius was just nineteen years old. Together they defeated Brutus and Cassius at the Battle of Philippi. Mark Antony, Octavius Caesar and Lepidus shared out the Roman provinces between them. Antony agreed to pacify the East and raise revenue, while Octavius Caesar returned to Rome to suppress Sextus Pompeius, who had taken Sicily, Corsica and Sardinia and was endangering the food supply of Rome itself.

Antony embarked on an expedition against the Parthians. On his way to the eastern frontier, he summoned Cleopatra to appear before him to explain why she had supported Cassius in the struggles following Julius Caesar's death. Their chosen meeting-place was Tarsus on the River Cydnus in Cilicia. Cleopatra was more than a match for Antony. As the splendid royal yacht carrying its magnificent queen sailed into the harbour, the people left Antony's court of justice and flocked to see Cleopatra. Like Julius Caesar before him, Antony was enchanted.

Antony's supporters in Rome (notably Antony's wife Fulvia and his brother Lucius Antonius) at one stage forced Octavius to flee the city. Matters were temporarily resolved when Antony came back from the East and reached a new working agreement with Octavius.

At Misena in 39 BC, Octavius was reluctantly obliged to recognise Sextus Pompeius's claims to Sicily, Sardinia and Corsica. But shortly after, with a strengthened fleet, Octavius crushed Sextus Pompeius, then turned against his own ally Lepidus and defeated him.

Talk together about how Shakespeare makes use of the stories of Julius Caesar, Pompey the Great, Brutus, Cassius and Crassus in the play. Look especially at:

Act 1 Scene 2, lines 176–85   Act 3 Scene 1, lines 1–5
Act 1 Scene 4, line 55   Act 3 Scene 2, lines 55–9
Act 1 Scene 5, lines 30–5 and 69–79 Act 3 Scene 7, lines 31–2
Act 2 Scene 2, lines 237–8   Act 3 Scene 11, lines 35–40.
Act 2 Scene 6, lines 8–29 and 62–72

Sole mastery of the Roman empire

Rome and its provinces now had only two masters. It was inevitable that Octavius and Antony would come into conflict. The attempt to cement the alliance with Antony's marriage in 40 BC to Octavius's sister, Octavia, failed.

Octavius's legions had given him supreme power in Rome and the western provinces. Supported by Agrippa, an able military commander, and Maecenas, a rich and clever Etruscan, he carefully cultivated the loyalty and support of the Roman citizens. Meanwhile, Antony's activities in Egypt were viewed with increasing anger in Rome. Antony was appropriating large slices of territory from the Roman provinces in Asia and Greece to form kingdoms ruled over by Cleopatra, their three sons and Caesarion (Cleopatra's son by Julius Caesar).

Octavius therefore launched a propaganda campaign in Rome which forced the Roman Senate to declare war on Cleopatra. The decisive battle was off the coast of Actium in Greece in 31 BC. In the midst of the battle, Cleopatra and her fleet fled, followed by Antony. The two retreated to Egypt, where Antony committed suicide. After Cleopatra had become Octavius Caesar's prisoner, she too committed suicide, allegedly by the bite of an asp. Egypt then became a Roman province. Octavius (later called Caesar Augustus) was now the unchallenged ruler of the Roman world, the first Roman emperor.

See the 'sweep of empire'

Use the historical background on pages 240–2 to make a time-line (a long wall-chart plotting the historical events described). Include quotations from the play.

Shakespeare's use of Plutarch

Shakespeare's main source for *Antony and Cleopatra* was Plutarch's *Lives of the Greeks and Romans*, which was translated into English by Sir Thomas North in 1579. Shakespeare plundered North's translation for numerous facts, details and phrases, but he did not merely take over the story. After all, he was concerned with writing a play not a meticulously accurate historical account. Here are just a few examples of how Shakespeare used North's Plutarch:

a He uses details from Plutarch to give dramatic life to a character or situation. For example, the story of the eight roast boars before breakfast or Cleopatra's trick with the salt fish.

b He rearranges and changes to create a special significance. According to Plutarch, Antony issued his challenge to Caesar *after* his successful skirmish outside Alexandria. It was Bacchus, the god of wine, who abandoned Antony on the night after the battle outside Alexandria.

c He compresses historical incidents. In Plutarch, over ten years elapsed between Antony and Cleopatra's first meeting and their deaths, while Antony's final defeat was many weeks after the Battle of Actium.

d Some events are omitted entirely (such as Antony's disastrous personal campaign against the Parthians, and the fact that Octavia lived with Antony for several years, bearing him several children).

e He expands and develops scenes or invents completely new ones. Most of the invented scenes concern Cleopatra (for example, Act 1 Scene 5 and Act 2 Scene 5). The role of Enobarbus is also extensively developed by Shakespeare.

Decide why Shakespeare might have made each of the changes to Plutarch's account mentioned in b–e above.

Compare Act 5 Scene 2, lines 274–322 with the following extract from North's translation:

When they had opened the dores, they founde Cleopatra starke dead, layed upon a bed of gold, attired and araied in her royall robes, and one of her two women, which was called Iras, dead at her feete: and her other woman called Charmion halfe-dead, and trembling, trimming the diademe which Cleopatra ware upon her head. One of the souldiers seeing her, angrily sayd unto her: Is that well done Charmion? Verie well sayd she againe, and meete for a Princes discended from the race of so many noble kings. She sayd no more, but fell downe dead hard by the bed.

The language of
Antony and Cleopatra

The language of the play is delicate yet strong, rich yet simple, varying with each changing mood and moment, building to the sustained intensity of the final death scenes of Antony and Cleopatra.

Dazzling, iridescent imagery

Ever-shifting clusters of images reflect and intensify the play's many complex themes. 'Images' in this sense refers to vivid words and phrases that conjure up emotionally-charged pictures with a powerful significance, far deeper than their surface meaning. Collect examples (with line references) of the following image-clusters as they occur through the play:

Images of imperial power and magnificence: war, empire, honour, armies, ships, treasure (look out for architectural images, such as pillars and arches).

Physical, sensuous and erotic images: sounds, sights, smells, eating, feasting, drinking, playing, loving and lusting.

Natural and elemental images: animals, insects, fertility, earth, mud, slime, river, sea, clouds, rain, sun, fire, air (the mingling of the four elements of earth, air, fire, water was thought to breed life – see also pages 172 and 222).

Images of Fortune and destiny: fate, chance, accidents, gaming and luck.

Images from myth and legend: Mars, Venus, Isis, Hercules, gods and goddesses.

Images of dissolution: melting, fading, dissolving, discandying, disponging and dislimning.

Cosmic and transcendental images: sun, moon, stars, heavens, spheres and worlds.

a Talk about the varying effects created by these image-clusters as they occur through the play.

b Find the images most frequently associated with Antony and Cleopatra.

c Earth and water were 'baser', more material elements; fire and air were the higher, more spiritual elements. Earth–water images used of Cleopatra in the early acts become fire–air images in the final scene. Find examples of these images and describe the changing visions of Cleopatra that they create.

d Find the melting–dissolving and cosmic–transcendental images in Act 4 Scene 15 and Act 5 Scene 2. What qualities do these images bring to the deaths of both Antony and Cleopatra?

The interplay of images

The image-clusters in the play interact with each other to echo and reflect the play's many oppositions and paradoxes. Collect examples of the following and design charts to show the oppositions:

• Images of Rome and Egypt: Rome evokes images of restraint, calculation, war, business, coldness. Egypt is associated with abundance, warmth, fertility, luxury, ease.

• Images of irreconcilable worlds: life–death, heroic past–tarnished present, fertility–corruption, measure–overflow, seriousness– sport, measurable–infinite, myth–reality, worldly change–eternal changelessness.

From honest plainness to magnificent hyperbole

Antony's soaring opening words in Act 1 Scene 1: 'Then must thou needs find out new heaven new earth', plummet immediately to an irritated reality: 'Grates me! The sum'. Shakespeare's language can swing a scene from one mood to another with such speed and ease.

Hyperbole (extravagantly exaggerated language) mirrors Antony and Cleopatra's larger-than-life characters. Do you ever believe their hyperbole? Compare their hyperbolic language in Acts 1–3 with their language in Acts 4–5.

Biblical images

Antony and Cleopatra's language at times echoes the Bible's vision of the end of the world. The book of Revelation speaks of stars falling and worlds shaking and cracking. Echoes of this vision are particularly strong at Antony's death (see pages 184 and 188) and also in Cleopatra's dream of Antony (Act 5 Scene 2, lines 78–91). Compare her words here with Revelation 10:1–6.

Parallels

Read again the deaths of Antony and Cleopatra (Act 4 Scenes 14 and 15 and Act 5 Scene 2). Find the parallels and echoes in the language. Another dramatist might have felt it necessary to contrast the two deaths. Why should Shakespeare deliberately echo them?

Shakespeare's verse

Over ninety percent of *Antony and Cleopatra* is in blank (or unrhymed) verse. Blank verse may be defined as unrhymed verse made up of five pairs of light (x) and strong (/) stresses (iambic pentameter):

x / x / x / x / x /
'The hand could pluck her back that shoved her on'

x / x / x / x / x /
'I must from this enchanted queen break off'

Blank verse can sound stiff and regular, with pauses at the end of each line (end-stopping) as well as regular mid-line pauses (caesuras). But such regularity is rare in *Antony and Cleopatra*, because Shakespeare insistently runs on the sense and rhythms from line to line ('enjambement' or run-on lines), continuing sometimes into long sentences. He varies the placing of the 'caesura', or has no mid-line pause at all. He adds to a line's length with 'feminine endings' (extra end-of-line unstressed syllables), or varies the line's basic iambic (x /) rhythm. Lines are very frequently 'loosened' by dividing them between one or more characters ('shared lines').

a Turn to the moment when Cleopatra helps Antony arm himself for battle (Act 4 Scene 4, lines 1–23). In pairs, speak these lines several times. Find examples of the verse-variations listed above. Talk about how these variations help to intensify the drama of the moment. Then find moments where a more regular verse pattern is used. What effect does it create?

b In pairs, read the scene between Cleopatra and the Messenger (Act 2 Scene 5). How do the shared lines help to create the tension in that meeting?

c It is a well-established stage convention that shared lines are spoken with little or no pause between speakers. Speak some of the many shared lines in the play (for example, Act 2 Scene 2, lines 73–109, Act 3 Scene 7, lines 3–30, Act 3 Scene 11, lines 50–69 and Act 3 Scene 13, lines 46–63 and 155–71). Does this pausing convention apply to *Antony and Cleopatra*?

Language, mood and character

The play's flexible dramatic-poetic speech creates many moods and emotions, from the brisk and business-like Octavius in Act 1 Scene 4, lines 74–7, to the sad pathos of Antony's farewell to his servants (Act 4 Scene 2, lines 25–34), or the steady intensity of Cleopatra's final commands (Act 5 Scene 2, lines 274–5). In pairs, take turns at reading the following lines several times. Describe in a word or short phrase each character's mood or emotion:

Act 2 Scene 7, lines 113–20	Act 3 Scene 7, lines 15–19
Act 3 Scene 11, lines 68–73	Act 3 Scene 13, lines 91–5
Act 4 Scene 4, lines 36–8	Act 4 Scene 9, lines 12–23
Act 5 Scene 2, lines 45–7	Act 5 Scene 2, lines 308–13.

Shakespeare's prose

Less than ten percent of the play is in prose, but it is used to great effect, as the dialogue shifts easily from verse to prose and back again. In the theatre, it is not easy to be sure if the actors are speaking very free verse or very poetic prose. Look at Act 4 Scene 3 and Act 4 Scene 14, lines 105–14 to see how much like verse the prose can sometimes be.

a Prose is generally used by low-status characters, by higher-rank speakers in more relaxed moments or for comic scenes. Identify one example of each of these uses. More interestingly, find exceptions to these 'rules' and say what effects are created.

b Sometimes a character will shift away from or 'resist' the verse/ prose form that others in the scene are using. In Act 2 Scene 2 for example, Enobarbus the down-to-earth soldier speaks in prose to show how different he is from the 'impressive verse' speakers around him. But why should he move into verse at line 200 when the others have relaxed into prose?

c Follow Enobarbus's shifts from verse to prose elsewhere in the play. How do these shifts reflect his changing state of mind?

d Talk about similar shifts from (or resistances to) the current prose/verse forms by other characters in Act 1 Scene 2, Act 2 Scene 7, Act 3 Scene 5 and Act 5 Scene 2.

The play in the theatre

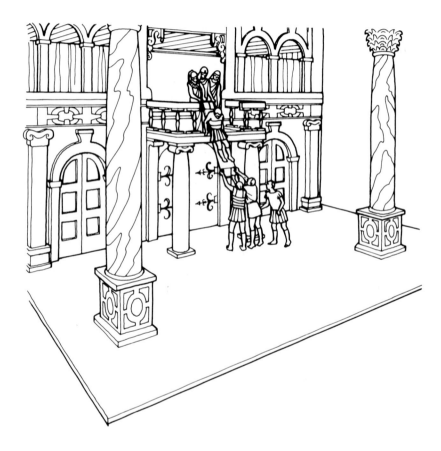

This is how Antony's death (Act 4 Scene 15) might have been presented by Shakespeare's company. Identify the characters. Work out how you would stage this scene on your school or college stage.

Nothing is known about the performances of *Antony and Cleopatra* in Shakespeare's lifetime. For the best part of 200 years after his death, there is just one recorded production of the play, using a script largely as it appears in this edition. Far more popular with seventeenth- and eighteenth-century audiences were reduced versions of the Antony and Cleopatra story focusing on the lovers' final hours. The most famous of these adaptations was Dryden's *All For Love*, first performed in 1678, which set the action in Alexandria throughout, used a small cast of actors and had more female roles.

Antony and Cleopatra was performed more frequently in the nineteenth century. Action and star performances were all-important, and the script was usually heavily cut to focus on a small number of convincingly 'realistic' scenes. One production recreated the Battle of Actium with opposing crews from two galleys firing arrows at each other.

In the twentieth century, productions have increasingly attempted to stage the full script of the play. The 1972 Royal Shakespeare Company production was influenced by the glittering treasures of the Tutankhamun exhibition of the same year. The Egyptian court was sensuous and colourful with canopies and silk cushions (see page 6). Back-projections showed outlines of mountains with clouds which altered and re-formed. Their changing patterns reflected Cleopatra's ever-changing moods. When the action turned to Rome, brilliance was replaced by austerity. On the back wall was a huge map of the Roman empire, the Roman Senators wore formal togas, and the marble walls of the Senate were cold and white (see page 54).

The 1978 Royal Shakespeare Company production emphasised the small, intimate world of the lovers. Events unfolded in a semi-circular area framed by large glass screens (see page 86). Lighting changes could create an opaque, closed interior, or a translucent, open landscape of change and violence. In one battle scene, the glass panels were suddenly spattered with blood. Eventually the glass panels cracked as the forces of the outside world broke through.

- How would you use a back-projector that created images of mountains and clouds to reflect Cleopatra's moods in Act 1 Scenes 2, 3 and 5 and Act 2 Scene 5?
- In the 1978 Royal Shakespeare Company production, at what moment would you have spattered the glass panels with blood? At what point in the play do you think the glass panels finally cracked?

A director's thoughts

John Caird, the director of the 1992 Royal Shakespeare Company production, had the use of hydraulic stage machinery which enabled him to move huge 'stone' slabs silently about the stage (see page 188). He describes some aspects of his production:

> There has to be a powerful distinction between the world of the Roman empire and the world of Egypt. Rome is where Antony finds himself cornered by his duties, by his military campaigns, by his marriage. Here he is surrounded by high walls, and there are formal tables of silver covered with paperwork to be filled in. No sky or bright light creeps in. Egypt is looser, much more timeless and very exotic. The stone walls roll back to reveal blue sky and huge bright parasols are carried in. Here we use low informal tables and bright rugs …
>
> I see strict behaviour patterns in Rome, strict military codes of behaviour and honour. People hold themselves stiffly, walk in straight lines. Messengers are brought in, paperwork is filled in and everything is clearly defined – like our own British empire. While in Egypt there is a completely different body language that Antony loves …
>
> The play creates more powerfully than any other Shakespeare play its geographical locations and its atmospheric effects, its sounds, its smells, its vision, from an extraordinary interlacing of words … .

a Using John Caird's comments above, sketch sets for a Roman scene and an Egyptian one. Draw in the characters and write the lines from the script that go with each sketch.

b Choose ten lines from an early scene with Antony in Egypt and ten lines from a contrasting scene where he is in Rome. Present these two scenes emphasising the differences in body language and movements.

c Construct a senses chart for the worlds of Rome and Egypt to illustrate John Caird's comment about how the play creates 'its atmospheric effects, its sounds, its smells, its vision, from an extraordinary interlacing of words'. You might do it like this:

Egypt	Rome
Smell: 'a strange invisible perfume' 2.2 **Hear:** **See:**	'knaves that smells of sweat' 1.4

Planning and staging your own production

What period and place?

Antony and Cleopatra has rarely been set outside its own place and time. This contrasts strongly with *Julius Caesar*, which has been staged in settings other than ancient Rome (strife-torn Lebanon, fascist Italy, a twentieth-century office). Talk together about whether or not you think there could be other possible historical periods and geographical locations in which to stage your production.

What publicity?

- Design a poster. It should make people eager to see your play.
- Work out a five-minute presentation to show potential sponsors.
- Plan some publicity photographs for your production.
- Video (or script) a two-minute advertisement for your production.

How to present your cast list

Early cast lists for *Antony and Cleopatra* placed Cleopatra and the other women after all the other actors (in Shakespeare's time women's parts were played by boys). Designing your own cast list can help your audience's understanding of the structures and relationships in the play (the list of characters on page 1, for example, is divided up into Egypt and Rome). Devise a cast list that you think would be most helpful to your audience.

Would you use a 'governing idea'?

In every stage production, director, designer and actors work together to bring a script to life in public performance. Some directors feel it is important to approach the script with no preconceived ideas, and to allow Shakespeare's language and characters to create their own atmosphere. Others are strongly influenced by a 'governing idea' (or concept) that they believe is centrally important to the play. One production of *Antony and Cleopatra* emphasised the influence of fate and chance, with the Soothsayer appearing on stage at crucial moments, then returning as the Clown to give the fatal asps to Cleopatra. Another production played down the political dimensions in order to focus on the love story, cutting, for example, the scene on Pompey's galley.

Decide whether you would use a 'governing idea' if you were directing *Antony and Cleopatra*. Write notes to justify your idea and suggest how it would affect the staging, the music and sound effects, and the casting and performances of the major characters.

William Shakespeare 1564–1616

1564 Born Stratford-upon-Avon, eldest son of John and Mary Shakespeare.
1582 Marries Anne Hathaway of Shottery, near Stratford.
1583 Daughter, Susanna, born.
1585 Twins, son and daughter, Hamnet and Judith, born.
1592 First mention of Shakespeare in London. Robert Greene, another playwright, described Shakespeare as 'an upstart crow beautified with our feathers ...'. Greene seems to have been jealous of Shakespeare. He mocked Shakespeare's name, calling him 'the only Shake-scene in a country' (presumably because Shakespeare was writing successful plays).
1595 A shareholder in 'The Lord Chamberlain's Men', an acting company that became extremely popular.
1596 Son Hamnet dies, aged eleven.
Father, John, granted arms (acknowledged as a gentleman).
1597 Buys New Place, the grandest house in Stratford.
1598 Acts in Ben Jonson's *Every Man in His Humour*.
1599 Globe Theatre opens on Bankside. Performances in the open air.
1601 Father, John, dies.
1603 James I grants Shakespeare's company a royal patent: 'The Lord Chamberlain's Men' became 'The King's Men' and played about twelve performances each year at court.
1607 Daughter, Susanna, marries Dr John Hall.
1608 Mother, Mary, dies.
1609 'The King's Men' begin performing indoors at Blackfriars Theatre.
1610 Probably returned from London to live in Stratford.
1616 Daughter, Judith, marries Thomas Quiney.
Dies. Buried in Holy Trinity Church, Stratford-upon-Avon.

The plays and poems
(no one knows exactly when he wrote each play)

1589–1595 *The Two Gentlemen of Verona, The Taming of the Shrew, First, Second and Third Parts of King Henry VI, Titus Andronicus, King Richard III, The Comedy of Errors, Love's Labour's Lost, A Midsummer Night's Dream, Romeo and Juliet, King Richard II* (and the long poems *Venus and Adonis* and *The Rape of Lucrece*).

1596–1599 *King John, The Merchant of Venice, First and Second Parts of King Henry IV, The Merry Wives of Windsor, Much Ado About Nothing, King Henry V, Julius Caesar* (and probably the *Sonnets*).

1600–1605 *As You Like It, Hamlet, Twelfth Night, Troilus and Cressida, Measure for Measure, Othello, All's Well That Ends Well, Timon of Athens, King Lear.*

1606–1611 *Macbeth, Antony and Cleopatra, Pericles, Coriolanus, The Winter's Tale, Cymbeline, The Tempest.*

1613 *King Henry VIII, The Two Noble Kinsmen* (both probably with John Fletcher).

1623 Shakespeare's plays published as a collection (now called the First Folio).